Academic Motherhood

Academic Motherhood

How Faculty Manage Work and Family

K ELLY W ARD AND L ISA W OLF-W ENDEL

RUTGERS UNIVERSITY PRESS

NEW BRUNSWICK, NEW JERSEY, AND LONDON

Library of Congress Cataloging-in-Publication Data

Ward, Kelly (Kelly Anne)

Academic motherhood : how faculty manage work and family /
    Kelly Ward and Lisa Wolf-Wendel.

     p.   cm.

Includes bibliographical references and index.

ISBN 978–0–8135–5384–9 (hardcover : alk. paper) — ISBN 978–0–8135–5385–6
(pbk. : alk. paper) — ISBN 978–0–8135–5321–4 (e-book : alk. paper)

    1. Women college teachers—United States—Social conditions.   2. Women in
higher education—United States—Social conditions.   3. Work and family—United
States.   4. Working mothers—United States.   I. Wolf-Wendel, Lisa. II. Title.

   LB2332.3.W37 2012

378.082—dc23

                                                 2011049382

A British Cataloging-in-Publication record for this book
is available from the British Library.

Visit our website: http://rutgerspress.rutgers.edu

Manufactured in the United States of America

CONTENTS

Acknowledgments   vii

1. Motherhood and an Academic Career: 1
    A Negotiable Road

2. Origins of the Study   13

3. Understanding the Existing Narratives   28
    and Counternarratives

4. Managing Work and Family in the Early Career   47

5. Mid-Career Perspectives on Work and Family   63

6. The Role of Disciplinary and Departmental   88
    Contexts

7. Institutional Type Differences   110

8. Social Capital and Dual Careers   149

9. Leaving the Tenure Track   165

10. Policy Perspectives   179

11. Conclusions, Recommendations,   212
    and Parting Thoughts

References   247

Index   259

ACKNOWLEDGMENTS

We would like to acknowledge the many people who have provided support for us throughout this project. We both had the support of our institutional colleagues, who discussed ideas with us, encouraged us, questioned us, and pushed us to think about work and family in new and different ways. We also want to thank the graduate students (and former graduate students) who helped us over the years. They kept us organized, helped us to collect or transcribe data, and generally served as a sounding board for the many ideas we came up with as a result of our data collection and analysis. We would not have been able to complete this project without their help.

The Alfred P. Sloan Foundation and the American Association of University Women both provided funding for the data collection aspects of this project—and without their support we never would have been able to write this book. Kelly also expresses her appreciation for the Ben and Nancy Ellison Faculty Fellowship at Washington State University and the support it provided her for carrying out this project.

We also owe a huge debt of gratitude to our spouses and our children (Daisy, Lucy, Henry, Addie, and Lily), who put up with our periodic satisficing and lack of balance that we needed to get this project completed. They also provided us with ample perspective and insight. A special thanks to Gene Solomon for his useful and necessary editing of the book.

We also want to thank the academic mothers who we interviewed in this project. We appreciate them for their honesty, for their time, for their dedication, and for their role modeling of how academic women can manage both work and family. The ultimate acknowledgment of this book goes to these women. We hope their stories inspire others to follow in their footsteps.

Finally, we want to dedicate this book to our friend J. Douglas Toma, who despite being a guy, epitomized how to achieve academic success and personal happiness and how to integrate the two. We miss you, Doug!

Academic Motherhood

CHAPTER 1

Motherhood and an Academic Career

A NEGOTIABLE ROAD

Academic women courageous (or foolish) enough to mention to their colleagues an interest in children and family are often met with a barrage of bad news, the received wisdom of the challenges of a journey fraught with difficulties. The general narrative suggests that both faculty life and parenthood are all consuming and irreconcilable, and that only a fool would attempt to balance a tenure-track academic career with the desire for children and a family life. Any encouragement usually falls in the form of a warning: You can have a faculty career and a family, so long as you time everything perfectly, perform at an unreasonably high level, learn to function without sleep, neglect any personal needs, and forgo happiness and sanity—at least until you get tenure.

If you have heard these messages, or if you have repeated them to others, this book is for you. We explore the origins of these beliefs and stories, and then offer a counternarrative, demonstrating that academic women with children can do more than simply survive the rigors of the tenure track—they can find satisfaction and success in all of their many roles. While acknowledging the realities and difficulties that motherhood and academic work entail, we hope to provide an institutional and cultural context within which women who are both professors and mothers (and the administrators and policy makers with whom they interact) can view the decisions and choices they must make, and can realize that motherhood and scholarship are not mutually exclusive or antagonistic.

Here are the stories and the lessons learned of real women, neither foolish nor perfect, who have managed to merge successfully their academic and family lives. The stories of these academics and their families, and the personal and policy choices they suggest, counter the traditional tales of trauma and travail by highlighting a narrative of promise and possibility.

Countering the negative narrative is important because its pervasiveness may have ill effects on the choices women make. It may influence women, for example, to forgo or delay having children in order to pursue an academic career. It might encourage women to avoid academic careers altogether or opt out of full-time tenure-track careers or into positions that are different from those they might otherwise desire because they see motherhood as irreconcilable with academic career success. These decisions could have long-term personal ramifications for individual women. These choices could also affect the quality of the academic profession and the ability of colleges and universities to recruit and retain the best and brightest, regardless of their gender or family status. This book explores the choices women make and attempts to contextualize and even problematize them by highlighting the way women who have made the choice to be both mothers and tenure-track faculty members, in all its messiness, have made their lives work. This book shows how choices are constrained by gendered and academic workplace norms and how women manage these norms to manage their multiple roles.

Before moving on, it is important to delineate the parameters of this book. It is based on a longitudinal study of women faculty members with children. These women were initially interviewed starting in 1998, when they were in their early careers and had young children (under the age of five). We then conducted follow-up interviews with the same women starting in 2008, to examine career and family progression at mid-career. The women in the study represent an array of disciplines and institutional types within academia. The focus on women is purposeful, as societal expectations of women, especially in terms of the demands of childbirth and taking care of young children, are very different from those for men. This is not to say that men may not experience these issues or are not important, but they are not the focus of this book. The choice of interviewing women on the tenure track is also intentional. Although it is true that many women faculty members are in non-tenure-track positions, the institution of tenure as the marker of a successful academic career is undeniable and makes the focus on achieving it all the more important. Recognizing that institutional context shapes the tenure process specifically and academic life in general, we also took care to include faculty members from different institutional types. While acknowledging that we left out the stories of others who are important—including men and non-tenure-track faculty members—and while acknowledging that there are a myriad of ways to study work and family in an academic context, the focus here is intentionally limited to how academic women manage work and family in early and mid-career stages of tenure-line positions.

A Brief Introduction to the Academic Profession

We think it would be helpful to provide some basic background information about the academic profession. A typical academic career begins when an individual earns a doctorate in a specific field and then applies for an academic position. As any academic knows, a doctorate is a serious investment. Preparing people for academic careers is one-at-a-time, deliberate, expensive, and slow—sometimes extremely slow—the average time to degree after earning a baccalaureate degree is 7.5 years, The rewards for such an intensive expenditure of time, energy, and resources come at the end of the path, when a person is hired as a professor and then subsequently achieves recognition in a research field and facilitates student learning as a teacher in the discipline. Another reward that drives individuals to invest in an academic career is the security of tenure.

In some fields, individuals will hold postdoctoral positions before starting a tenure-track position. This adds to the already impressive investment of time and energy undertaken by the prospective faculty member. The academic labor market varies greatly by discipline. In the last several years, the market has been tight—there have been too many individuals with advanced degrees and not enough full-time, tenure-line positions available. Many tenure-track jobs have been converted to non-tenure-track positions, making tenure-track positions all the more coveted and, at times, quite competitive.

Assuming a tenure-track position, which is not necessarily a safe assumption but, nonetheless, the focus here, the initial rank for a newly hired professor is assistant professor. Typically, a person maintains this rank for five to seven years before going up for promotion to associate professor with tenure. This probationary period is fairly fixed—and there are not many deviations allowed within this timeline. Unless they stop their tenure clock, tenure-track faculty members must go up for tenure by year seven. Tenure is determined by the ability of the assistant professor to demonstrate that she has achieved a certain level of distinction in the activities valued at her institution. Such academic activities and duties vary greatly by field and institutional type. Faculty members at research-oriented institutions will do some combination of teaching, research, and service. Faculty members at institutions with a teaching focus will mainly teach courses and engage in professional service, with fewer expectations for research. In any case, tenure is a high-stakes proposition. The tenure decision is an "up or out" one—if an individual is denied tenure, she has to leave the institution.

The American Association of University Professors (AAUP) established tenure, as we know it, in 1940. By design, tenure is intended to guarantee the right to academic freedom and to protect faculty members in terms of exploring new or unpopular lines of research or teaching. Tenure allows faculty members intellectual autonomy to investigate and teach topics about which they are most passionate without fear of reprisal. Tenure also allows faculty members to fully participate in campus governance and policy making without fear of losing their jobs. Many argue that tenure helps attract the best individuals to the career and helps to compensate for the relatively low pay afforded to faculty members, at least as compared to professionals in other fields such as medicine or law. There are, however, many critics of tenure. Some suggest, for example, that it is an expensive proposition; it can cost an institution of higher education over 2 million dollars per faculty member over the course of a thirty-year career (Taylor 2010). Others suggest that it does not allow institutions to be agile and flexible in a way that hiring non-tenure-track faculty might. Further, tenure, some argue, protects those individuals who are "deadwood" and are no longer productive. We should note that it is possible to be fired even if one has earned tenure—faculty members can be terminated for failure to perform their job, for moral turpitude, for reasons of financial exigency, or due to program termination. However, it is relatively rare for institutions to terminate tenured faculty members. The purpose of this book is not to critique tenure, although we will offer some suggestions for ways to amend it. Rather, tenure provides the context in which discussions about academic motherhood take place—especially for the women in our study—so it is important to have a basic understanding of what it is and how it works.

Once tenured, there is no set timeline for faculty members to move from associate professor to full professor. Going up for promotion is an option, not a requirement. Often there is a minimum amount of time that individuals are expected to stay in rank—five years or so—but there is huge variation in how much time people remain at the associate professor level. Some faculty members might stay at the associate professor level throughout their entire careers. Others achieve the rank of full professor relatively quickly.

Academic life is different from other professional fields in that the motivation and drive to progress professionally is largely internal. Faculty members do not really have a "boss"—though they do have a department chair and a dean who assign teaching loads and work duties. Faculty life is known for its autonomy: the work can be done anywhere and almost at any time. Research on faculty members suggests that they are hard workers who put in long hours. By some estimates, the average faculty member works well over fifty hours a week (Jacobs & Winslow, 2004). This is necessarily an estimate, because professors do not often have fixed hours of work in the office or laboratory and because their schedules are usually not based on an 8 A.M. to 5 P.M. workday. Perhaps this lack of structure leads to overestimations about time spent working, but it could also lead to underestimations. It certainly appears that faculty members not only work hard themselves but also set expectations for others that are difficult for many people to achieve, especially individuals who have responsibilities outside of work.

There are two extreme stereotypes that influence how tenure-track faculty members live their lives and are perceived by others. At one extreme is the deadwood professor—waking late in the morning, mowing his lawn at 11 A.M., going for a bike ride at noon, stopping by campus to teach a class, reading a book in the late afternoon, and generally getting paid for doing little or nothing. No faculty member wants to be viewed as deadwood. Faced with this stereotype, faculty members are loath to admit that their jobs are enjoyable and rewarding for fear that someone (the public, students, legislators, boards of trustees, administrators, students, colleagues) will equate their satisfaction with slacking off and not working hard enough. Faculty members may very well enjoy their lives—especially the intellectual rigor, the challenge of their work, their ability to influence students and the field, and even the flexibility and autonomy that comes with the position—but talking about the career in positive terms can too easily be misinterpreted as slacking, so instead most academics stress the difficulties of their work rather than highlighting the joys of it.

The other extreme picture of the professorial lifestyle is that of the ideal professor, a variant on what Arlie Hochschild (1995) called the "ideal worker"—focused on the task at hand without outside responsibilities or distractions. Hochschild's ideal worker is one who is dedicated solely to the workplace without interruption from outside influences. This ideal worker works free from family concerns or issues in his private life. The absent-minded professor is an extreme variation on this, as he is so focused on his research that he (or occasionally she) forgets the basic niceties of polite society—changing clothing, eating, outside appointments, and the like. Although this image is neither realistic nor even ideal, the legacy of the concept permeates many contemporary academic workplace cultures. Many employers, even well-intentioned ones, view a single-minded dedication and commitment to work, above all else, as the ideal employee attribute and as the way to create efficient and effective workplaces.

Historically, the professorship arose from the clergy class, where vocation and avocation were often united (Finkelstein 1984). This ideal professor was not expected to be bothered by family or other domestic demands—those were presumably to be handled by a support system at home—wife, mother, domestic help, or some combination thereof. The assumption was that a professor was male and dedicated solely to his job, and the system and culture of tenure was created in light of this assumption. If the professor did have children, he had a wife at home who managed the household and dedicated herself to the family with the same dedication that her husband applied to his job. Although men are increasing their share of responsibility for family life, women still tend to be primary caregivers for young children and aging parents (Hochschild 1989). In addition, women tend to be in charge of the "second shift" (family care and house care) after working their "first shift" at the job. The second shift impacts the time women have available for work and also creates a divided set of loyalties that men often do not encounter to the same extent.

A faculty member looking to establish her career in the face of conflicting time demands between workplace and home may not be able to be an ideal academic worker. This clash of ideal expectations is, in large part, what makes the prospect of a woman being successful in a tenure-track academic career if she has children seem impossible to achieve. The concepts of the ideal worker and gendered norms are revisited throughout the book.

THE CASE FOR STUDYING ACADEMIC MOTHERHOOD

We are often asked why our research only focuses on the experiences of women, given that both men and women are parents and professors. There are two elements that compel us toward the study of women—the history of the academic profession and the physical realities of having children. The traditional wisdom in academe has been that women who are serious about their careers ought to forgo having children or have a baby after tenure (Armenti 2000; Drago & Colbeck 2003; Tierney & Bensimon 1996), but from a fertility standpoint, delaying childbirth this long can create difficulties (Drago & Williams 2000). Women with doctorates earn them, on average, at the age of thirty-four, and female fertility declines significantly around the age of thirty-five (Varner 2000). Even with a straightforward six-or-seven-year period pursuing promotion, the average female professor will not achieve tenure until around the age of forty. This landscape can present a woman who enters the academic ranks childless, but wanting children, a feeling that she confronts what can seem like irreconcilable differences between parenthood and a career as a tenure-line faculty member. For many academic women, the tenure and biological clocks tick simultaneously.

There are additional elements of the academic profession that make it unique and emphasize the importance of studying women in this profession separately from other groups of women. Women in all areas of society have experienced societal changes and work force shifts that arose from external forces, including involvement in world wars and broader access to child care and education, combined with the women's movement with its attention to equity in the workplace, birth control, and the expansion of traditional gender roles. Together, these shifts have led to a continued increase in the numbers of women in the professions, including those within the academic workplace and professorial positions at all types of colleges and universities.

The number of women serving as professors has expanded much more quickly than changes in the expectations and role of the professoriate. These changes in the demographics of the academy have provoked some changes in policies and provisions, but for the most part the traditional, normative view of the professor—as a single-minded academic resource, free from external distractions—has remained.

Given the physical realities of having a baby, it is not an "outside interest" that a woman can easily overlook. Having a baby makes gender salient, and often causes a woman be viewed as not just a professor, but a female professor with a child. This label clashes both with the singularity of her purpose and with external expectations of what it means to be a professor (Ridgeway & Correll 2004). While "average" professors have changed from being almost exclusively male to including more females, the general view of a professor as a single-minded and dedicated academic monk has changed little, leaving female faculty members between old expectations and new realities.

The inroads women have made in higher education has been impressive. Looking at the numbers superficially, one sees great progress. Across the board, women make up a majority of undergraduate students and, in some areas, graduate students as well. Many incoming cohorts of faculty are also majority female. According to the 2010 *Digest of Educational Statistics*, women now account for 43 percent of full-time professors on American college campuses, with representatives in every academic discipline. But when the numbers are viewed more closely through the lenses of discipline, institutional type, position, and rank, the gains are not as clear. The higher the academic rank and the more prestigious the institutional type, women are increasingly underrepresented. They are also underrepresented in some fields, including science, technology, engineering, and mathematics (STEM). A simplistic pipeline metaphor would suggest that an influx of women into assistant professor positions will lead inevitably to a greater number of women in associate, senior, and administrative ranks. A detailed analysis shows, however, that while women have made progress in many fields at the incoming levels, they do not steadily progress into associate and senior ranks (NCES 2010).

In terms of achieving numeric parity with their male colleagues, faculty women have experienced considerable "demographic inertia" in their progress, which is shaped in part by the academic labor market and also by the age and sex composition of faculty (Hargens & Long 2002). Assuming no gender discrimination, constant faculty size, and equal ability of faculty (a difficult assumption to make), given the current make-up of faculty ranks it would take thirty-five years for the sex composition of the faculty to equalize at the senior ranks (Hargens & Long 2002). In fact, there are a number of factors that make this parity projection unlikely, including delayed faculty retirements, often due to economic factors, and the replacement of vacant tenure track positions with part-time and/or adjunct faculty on annual contracts (Kezar & Sam 2010). In addition, women tend to be older than men when they receive their doctorates, and therefore enter the academic workforce later. Women also enter into faculty positions at a slower rate than men, relative to the number of doctorates earned (Hargens & Long 2002). This slower entry rate is partly attributed to dual career couple constraints; women are more likely than men to subordinate their professional ambitions to their husband's and to be the "trailing" spouse. This is especially likely if both members of the couple are academics (Schiebinger, Henderson & Gilmartin, 2008). These demographic conditions make it unlikely that the academic ranks will ultimately achieve gender parity simply on the basis of time elapsed.

Much of the research into the professional and personal lives of women faculty members has focused on the challenges they face in their chosen profession. The literature highlights the struggles of women to meet professional expectations, including consuming dedication to students, department, college, and discipline, while trying at the same time to raise families and maintain rewarding relationships. Indeed, there has been a tendency to focus on the problems women face as faculty members—they are underpaid, overrepresented in non-tenure-track positions, and likely to carry disproportionate service and teaching loads compared to their male colleagues. The portrait of academic life painted by many contemporary researchers suggests a career of pain and suffering not intended for the weak-willed, faint of heart, or those with (or wanting) a family. The negative tone in the literature about female faculty was cemented by Nadya Aisenberg and Mona Harrington's foundational work, *Women of Academe* (1988), a book that was one of the first to focus on women faculty. Unfortunately, much of the data and the personal accounts in the book are focused on women who were denied tenure and subsequently left academe and the tenure ranks. The negative undertone of Aisenberg and Harrington's work was warranted, given the realities of many women (although certainly not all, as the book suggests) wanting to meld into a largely male-oriented workplace. But as a result, their book failed to capture the stories of those who had succeeded in the academic context, a gap we hope to address in this book.

Looking Forward

The chapters to follow focus on the female faculty members who are at the center of our study. We start in chapter 2 by providing more details about ourselves as researchers, mothers, and professors in addition to information about the study origins and methods. Chapter 3 provides context and perspectives about the academic profession, the norms that guide faculty life, and the choices faculty members make about their careers. Recognizing that change does not always come easily or smoothly in academic contexts, this chapter draws upon theories related to ideal worker norms, life-course development, feminism, and gendered views of work, to prompt readers to think in expanded ways about work and family dilemmas in higher education.

Chapters 4 and 5 highlight the findings from our interviews with early and mid-career faculty members, respectively. We draw on the experiences of the women in the study to present the counternarrative about work and family. Their stories highlight the view that academic life is challenging, but also very rewarding. The academic career provides the opportunity to do work that is intellectually stimulating, satisfying, and that contributes to the development of the next generation of students and scholars in their discipline. Yes, the career is demanding, but it is also flexible. In these chapters we focus on how the roles of faculty members differ at different stages of the academic career.

Although there is much commonality of experiences for tenure-track faculty women with children, there are important contextual differences that are also worth noting. Chapter 6 looks at faculty in the study from the perspective of discipline, and chapter 7 from the perspective of differences in institutional type. Chapter 8 looks at the influence that family background and marital status has on how one balances work and family within an academic career. Chapter 9 explores the experiences of those women who either were denied tenure or opted out of tenure-track positions. Chapter 10 is dedicated to a discussion of departmental and institutional policies and practices as experienced by the women in the study, and suggests ideas for using theory and practice to create and influence change on college and university campuses, with the ultimate goal of making campuses more welcoming, supportive, equitable, and rewarding for professors with families, as well as for all faculty, administrators, and students. We wrap up the book in chapter 11 with recommendations and conclusions from this study.

We believe strongly that the knowledge and experience of the women who make up our study, along with the analysis of academic policies, both in place and proposed, provide insights into the balancing act that is the life of the faculty member with a family, and offer a vision for a future where faculty mothers will find both their professional and private lives more fulfilling and more rewarding. There are now tenure-track women faculty members with young children who do it all and find success. These women who are managing both their personal and professional lives admirably work in a variety of disciplines and a variety of institutional types, and their journeys are individualized but often overlapping. The academic workload may be unending, but tenure-track academic positions offer flexibility and autonomy that make this a viable career choice for those who have a passion for education, research, and service. Admittedly, the success of these women is more often due to their own agency and choices than to the support of their academic institutions. However, there is an increasing recognition by colleges and universities that being "family friendly" is beneficial to institutional mission, success, and productivity. Still, institutions of higher education could do more to be supportive and to make their climates more hospitable, accepting, and facilitative of the success of all their faculty members.

Another theme of this book is that although women make choices about how to live their lives both personally and professionally, these choices are at least partially constrained by societal and institutional expectations of what women should do in the best interests of their families and their careers. Institutional expectations about what it means to be a good professor combine with gendered norms about what it means to be a good mother, and these two norms clash and influence the choices that women make and how they live out their lives. These cultural and gendered institutional expectations mean that colleges and universities need to do more than just have work/family policies on the books. If campuses (and the higher education system as a whole) want to recruit and retain the best faculty, men and women, then they must not only implement policies but they must also create environments that are conducive to using policy. In addition, there is more to an academic career than just the pretenure period and more to parenthood than just taking care of an infant—careers and parenthood are lifelong propositions. Attending to the needs of faculty members at early, mid, and even late career is essential. Colleges and universities need to establish policies and practices and a culture that encourages all faculty members to be productive, successful, and happy institutional citizens. This is necessary in order to recruit and retain the most qualified, generative, diverse, and productive faculty. It is the individual and the institution that together make an academic career and motherhood a viable combination.

CHAPTER 2

Origins of the Study

Before providing more detail about our research study and presenting the findings from the interviews, we thought it would be helpful to present more information about our lives as academics and mothers to provide perspective and background information. We have both spent our careers dedicated to informing practice and theory related to faculty careers and also to creating equitable and just environments for women and people from historically underrepresented groups. We also both became tenure-track professors and mothers along the way, leading us to question some of the traditional notions about faculty life. It is with these perspectives that we now share more information about ourselves as mothers, professors, researchers, and people by way of introducing the study.

OUR STORIES

As authors of this book, we have lives and careers that parallel those of the women described here. Because our own experiences as mothers and scholars have influenced how we came to envision and execute this research project, we present each of our academic and parental stories, in the hope that these narratives provide insight and context for the data and findings that follow.

Lisa's Narrative

I love colleges and universities and have since the moment I set foot on one as a prospective undergraduate. When I graduated from college, after having attended Brown for two years and Stanford for two years, my only goal was to stay on a college campus. I had worked as a resident advisor—a "dorm-mom," as my relatives used to tease me. At the time, someone told me that there was a graduate degree you could get that would help you to understand how institutions of higher education worked and how to be a successful administrator. I found a number of such programs around the country and applied to them. I was pretty naïve and very young—I didn't really know what I was getting myself into, but I figured that a graduate degree focused on the ins and outs of higher education would be a good fit for me. I was right. I attended Claremont Graduate School, where I had the pleasure of working under the tutelage of Daryl Smith, a noted scholar on diversity in higher education, and Jack Schuster, one of the foremost experts on the professoriate. I soaked up everything they offered me—and worked multiple jobs, including one as the coordinator of Residential Education at Scripps College. I started my graduate degree program with the desire to be a dean of students and help students get the most out of their college experience. About mid-way through the program, however, I made a strategic shift in my thinking and career plans. After being a teaching assistant for a statistics class, working on some research projects, and reading more about colleges and universities, I decided I wanted to be a professor. It helped that both of my mentors were parents as well as successful academics. I never talked to them explicitly about how to combine the two paths, but watching them showed me it was possible.

Around this time I met Kelly Ward. She was also a graduate student studying higher education, although she was at Penn State. We met at an academic conference and bonded immediately. Kelly had similar goals and experiences. We didn't know how, but we knew that we were going to collaborate on something at some point in our careers.

Meanwhile, I met a man, Doug, who said he was willing to follow me anywhere if I were to get a faculty job. We dated for five years and then decided to get married right before I graduated with my doctorate. Within a single month, I earned my doctorate in higher education, was offered a faculty position at the University of Kansas, married Doug, packed up our cats, and moved to Kansas to begin life anew as a professor. Doug went back to school to get an MBA, and I settled into life as a not-yet-tenured assistant professor. I experienced the usual types of pretenure traumas—it took me a while to figure out how to teach graduate students, how to use my time effectively, how to get projects done, how to navigate departmental and university politics, and so on. After the first year or so, I felt I had a pretty good handle on things. I would go to my annual academic conference and check in with Kelly and she, too, seemed to be surviving the perils of pretenure. I think it helped that both of us were familiar with the academic profession—not just on the basis of our own experiences but also from the research that we read, taught, and conducted. We knew, better than most assistant professors, what the reality of the academic profession was like.

At some point in my pretenure state, Doug and I decided that we wanted to have children. This turned out to be not as easy as we initially thought it would be—or as they had warned us about when we were younger. It turned out that I had difficulty carrying babies to term; I had two miscarriages in a row and was worried that I wasn't going to be able to have a baby. I had initially thought about timing the birth to come in the summer—but once I experienced the difficulties, I gave up on timing concerns and just hoped to have a baby. After two years of trying unsuccessfully, I learned that I was pregnant again. This time everything turned out well, and I gave birth to a baby girl, Addie. She was (and is) healthy, and we did it—we had a baby while I was on the tenure track.

For the few years that I tried unsuccessfully to have a child, I still carried out my academic work. I wrote articles, I presented papers at conferences, I networked with colleagues across the country, I taught graduate classes, I did service work for my department, school, and university, and I loved every second of it (well, maybe not every second). But I loved my job and I thought it gave me great refuge from the difficulties I was having with trying to have a baby.

Addie's timing turned out to be impeccable. She came the summer before I earned tenure. I gave birth to her and shortly thereafter turned in my tenure dossier. I took no maternity leave, didn't stop my tenure clock, and took no advantage of any policy or practice at my institution. I am no superwoman. The timing and support of my husband and friends made all of this doable. I earned tenure when Addie turned nine months old. I had managed to have a baby (which turned out to be the hard part) and got tenure (which just felt like the natural reward for all of the hard work that I had put into the job).

My life didn't change much post-tenure—I continued to work hard, publish, teach, serve, and so on. Doug took a job on campus at the university theater, and we both obviously had additional responsibilities taking care of Addie, but we seemed to manage pretty well. I hired someone to clean my house (that was great). I hired babysitters to watch Addie (they were wonderful). I pumped breast milk at work—often while typing or even talking on the phone, frequently with Kelly on the line. I had a mommy's group that was made up of a number of women in our community who all had children at the same time; we were all in our late thirties and all worked full time. We had a lot in common and were a constant source of support for one another.

In terms of the effect of having a baby on my work, I think it made me more productive and efficient. I would work really hard during the day time and then rush home to Addie and Doug—and then work really hard at being a good mom until it was time to go to sleep. I recall feeling pretty tired, but also gratified that I had chosen a career that allowed me to succeed in both my personal and professional life.

Two years later (with a third miscarriage in between), I gave birth to Lily. She was born on a Monday in February. I cancelled class that day and returned one week later to teach that class (classes only met once a week). I made no arrangements for maternity leave, and didn't want to impose upon my colleagues to cover for me, although I am sure they would have if I had asked. I felt supported, but also felt I had few options for how to deal with my course load and my new baby. I taught both of my classes with Lily in tow. She was an easy baby, and except for the few times when I had to nurse her while lecturing, I think we did pretty well. I did get a few comments on my class evaluations about seeing my breasts (I tried to be discreet, but it's not easy when you are breastfeeding an infant while teaching). In retrospect, I should have sought a different solution during that semester, but I had a department chair who was interim and he didn't know how to help, and I wasn't sure what to suggest, either. It wasn't an ideal situation, but I still felt lucky that I could do both. I know now, hindsight being 20/20, that I should have asked for more of an accommodation and that I had a right to such assistance. At the time, I just did what I thought I was supposed to do. I didn't help that I was the only woman in my department with young kids at the time, and it didn't help that I am not good at asking for help when I need it.

I survived that semester and then took a well-deserved sabbatical. At this point, Kelly and I had several conversations about ways that we could collaborate. One late night at a conference, we were both talking about how happy our lives had turned out to be. We had jobs we loved, we had families we loved, we had great friends, and great lives. Stories of women who were like us, however, were shockingly absent from the literature we knew about and taught in higher education. Stories of how impossible it was to have a family and an academic career on the tenure track were legendary and prominent. We had seen all the evidence that women faced discrimination, feared using family-friendly policies (even when they were present), and were choosing less-demanding careers. And some of these things we had experienced ourselves. But the overall narrative of how to make it work—not "you can't make it work"—seemed to be missing. We wondered: How do other women faculty balance work and family? How do the different choices that women make about where to work, and when to have to children, get played out in everyday life? This, we decided, was what we wanted to study. We wanted to find real women who were balancing work and family. We wanted to tell how women made it work—not skipping over the hard parts and not pretending that all is rosy—but still presenting this life that we had chosen as possible, doable, and enjoyable.

Kelly's Narrative

When I was a work-study student in Main Hall at the University of Montana, it occurred to me that I wanted to always work on a college campus. Working on a campus is not a career per se, so I started asking around about the different career options. At the time I did not have faculty life in mind, but was interested in some combination of student affairs and academic administration. After some conversations with my undergraduate advisor and a senior administrator on campus, I was off to graduate school. I had a few diversions along the way—one to the ski slopes, one on a cross-country jaunt, and one to a change in graduate school direction—but at some point in the journey I opted into a program to study higher education at

Penn State University. While there, my mind was turned up, down, and all around with all the possibilities that colleges and universities offer as a place to work—Work with students? Work as a faculty member? How about strategic planning? All presented themselves as options to me.

At a conference during my Ph.D. program I sat in a session watching my advisor present a paper, and I had the epiphany that I wanted to teach, do research, and be a faculty member. I also had the realization that I somehow wanted to do it my own way because the research pressures I saw faculty members encounter—sometimes gracefully and sometimes in a pile of stress—intimidated me. I wanted to be a faculty member, but I wanted to do so in a way that comprised a life that included some fun and balance. I'm sure my professors at Penn State had fun and had outside lives, but from my vantage point as a graduate student it didn't seem that way. All that I saw was that their work lives dominated all else.

As I got close to graduation, I was invited to apply for some faculty positions and although I did, I felt fundamentally that I was not ready for such an endeavor. I was young and inexperienced, and heeding some sage advice I got from a friend and colleague, I decided I'd ultimately be better off in my career if I gained some much-needed professional experience working as an administrator before I went on to work in a program that primarily prepares people to work in administration. Good advice. My partner, Gene, was willing to go with me on my adventure, so off we went to my alma mater to work in the same Main Hall that had inspired my desire to work on a college campus to begin with.

As an administrator leading faculty development and community service initiatives, I had an intimate glimpse into faculty life and the tenure process, experience with writing grants, and was able to establish myself as a researcher. After four years I finally felt ready to be a faculty member. I got some teaching experience, which clarified to me that I wanted to teach as a profession, not as a side. I was still intimidated by the whole tenure process, and I continued to feel unsure I could successfully navigate it. I applied for a faculty job, and at about that same time I found out that I was pregnant. I had actually not considered a conflict between work and family/baby and job prior to getting pregnant (although I did plan for a December baby), but as soon as the interview and the pregnancy appeared on the same radar I was instantly concerned. Should I tell them I'm pregnant? If so, when?

Do I need to be worried about this? In short, I felt instantly censored and initially didn't tell anyone I was pregnant for fear it would compromise my chances for an academic job.

I ended up in a different faculty job at the University of Montana, and I did not tell anyone that I was pregnant during the job search process. At our department meeting at the beginning of the school year we did introductions that involved sharing something no one knew about us. Convenient. I shared that I was pregnant and everyone appropriately fawned over me. My pregnancy went on uneventfully, I had the baby, my partner opted to stay home to be a full-time/stay-at-home dad, and I returned to work in January without a hitch. I did not take any leave or miss any work or activate any work/family policies. I did not even know that any existed.

I did not seek to hide my baby, but I felt acutely aware that I needed to have my baby not interfere with my work—and she didn't seem to. When talking to other women on campus, they all told stories of combat and fatigue, so I was a bit spooked by the whole combination of baby and faculty enterprise. I didn't say much and focused on my work. It certainly helped that my husband stayed home so that I was able to focus on work without having to worry about daycare. I was able to do my work guilt free, and I had the luxury of my husband bringing me my baby to feed on the nights I taught.

I took my daughter to conferences with me, which created a new domain to navigate. It was interesting how having a baby put me in conversation with some people who had never before talked to me, and how it removed me from certain other conversations, as well. In some ways I was very public with baby in tow and in other ways quite invisible. Meanwhile, back at the University of Montana there was an unexpected change, and I ended up losing my job due to program realignment (aka "you're fired"). I was crestfallen. I had expected to spend my entire career in Montana, to have a new baby, and be the primary breadwinner for our little family; to have my position eliminated—I was at a loss for what to do. I didn't want to leave. Life was good. This was not supposed to happen to me! My options were to stay in Montana in a non-faculty position—something I did not want to do since I loved faculty life—or leave for another position. I had a year to think about it, and knowing I wanted more than one child, I figured the "terminal" year at Montana would be a good time to have another baby. (I had one colleague who apparently didn't think my having a baby was a good idea because he asked me if I knew what "caused" babies.) I also applied for faculty jobs. In my calculations, I had not factored in a death in the family and interviewing while seven months pregnant. I had some tough days and the occasional bout of tears, but somehow it all worked out and I ended up in a faculty position at Oklahoma State University. I moved to Oklahoma on a very hot August day with an eighteen-month-old and a newborn.

At the time, I felt that having babies didn't affect my career very much. I felt the merging of work and family/baby for me was pretty fluid (certainly aided by a stay-at-home partner). In the midst of all these transitions, my research was focused on faculty development, and there was an increasing national conversation at this time (late 1990s) about how female faculty reconcile work and family (or don't). I had done my dissertation on faculty, and the predominant discourse of the time focused on the negatives of faculty life for women (low pay, dissatisfaction.); the findings of my own research confirmed much of the same. Children were not really part of the equation of my own research or of research about faculty life in general. I'm not sure if it's because I didn't have children when I worked on my dissertation, so didn't see research that addressed the topic, or if it's because children weren't mentioned. When I look back at some of those articles and my own research, it was a little bit of both.

I continued to study faculty, and at a conference I was sitting in a session on female faculty with my nursling nearby, and the negative tone of the session really hit me. I was a female faculty member, sitting with other female faculty members, including Lisa, thinking: "This is a pretty good gig. I'm here at a conference, in a nice city, getting to present my research; I like my job—what's not to like?" It occurred to me that a faculty job is actually a good job for a person who wants to combine a meaningful career and family life. At that moment it seemed to me that a lot of the research was focused on faculty members who faced insurmountable challenges in their careers, many of whom did not stay. I certainly didn't want to negate this story, but I also felt there was another story to tell—that of people, and in particular women, who maintained tenure-track academic careers while raising children. What if we asked women how they managed work and family? What might they say? And so was born a research agenda related to work and family, and a very fruitful collaboration with Lisa as a colleague, fellow mother, co-researcher, and friend.

At the time, the Sloan Foundation was funding projects about work and family, and we were able to obtain support to conduct research to see how female faculty in different institutional contexts managed work and family. We intended to focus on how people managed. We also intended to look at faculty from all different types of institutions, since the preponderance of research in this field focused on research institutions. Over the course of two years (1998–2000) we collected data from women at research universities, liberal arts colleges, community colleges, and regional institutions. We also expanded our work to include a study of department chairs and an investigation of work/family policies.

Meanwhile, my own life went on. I had another tenure-track baby while I was at Oklahoma State, much to the consternation and amazement of many of my colleagues. Three babies! I had a fruitful time at Oklahoma, obviously, and it was a very good time for my career. Then, given an opportunity to migrate back to the Northwest, I moved from Oklahoma to a position at Washington State University. As I evolved professionally and personally, so did my research. Initially I did not see that Lisa and I were participants in our own study, and we did not approach our research that way. However, as we moved along the pipeline—got tenure, earned promotions—just as our participants did, I started to see many of the same milestones we were encountering in our own careers. As we were asked to take on increasing roles and responsibilities at our institutions, we figured that other people were moving along in their career as well.

In 2007 I had a fortuitous conversation with a member of the American Association of University Women about women in the science, technology, engineering, and mathematics (STEM) pipeline and the "leaks" that often take place at critical turning points. I had realized that research focus on the pipeline tends to look at dropout points at the undergraduate, graduate, and early career levels, but not so much at the senior levels. I also knew that at my own institution, as at most across the country, the number of women in the senior ranks was limited and that women do not progress from junior to senior levels at a steady rate. I started to wonder what role family plays in this equation.

Lisa and I had been presenting and publishing our work on early-career faculty women steadily throughout the time of doing this research, but we did not see many people looking at work and family at different stages in the career path. And so we added a longitudinal component to our research.

So here we are. We have both been promoted to full professor. We both have happy and healthy families and strong marriages. While our purpose is not to say, "We did it, you can, too," we do feel that academic motherhood experiences have been underreported and those available are negative in tone. We always have eager graduate students wanting to know when the best time is to have a baby and wanting the recipe for to how to make it all work. Neither question can be given a simple answer. This book, like our own journey, is a testament to the ability to meaningfully combine work and family, a journey that is sometimes smooth and sometimes challenging. We have grown and evolved with the women in this study. In many ways their story is our story, too. With our stories in mind, we now turn to a more detailed description of the study that is the focus of the book.

STUDY METHODOLOGY

Although much of the research on women in higher education has focused on the challenges faced by female faculty, our research and our personal lived experiences suggest that many women have found ways to negotiate the balance between a satisfying and productive academic career and a full and fulfilling family life. Although the professor's job is very challenging on many fronts, we believe that there are many aspects to the position (such as autonomy, flexibility, academic year contracts, and so on) that make motherhood and professorship compatible. We have encountered many women who have disregarded the conventional wisdom and had children while on the tenure track, and contemporary research has begun to acknowledge the existence and experiences of these women (Evans & Grant 2008; Hollenshead et al. 2005; Mason & Goulden 2009; Philipsen & Bostic 2010).

To gain a greater insight into the professional and private lives of mothers on the tenure track, we initiated a study in 1998 to find out more about the experiences of these women, with multiple goals in mind. We believed that information about what academic mothers were encountering in their family and academic lives would provide direction and validation for women in similar situations and for women contemplating combining their desires for families with their aspirations to work in higher education. We also believed that the information gathered would help to provide direction for practices and policies that could improve working conditions for these and other women and their departments and colleges and universities.

The initial study successfully met all of our goals, and eight years later we added a longitudinal component to the study, following up on the professional and personal stories of our participants as their careers progressed. The insights gained from both aspects of the study form the basis of the present book.

Initially, we set out to address the question: How do female faculty members manage work and family while on the tenure track? To address this question, the study initiated in 1998 relied on interviews with women assistant professors who had children aged newborn to five years. The respondents came from research universities, comprehensive/regional institutions, liberal arts colleges, and community colleges. We interviewed approximately 30 women from each institutional type, for a total of 120 participants. The participants in the study represent a range of disciplinary backgrounds (hard sciences to the humanities to the professional schools).

The vast majority of the study participants are European Americans in heterosexual marriages; we did interview one woman in a lesbian relationship (at a comprehensive institution) and three single mothers (two at community colleges and one at a comprehensive institution). We also interviewed several women of color (three at research universities, three at comprehensive colleges, three at liberal arts colleges, and six at community colleges). Although the numbers do not allow for any type of generalization for women in particular circumstances, we are careful to take into account their unique experiences in the analysis.

In the first phase of the study (1998–2000), the average age of women in the research universities was thirty-six; the average age of women at the community colleges was thirty-four. The average age for the women in the liberal arts colleges and at the comprehensive institutions was thirty-seven. The average number of children of faculty at the research universities was 1.5 (with 53 percent having only one child); the average number of children for women at the comprehensive institutions was 1.8 children each (with

32 percent having only one child). The average number of children for women at the liberal arts colleges was 1.7 (with 60 percent having only one child), and the average for women at community colleges was 1.9 (with 40 percent having only one child). The sample configuration supported the goal of the study: to learn more about how faculty members manage the dual roles of faculty and motherhood of young children within different institutional contexts.

The institutions in the study also represented variety in terms of geographic location and institutional prestige. Approximately half of the research university faculty members we interviewed were from member institutions of the prestigious Association of American Universities (twelve out of twenty-seven); the other half were from research universities (I or II) as classified by the Carnegie Classification scheme in 1994. The most recent Carnegie Classification schemes do not allow for appropriate institutional comparisons, so we rely on the 1994 criteria. Research I institutions are those that offer a full range of baccalaureate programs, are committed to graduate education through the doctorate, give high priority to research, and annually receive $40 million or more in a federal support. Research II institutions have essentially the same mission as Research I's, but grant fewer doctorates and receive less research funding. Two-thirds of the faculty members from liberal arts colleges (twenty out of thirty) worked at institutions listed as "prestigious" according to *U.S. News and World Report*. These institutions attract a national student clientele, are quite selective in admissions, and have ample financial resources. The other faculty members worked at liberal arts colleges that are more regional in nature, have more modest endowments, and are tuition dependent. The comprehensive colleges were a mix of public and private institutions that offer both undergraduate and master's degrees; they all attract a regional student clientele. On a post-hoc basis, based on the interviews, we labeled some of these comprehensive institutions as "striving" because they seemed to be emulating more prestigious research universities (eleven out of twenty-seven). We will talk more about this in chapter 7. The community colleges in the study included a mix of urban, rural, and suburban institutions, varying greatly in size and resources. Ten of the participants from community colleges were at institutions that were founding members of the League for Innovation, typically the most well-known, largest, and resource-rich institutions within the community college sector.

We identified participants through existing networks, on-campus child care centers, and by asking participants to identify colleagues who also met the inclusion criteria (women, on the tenure track, pretenure, with children under the age of five). Interviews lasted for approximately 1.5 hours and were guided by a semi-structured interview protocol. Questions focused on the relationship between professional life and parenthood, sources of support, sources of tension, prospects for tenure, and strategies for maintaining balance and sanity. We detail the findings of this first phase of the research in chapter 4. These interviews took place from 1998 to 2000. In addition to using data from the interviews of the participants throughout the book, as is common in qualitative research, we also created vignettes that combine the stories of multiple participants to tell a more compelling story that cuts across the individual interviews to illustrate key points. Vignettes are described by the researchers Ely, Vinz, Anzul, and Downing (1997) as vehicles that "carry within them an interpretation of data" (10). The vignettes emanate directly from the interviews and combine quotes with paraphrases. The vignettes are a nontraditional way of representing qualitative findings, which we chose because we believed it would make the results more readable and accessible. Vignettes are a means of conveying shared experiences, demonstrating patterns and trends of many people simultaneously. In addition, we use more traditional qualitative techniques to provide individual voices and share experiences beyond the composite vignettes.

Knowing that careers and families are both dynamic, and also seeing that the focus on work and family research for academics was focused on early-career faculty members, starting in 2008 we added a longitudinal component to our study by following up with women from the initial study to see how their careers and families were evolving. We were able to conduct interviews with 87 of the initial 120 women. A combination of factors prevented us from interviewing all the initial women, including logistical challenges of conducting the interviews (such as sabbaticals in distant lands), the inability to find some of the women who had left their initial positions, and the preference of some who did not want to be interviewed either for personal reasons ("I don't want to talk about life right now") or logistical ones ("I'm too busy to talk").

The breakdown of the 87 women we interviewed a second time was as follows: 23 women from research universities, 19 from comprehensive universities, 23 from liberal arts colleges, and 22 from community colleges. The second phase of the study was guided by the following research questions: What happened personally and professionally to the women since the initial study? And what ideas do study participants have about their dual roles now that they are more firmly established in their careers? The focus of chapter 5 is the findings from this phase of the study.

A longitudinal perspective is unique in work and family research related to higher education and affords insight into the ongoing interaction between work and family and about how having children shapes decisions about the academic career over time. Such information is important to help guide policy, inform decisions about pursuing an academic career, learn about different time-based aspects of the career (that is, achievement of tenure, pursuit of promotions), and learn how the interaction between work and family persists as children grow and careers develop. A longitudinal perspective is also helpful given the pipeline perspective that permeates research related to faculty life. As stated earlier, conventional wisdom suggests that as more women enter the workforce as assistant professors, ultimately there will be more women rising into associate and full professor levels and also into administration. On the basis of our own experience as well as evidence from related research about the academic career and the pipeline (e.g., Mason & Goulden 2002, 2004), we suspected that the path from incoming assistants to senior chairs might be more complex than a simple progression from one stage to another. In addition, knowledge gained from the initial study into the complexities and nuances of families and the progression of life with children led us to believe there was much to learn from and about women as they progressed throughout their careers.

This book also incorporates data, findings, and perspectives that emerged from two additional studies related to work and family with which we were involved. One was an examination of policies at the different institutions where we conducted the interviews. The second study involved four case studies of particular institutions where faculty women in the initial study worked. These cases were studied and analyzed as a way to garner other perspectives than those of the women in the study. We interviewed department chairs, senior and junior faculty, male and female faculty, and faculty with and without children as a way to gather more complete information about departmental contexts and to get multiple perspectives on academic motherhood. Although the case study project data are not the focus here, these data are referenced throughout the book.

Following this explanation of our backgrounds and perspectives and the methodology that we use as the basis of this book, the following chapter turns to a more thorough discussion of the theories and ideas that guided our thinking as the project and data analysis evolved. Some of these theories and ideas were introduced in chapter 1, and all of them are used throughout the analyses in the book. Although we hesitate to have this next chapter read like a "literature review" from a dissertation, we are believers in the idea that good research owes its origins to the work that comes before it, and therefore feel it is important for readers to be aware of the existing relevant theory and research that informs this book.

CHAPTER 3

Understanding the Existing Narratives and Counternarratives

There is a "narrative of constraint," reinforced in the research literature and in academic lore, which suggests that tenure-track faculty life is not compatible with outside pursuits, like motherhood. The label was introduced by KerryAnn O'Meara and her colleagues, Aimee LaPointe Terosky and Anna Neumann (2008), who pointed out that the tone of existing research imposes internal and external constriction, control, and limits on how people view academic work. Although their monograph maintains that there are important experiences that counter the narrative of constraint, when one reads the academic literature on the topic of work and family (in all domains, but in higher education in particular), a narrative of possibility is hard to find. The existing narrative is clear that motherhood and work as a tenure-track faculty member are difficult propositions separately, and are especially challenging when taken together. It is helpful to understand the perspective that emanates from the literature, even though it is negative, because it provides an opportunity to explore the strongly held beliefs in the field. Dominant norms and existing literature, as in most research, provide important reference points for understanding the phenomena under study, even though they can also be limiting in terms of how people think about particular problems.

The goal of our work is to present a counternarrative of what it means to be an academic and a mother. To get to this counternarrative we rely on the stories that emanate from the personal experiences of women who have managed the rigors of academic life and the realities of motherhood in early and mid-career. We also use theory as a way to help us think differently about these experiences. It is superficially easy to rely on pipeline arguments—as more women enter the academic workforce and have children, the problems associated with work and family will dissipate. Yet our research, as well as the research of other scholars, points to the flaws in this line of thinking. We have found theory to be helpful to guide and broaden our thinking as we grapple with the different aspects of what it means to be a mother and an academic.

We note that initially, the role of theory in the project was minimal. We went into the study focused on faculty career stage and institutional type, and intentionally selected participants who met our criteria in these areas; as such, we analyzed the data mindful of these perspectives. We also wanted to be sure to include women from different walks of life in terms of demographics and other background characteristics. Beyond that, in the initial stages of the project, we had not been very attentive to other theoretical perspectives. Although we both consider ourselves to be feminists, we did not set out to deliberately take on a feminist project. Tenets of feminism were part of the project in terms of the questions we asked and the assumptions we had about women and work, but it was not a deliberate focus and not integrated into our early analyses. Once we started conducting the interviews, however, we continually came across situations and findings that defied simple explanation. We needed more explicit theoretical frameworks to help us fine-tune how to make sense of what it was that we were starting to find. Accordingly, we turned to existing research to find theoretical grounding.

There are four different theoretical perspectives we now use as lenses in our work. The first lens is rooted in the writings about ideal worker norms. We present it as a means to understand the negative narrative. The other three frameworks provide a means to grasp more fully what is involved to get to a counternarrative. The first of these is focused on life-course perspectives, which is especially important because our study looks at women in two distinct periods of their lives, early career when their children are young, and mid-career when their children are school aged. Parenthood and careers are not static. Understanding how career and life development, with special attention to the career stages of an academic life, may influence these women's perspectives and experiences is very important to provide a holistic (and realistic) view of career development and family formation. The next theoretical lens, feminist theory, helps to frame the lives of women in a larger societal context where gender and power shape how people interface with the workplace and the roles they play in their families. We look specifically at two types of feminist theory—liberal feminism and poststructural feminism. The two frameworks provide different and important perspectives to contextualize and help us better understand our findings. The fourth lens, although not a theory per se, comprises a set of constructs we categorize as "gendered views" of work and family to provide theoretical grounding. Many of these constructs are informed by feminist theory, and they offer important perspectives for us to consider as we make sense of the findings as they relate to academic life and motherhood in contemporary settings.

The Negative Narrative: Professorial Mystique and Ideal Worker Norms

As we noted in chapter 1, the academic career is imbued with mystique and particular workplace norms about what it takes to be successful. Faculty career mystique and faculty ideal worker norms set up an expectation that make it difficult to imagine how a mother in today's society would be able to balance work and family, especially in a tenure-track position. In our research it has been particularly important to maintain awareness of the intricacies of the tenure quest and the strength of ideal worker norms, given how these nuances and norms shape what it means to be an academic in the contemporary academic workplace.

The tenure system favors ideal workers—those who can dedicate them-selves to their academic pursuits above all else. The professorship is based on a monastic tradition, and the tenure system tends to reward those who sublimate private concerns to their jobs (Finkelstein 1984). As noted earlier, achievement of tenure is typically a six- or seven-year process that introduces faculty members to their positions through a probationary process wherein they have to prove themselves to maintain their position. The reward for success is considerable—a continual contract, the protection of academic freedom, job security, and the lifelong right to due process. But the up-or-out nature of the tenure process creates considerable pressure for novitiates. It means that faculty members either advance through the academic ranks and achieve tenure or they fail to advance and lose their positions.

The culture of tenure has created an environment of competition that appears to reward dedication to the position—the professorship—above all else in life. This is the very description of the ideal worker. These norms are characteristic of the notions put forth by Phyllis Moen in her work on career mystique (Moen & Roehling 2005). She argues that it is a myth that hard work leads to career success and that career failure is a result of simply not working hard enough. Faculty members, like individuals in other professions, have created an ideal expectation that does not allow individuals time out from their careers without being seen as nonproductive. Further, if they take too many breaks, workers (that is, faculty members) are viewed by their colleagues as not working hard enough. Moen explains that part of career mystique is the idea that "clocking in" and being present is often more important than actual productivity. This career mystique is particularly acute in the academic profession because of stereotypes and beliefs about faculty members held by those outside the profession (and even by some in the profession) that the career is easy and requires little commitment, and the need to counteract that belief by maintaining that it is a strenuous job requiring untiring commitment.

Clearly such an environment shapes how people think about their work. For women, in particular, this shapes how they think about their families in relation to work. Given the history of the academic workplace as a male enclave, it is important not only to consider norms that govern faculty life but to also keep in mind how gender plays into these norms. In our society, both men and women face gendered expectations and norms. One such norm faced by women is that if they are to have children then they must fulfill their role as primary care giver; they face the related expectations of what it means to be an ideal mother. As the literature portrays, ideal mothers are dedicated solely to the care of their children, a proposition that would exclude women from full participation in the workforce (Drago 2007; Somerville 2000).

The history and culture of work still today favor commitment to the public, rather than the private, sphere, and the history and culture of motherhood still favor commitment to the private sphere. The notion of public and private spheres is a very important idea to frame discussions related to academic work and family, because even in this era in which women have made great progress in their ability to access the workplace as professionals, women have *historically* been relegated to doing their work in the private sphere, in the home, while men were expected to do their work in the public sphere, outside of the home. Although there has been significant progress in challenging the expectation of clearly delineated and mutually exclusive private spheres for women and public spheres for men, the norms and history associated with these spheres are important to consider in any exploration of work and family.

We note here that the delineation of private and public is largely applicable to educated white men and women with middle- and upper-middle-class backgrounds. The focus on work and family, on how women can balance both, and on how their workplaces ought to be accommodating, is clearly an issue rooted in socioeconomic privilege (Williams 2010). For many groups of women, including historically disenfranchised racial and ethnic minorities, immigrant women, and women from lower socioeconomic statuses, work has always been a necessity—and there has been little or no attention paid to their concerns about work's effect on their family lives. These women have always had to negotiate the tensions of work outside the home and family within very different rules and expectations about what is private and what is public. The history and many of the observations that we make throughout this book, unfortunately, do not necessarily represent the experiences and perspectives of all women in the workforce—just those who are in the academic profession and who have the privilege and luxury of demanding a workplace that recognizes their multiple roles. This is a shortcoming of the existing literature and also a shortcoming of our own work in some regards. Despite this caveat, the specter of gendered norms and the primacy of gendered role expectations set up a potential disconnect with the norms and expectations of a tenure-track academic career.

The Counternarratives: Theoretical Considerations

Life-Course Perspectives

The life-course perspective suggests that, depending on an individual's life stage, different factors take on varying levels of importance (Han & Moen 1999; Roehling et al. 2001). This perspective highlights the "web of interdependence between the public (work) and private (family) threads of adult lives, the interactions between work family experiences of men and women, and the contextual nature of the work family interface over time and across multiple domains" (Han & Moen 1999, 99). A life-course view emphasizes the integration and interaction of different spheres. What happens in one sphere, such as the family, shapes what happens in other spheres, such as work. We rely on the focus on interdependence and integration in different life spheres and in different life stages to guide our understanding of work and family for female faculty members. It is necessary to adopt a holistic perspective in order to fully understand faculty life for women.

Life-course perspectives move beyond an emphasis on structure to an understanding of the simultaneity of different domains and how they unfold over time (Han & Moen 1999). This is an especially useful lens to understand the concepts of transitions and trajectories as they relate to academic career development. The different life domains of women academics (that is, work and family) are particularly important concepts to consider from a temporal perspective at times of transition within both professional and family trajectories.

With regard to motherhood, the life-course perspective takes into account that having a child and other family events influence individuals in multiple and complex ways, including a person's interface with the workplace. Becoming a parent is a sociohistorical event that is tied not to simply having a child but also to other things taking place in life. For professional women, in particular, having a child is often timed in relation to career and educational milestones, and is not always tied to a simple linear progression (such as marriage then children). In addition, the life-course emphasis is not simply on having a child but also on being a parent and how that changes over time. A lot of the discourse about work and family is focused on how people manage work and family when they have a baby and their children are young. Children, however, are lifelong propositions, and the life-course perspective acknowledges that parenthood, and in particular motherhood, given our focus here, evolves over time.

The life-course perspective also informs how people approach their work. The faculty career is typically viewed as a linear pipeline, from undergraduate degree, to graduate degree, to post-doc, to assistant professor, to associate professor, to full professor, to retirement. Each one of these stages has its issues and struggles and its own levels and layers of stress. Milestones and, therefore, growth and development in the academic professional sphere play an important role in how academics view their own aspirations and identities over time (O'Meara, Terosky, & Neumann 2008). A life-course perspective, however, takes a more fluid and holistic approach to understanding careers. For example, Roger Baldwin and Robert Blackburn (1981) build on research related to adult and career development and apply it directly to the academic career. Their focus is on career stages and development and they outline a linear progression. As a first step, Baldwin and Blackburn identify five career stages of faculty:

- Assistant professors in the first three years of full-time college teaching.
- Assistant professors with more than three years of college teaching experience.
- Associate professors.
- Full professors more than five years from retirement.
- Full professors within five years of formal retirement.

The intent of delineating these stages is to illustrate the hierarchy of the academic career and to understand some of the key turning points that define each stage. A fair amount of research has been done to understand early-career faculty members, including the transition from graduate school. Recognizing a paucity of understanding beyond early-career faculty, recent research (e.g., Baldwin et al. 2005; Britton 2009; Neumann 2009; Neumann & Terosky 2007) has examined the mid-career faculty stage more fully, although it continues to be an area that is not well understood. The associate professor category comprises a large group that includes newly tenured faculty members who are thirty years old as well as individuals who have been tenured for twenty-five years and are over sixty years old. Research by Baldwin and Blackburn (1981) and, more recently, Baldwin et al. (2005) suggests that there are important differences between early and mid-career faculty members. In particular, Baldwin et al. (2005) note that existing research suggests that "faculty work during midlife and beyond has a perceptibly different character than the work distribution of early-life faculty" (7). They also note that as professors gain control over their work, they seek more balance between their work and family lives. These authors acknowledge the complexity and also the challenges associated with studying faculty members at mid-career, which can encompass both associate and full professors, depending on how the broad category of mid-career is defined. A recent study by Anna Neumann (2009) on early-career associate professors (those who recently earned tenure and were promoted) showed that this group serve a very important role within colleges and universities and that they require more nurturing and support than they are receiving. In particular, Neumann concludes that this group of faculty often maintain active research agendas and play significant and active roles in institutional service; they are the life-blood of many academic institutions. However, they need attention and support in order to move to the next level within their career, or potentially they will face burnout.

Not only does work have stages but so does family life. Our research clearly indicates that decisions about academic work and decisions about family are not static nor are they independent of one another. They are also not limited to linear characterizations, especially for women, but may be more open and fluid. Although it is important to acknowledge academic career stages, a life-course perspective helps more fully capture the nuances that take place throughout the career and how other domains of life, including family, interface with the career. Although not all female academics have children, family formation and evolution nonetheless play a role in how women plan their careers and daily lives (and also how they are perceived by others). A life-course perspective allows us to simultaneously consider how work decisions shape family and how family decisions shape work throughout the career.

Feminist Theory

Feminist theory allows us to look at organizational and societal structures and how they shape understanding of academic work and family for female professors. A feminist perspective also provides a vehicle to look at women and gender as key analytic approaches to create change—a particularly important component of creating a counternarrative. Common to all theoretical perspectives that align with feminism are the following assumptions:

- Sex and gender inequality exists and is central to social relations and the structure of social institutions.
- Sex and gender inequality is not "natural" or essential but a product of social relations.
- Sex and gender inequality should be eliminated through social change. (Allan 2011, 18)

In spite of these commonalities, there are also different theoretical approaches that further define feminism. In our work (and also in existing research related to women, work, and family) two predominant approaches have been used and can be helpful. As we see it, to understand and call for change in higher education we need to look more closely at liberal and poststructural views of feminism. First, we introduce the theories of liberal feminism and poststructural feminism. Then, we use these lenses to look at some of the gendered aspects of work and family in higher education, especially with regard to policy, practice, and change. Later in the book we also use these lenses to help us analyze the data and make policy recommendations.

Liberal perspectives. Liberal feminism posits that women should be entitled to the same "natural rights" as men (Donovan 2000). This is a viewpoint that gives way to the contemporary notion of equal opportunity (Acker 1987). Liberal feminism is a response to a workforce and society that restrict women's full participation. For liberal feminism to be realized, women should be "free and equal" to participate in society unencumbered by traditionally defined gender roles, and women should be afforded full participation in the workplace. Liberal feminism is grounded in the notion that men and women are created equal and that policies and practices ought to level the playing field for them to compete on an equal footing (Donovan 2000). This is the predominant view used to create gender-equitable workplaces.

The thinking goes that if institutions create more equitable policies and workplaces, then women will perform and progress in ways that mirror men. Thus the liberal view of feminism is a predominant view used on campuses wanting to improve the conditions of the workplace for women, and is the basis for creating work/family-friendly policy. Elizabeth Allan's (2011) monograph on women in higher education uses the example of studies on gender pay inequities as an example of liberal feminism; the goal of such studies, she argues, is to discover if inequity exists and, if so, to redress it through policy or formal mechanisms within the institution. This lens offers some insight into understanding how institutions have responded to work/family needs in the past. Our research and that of many others, however, shows that this is clearly not enough, leading us to additional forms of feminist theory and more nuanced ways of looking at work and family in the academy and the underlying structures of colleges and universities.

Poststructural feminism. The feminist poststructural lens is helpful as one thinks about some of the constraints women still face as they seek to accomplish the dual roles of mother and professor. Although many campuses have instituted policies to mitigate these constraints, guided by a liberal assumption that women ought to have equal access to workplaces, and that creating policy will help create a level playing field, these policies and practices have been incomplete. A liberal view can obfuscate workplace structures that are foundationally inequitable. The poststructural feminist argument is that creating policies in workplaces that are fundamentally inequitable to women will be limited in their effectiveness because they only deal with the symptoms and not the disease. In contrast, a poststructural view of feminism focuses more on gender in relationship to foundations and structures. Feminist poststructuralism "is a mode of knowledge production which uses poststructuralist theories of language, subjectivity, social processes and institutions to understand existing power relations and to identify areas and strategies for change" (Weedon 1997, 40). Feminist poststructural analysis emphasizes understanding gender and gender differences in social structures through the lens of discourse and the power relationships that are manifest through discourse. Such a perspective allows for the examination of women's experiences and shows how these experiences relate to social practices and the power relations that support and structure them (Weedon 1997). Poststructural feminism focuses on language, meaning, power, difference, and subjectivity (Allan 2011; Allan et al. 2009; Ropers-Huilman 1998; Scott 1988; Weedon 1997).

A core element of a feminist poststructural theoretical position is advocacy for change—this is a framework that questions the status quo and seeks to address inequitable social systems and divisions of labor from the perspective of gender (Weedon 1997). The poststructural feminist perspective is particularly useful to us as it helps us think about our research as a vehicle to change higher education. In higher education, a poststructuralist view helps to uncover deeply held assumptions about the workplace and particularly how gender shapes those assumptions (Allan 2011). It is also a way to look at how overlapping identities interact and shape work and personal life. We refer to both liberal and poststructural feminism to help us understand our findings.

Gendered Norms and Cultural Expectations
Related to Work and Family

In addition to understanding life-course perspectives and liberal and poststructural feminism, there is also a body of literature that is often used in reference to work and family research that looks at gendered norms and cultural expectations of women and men. Although many of these perspectives have ties to feminism in that they look at power and gender, we group them separately because they focus more on the micro concepts that can shape how women with children experience the academic workplace. These perspectives are useful because they acknowledge how women operate in both the public and private spheres of their lives and the gendered norms of these spheres. They have also been helpful to us throughout this project as we look at how people change in their careers and in their families, in addition to the decisions people make about work and family.

Historically, women were excluded from the public sphere of work, leaving many of the normative structures of the workplace to be defined in male-oriented ways. This is particularly true of the academic workplace, where the structures and timing of tenure, for example, do not take into account issues of childbirth and external demands on a faculty member's time. The body of research that critiques the workplace using concepts of gender schemas, male time clocks, greedy institutions, bias avoidance, satisficing, buffering, and accumulative disadvantage are the focus of this section. The conceptual views presented here are perspectives that have been used in previous research as well as in our own research, as a way to guide our understandings and interpretations of how female faculty manage the complexities of work and family and how these structures are shaped by gendered positions.

Gender schemas. In an effort to understand the relatively slow advancement of women in higher education, Virginia Valian (1998, 2005) utilizes the social cognitive concept of gender schemas. Gender schemas are the hidden assumptions people hold about gender that tend to overrate men and underrate women. Gender schemas examine the "the moment-by-moment perceptions and judgments that disadvantage women" (Valian 2005, 200). These perceptions can undermine women's progress toward promotion, tenure, and career advancement within the academic career. Within the framework of gender schemas, strongly held cultural beliefs about what is possible and appropriate for women with regard to both work and family contribute to how women fare in hiring and promotion processes and are a way to explain why it is that women do not advance as readily as men in the academic workplace.

Since mothering is a gendered phenomenon that can lead to hidden assumptions about proper roles for women as mothers (for example, staying at home with children, being the primary caregiver, taking care of the house), gender schemas and perceptions held about women as mothers can thwart women's abilities to advance professionally once they become parents. Beliefs and perceptions about socially appropriate roles for women, many of them hidden, can undermine women in their quest for equity and advancement as faculty. Women can pay a "motherhood penalty" for deviating from prescribed behaviors based on their predefined gender roles, which can lead to, among other things, lower salaries and less workplace respect (Budig & Hodges 2010). Motherhood penalties stem from women displaying behaviors associated with workplace success that are out of sync with motherhood and caregiving. Interestingly, women who engage in these "successful" workplace behaviors are not only seen as neglecting their parenting roles but also as not as highly valued for their behaviors as men might be. Conversely, there is discussion in the literature about fatherhood premiums, which accrue to men who prioritize being a "good worker" over assuming caregiving roles. By being good workers, men are rewarded accordingly; they are also rewarded when they engage in "good parenting."

An example of this comes when men are praised for being a good father when they leave work early to pick up a child from daycare, while women who engage in the same behavior are seen as not committed enough to the workplace. Such beliefs are not only held externally but also might be internalized by the women and men about their own assigned gender roles. For example, women see themselves as "bad mothers" rather than as good workers when they place work obligations before family, and they feel they have to hide their mothering duties that might interfere with work.

Gender schemas are often present even in environments that outwardly seem to seek gender equity—which is often the case in higher education. There is a tendency in such environments to overlook the micro inequities that can accumulate to disproportionately hold back women in their careers. The beliefs people hold and the actions they take based on gender schemas accumulate over time to significantly disadvantage women. Taken individually, each inequity (such as a delay in promotion, a smaller raise) may seem innocuous, but the outcomes of these inequities compound over time (as in the case of salary), and they also accumulate to create imbalances in the senior and leadership ranks (see the section below on cumulative disadvantage).

In understanding gender schemas, it is important to recognize that colleges and universities are gendered organizations, meaning that they still hold expectations of people and positions based on gendered norms (Acker 1990; Britton 2009). People in these organizations hold perceptions of what it means to be successful, and many of these perceptions are based on traditional gender roles that dictate that to be professionally successful involves total commitment to the organization, to the exclusion of outside interests.

Male time clocks. A related theoretical explanation of women and their challenges as mothers in academic careers is one that posits that the tenure clock is based on a male time clock (Hochschild 1975; Williams 2000a). As one study explains: "The clockwork of the [academic] career is distinctly male. That is, it is built upon men's normative paths and assumes freedom from competing responsibilities, such as family, that generally affect women more than men." (Grant et al. 2000). The tenure timetable, given the realities of age and biological clocks and having to prove expertise in the first seven years of the career, is tuned to men who are presumed, ideally, to have no outside interests or responsibilities such as family, and is often in direct conflict with female clocks (Bailyn 2003, 2011). The idealized trajectory of a faculty career (from graduate school to assistant, associate, and full professor, in direct succession) may not describe the actual or expected career of an academic woman. For some women, the balance between work and family disrupts the standard timetable. In the interest of spouses, children, or personal commitments, women may extend or suspend their graduate school careers (the average age of women when they earn their doctorates is 34); they may wait to join the professoriate, or attempt to stop or slow the tenure clock (Ward & Bensimon 2002). This creates tension for faculty women who seek to combine work and family and can lead to the view that the two are mutually exclusive.

Greedy institutions. The concept of "greedy institutions" put forth by Lewis Coser is a helpful conceptual lens to understand the tensions that emerge from the simultaneous pressures of parenthood and the tenure track. Greedy institutions are those that "seek exclusive and undivided loyalty." Further, they "exercise pressures on component individuals to weaken their ties or not to form any ties, with other institutions or persons that might make claims that conflict with their own demands" (1974, 6). Academic organizations are greedy institutions, and faculty life and the tenure track, in particular, are marked by the call for an all-consuming commitment to conform to the ideal worker norms described above. The occupation of parenthood is also a greedy institution and, given the dynamics of the second shift, is particularly greedy for women. While both men and women have second-shift responsibilities, research shows that women disproportionately take on second-shift responsibilities related to child care and homemaking (Hochschild 1989). What happens when the greedy institutions of motherhood and academic life come face to face? Throughout our research we have grappled with this question.

Bias avoidance. Our research and other studies suggest that faculty members in general skirt issues associated with work and family policies by using bias avoidance strategies (Colbeck & Drago 2005; Drago 2007). In extreme cases, this means not having a baby at all or employing such strategies as having a baby in the summer or returning to work as soon after birth as possible without missing any (or very little) work (Williams 2004). The goal of such strategies is to avoid bias by eliminating the need to call upon the campus for support. Using such strategies, of course, assumes situations where a woman can plan her due date to coincide with the academic calendar, and where the baby arrives on time and without complications. Bias avoidance is rooted in fear. Faculty members, women in particular, are fearful that if they use work/family policies to assist them they will be seen as "weak" and will face negative repercussions. This fear is rooted in dominant discourses associated with tenure and academic culture. The fear is also triggered by the need for women to maintain legitimacy as faculty members. Women as "outsiders in the sacred grove" of the academy still occupy a tenuous place in the academic hierarchy (Aisenberg & Harrington 1988; Cooper & Stevens 2002). Dominant discourses prevail and dictate what the tenure process "should" look like, and these discourses do not allow for stopping the tenure clock or taking a leave without fear of bias and/or retribution. Women faculty members go to great lengths to avoid what they perceive as potential bias (Drago & Colbeck 2003), and do everything in their power to avoid taking advantage of policies or programs that might assist them in negotiating work and family demands.

Satisficing. One of the concepts that we have used in our work is that of "satisficing," an economic term used to describe decisions that are "good enough" though not necessarily optimal (Simon 1981, 35). When applied to people, in this case faculty members, satisficing is a coping mechanism used to do the best one can to meet responsibilities, knowing that it might not be possible to fulfill all of the responsibilities and expectations an institution places on its workers. In the case of women with children, satisficing is used as a way to manage work responsibilities to the best of their abilities and in ways they might not have had to if there were fewer roles to play and responsibilities to juggle.

Life on the tenure track calls for faculty members to engage in what can seem like an unending workload. There is always more work to be done, more grants to write, more articles to publish, more papers to grade, more committees on which to serve. Satisficing is one way to explain how people get their work done in the face of endless workloads, given the reality and limitations of time, energy, and resources. This phenomenon is not unique to women faculty with children, as all junior faculty members are constantly faced with deliberations over quality versus quantity in teaching and research (Boice 1992; Tierney & Bensimon 1996). We found, however, that it is likely that these pressures are compounded for junior women faculty with children, and that satisficing may be more prevalent among this group.

Buffering. Buffering is a moderating process that suggests the "negative effects of stress or failure in one role can be buffered by successes and satisfactions in another role" (Barnett & Hyde 2001, 786). Buffering provides time-out, perspective, and protection of self-esteem. As noted by Faye Crosby (1991), when stress accumulates in one sphere, people can buffer themselves by shifting their focus to concerns in the other sphere. Women who have children buffer themselves from the stress and the all-consuming nature of the academic career simply because they have to. For example, if a child gets sick, calling for the need to leave work, there are sometimes the hidden benefits of getting more time to complete a project or simply having a mandated time out from work—home life "buffers" work. Movement back and forth between spheres can give women in the workplace a positive sense of "time out," which eases stress and tension. On the other hand, for professional women, accomplishments in the workplace can buffer consuming stresses at home. The gratification of professional accomplishment can help put children's temper tantrums and household chores into perspective. In turn, the presence of a child can buffer women from the harsh realities at work.

In the academic setting, buffering is a particularly apt perspective given the finite nature of the tenure clock and the "up or out" repercussion of not achieving tenure. Having a life that includes a family can help buffer faculty women from work realities that can include not getting promoted. Having a child can help put into perspective successes and failures at work and is a mechanism to protect self-esteem. This is something we heard repeatedly from the women in our study and something we have experienced personally.

Engaging in multiple roles can also help buffer work and family realities by providing a broader frame of reference, as "multiple-role holders have many more opportunities to get perspective on their ups and downs than do single-role holders" (Barnett & Hyde 2001, 788). This is apparent for working women, especially those in faculty positions, who can use their multiple roles to keep the rigors of the tenure track, the ambiguity of tenure and promotion expectations, and the consuming nature of academic work in perspective. When unable to produce at high levels or when needing to satisfice, a child provides perspective and justification for doing so. A broader frame of reference also provides a mechanism to transcend fear of failure about tenure decisions and see a broad base of options. There are other ways to have a broadened frame of reference, to be sure, but research indicates that having children achieves this and expands notions of identity, especially for women.

While buffering and expanded frames of reference provide helpful coping skills, the ability to use family and work in this manner requires a delicate balance. Multiple roles can also lead to negative spillover (Sorcinelli & Near 1989) and create overload involving greedy institutions. When either work or home life is threatened or added to (by a sick child or ailing parents, for example, or when a paper is due), disequilibria, stress, and nonproductivity are likely. Quality of the professional role is crucial to enabling optimal functioning in other roles (Crosby 1991). If a professional finds herself in an untenable work situation, it is harder to reap the benefits of integrated roles, buffering, and an expanded frame of reference. Professional role quality hinges upon the opportunity for professionals to vie for success, and in the case of tenure-line academics to earn tenure, in ways that allow one to function fully as a professional and a mother. When the workplace calls upon people to make an unhealthy commitment to their career, especially in the case of tenure where the probationary period is finite, role quality can be diminished. Having buffers provides an important coping strategy.

Cumulative (dis)advantage. Women have made great progress in the academic ranks, but they continue to be significantly underrepresented in many disciplines, in the highest ranks, and at the most prestigious institutions. In part, this can be attributed to the concept of cumulative disadvantage. The earliest conceptualization of cumulative disadvantage related to female faculty was in a study conducted by Shirley Clark and

Mary Corcoran (1986) who theorized that, just as individuals accumulate and compound wealth, they can also accumulate and compound advantage and disadvantage in their careers. Success as a faculty member is really an accumulation of advantage over time, in which faculty members exploit small gains to obtain greater gains (Merton & Rossi 1968). This is also known as the "Matthew effect," where the "rich get richer and the poor get poorer." For female faculty, as Virginia Valian (2005) also points out, this means that small inequities can build over time to create fairly large disparities and inequities between men and women. Professional women, including faculty members who end up at a slight disadvantage in interactions with colleagues, senior faculty, department chairs, and deans, can accumulate a fairly significant disadvantage over time (Valian 1998).

For junior female faculty, the combination of work and family can contribute to part of the disadvantage they accumulate (Grant et al. 2000). This disadvantage is presented in two ways in the literature. First, from a comparative perspective, women are at a disadvantage when compared to male colleagues when the variable of parenthood is considered. For men, having a child actually increases productivity, whereas for women it has a negative effect (Hargens et al. 1978; Sonnert & Holton 1995). Second, the literature presents some general nuances of academic life and how they might disadvantage women in light of parenthood (Bailyn 2011). As we have said, women in the workplace have to fight workplace norms and have to prove their commitment and competence, especially if they have a child. These are both disadvantages, since although anything that people do that demonstrates commitment or competence advantages their career, things people do that could be viewed as threats to commitment or competence disadvantage their career.

The theoretical perspectives presented in this chapter helped shape the project and provided us with concepts and viewpoints to help us understand and grapple with what we have found from conversations with women at early and mid-career stages. In the next six chapters we turn to a more detailed discussion of the data from our research and we use the theoretical grounding presented here as a way to tell more fully the story of what it is like to manage work and family in early and mid-career stages. Although the findings from the data tell part of the study, a detailed theoretical analysis highlights underlying issues and critiques of the academy. Without digging deeper into the findings to uncover and complicate the gendered nature of work for faculty members in the academy, change is unlikely and academic hierarchies will persist in the exclusion of women.

‿‿‿

CHAPTER 4

Managing Work and Family in the Early Career

Amy is a thirty-six-year-old second-year professor at Flagship University and an emerging scholar in her field. She's been married for two years and has a new baby. She thought a lot about the timing of having her child, and she wasn't sure she was ready in terms of her career, but she felt ready in terms of her biological clock. Amy worried that if she waited to have a child her fertility might pass her by, especially since she wants to have more than one child. Amy initially wished for a May baby, but she found herself pregnant sooner than expected, and the baby came in February. Her husband, an attorney who recently joined a law firm in town, didn't feel he could take time off work to help with the baby. Amy didn't really want to take time off during the semester, but with the February due date life became complicated. She worked until she had the baby, and then she arranged to have someone cover her classes for the three weeks until spring break in March. Her mother came to visit to help with the baby, so Amy could go back to work after spring break until the end of the semester. If she can make it to the end of the semester, she figures she'll be fine. Amy will take the summer off from teaching but hopes to write. She plans to resume a full schedule in the fall.

Amy talked to her department chair about options for taking leave and was informed that she was free to take leave for the whole semester, but that it would be unpaid beyond what she has saved for sick time (which isn't much, since she is new). It's not a financial option for her to take unpaid leave, and she was nervous about depleting her sick time in case she or the baby got sick. She also worried about how it would look to take time off so soon after getting to campus. What would her colleagues think if she was not around all semester? She's asked about how other people have handled their pregnancies and learned of only one person who took a leave of absence, but she had left the university. At this juncture, Amy feels like she can do it all without a leave of absence. She noticed in the faculty handbook that there is a provision to stop the tenure clock for a year in the event of the birth of a child, but at this point she's thinking it is better to avoid that. She feels she is getting herself established, and since her department chair didn't mention stopping the tenure clock she figures it best not to, as well.

In terms of day-to-day life Amy feels she has things relatively under control. She is happy with the flexibility of her position and feels that both her work and her home life are satisfying. She feels the challenges are doable. While she can't use the word "balance" to describe her life, she certainly feels things are under control. Amy likes both aspects of her life—work and family—and derives fulfillment from both. She finds that having a baby gives her a sense of perspective that she didn't have before. She also only has finite time in her day, so she feels she is more efficient. In some ways, having a baby has made her more productive. Amy wishes there were more women in her department who were doing this—and she certainly is getting a lot of positive attention from her graduate students, who are watching her to see how it will all work out. On good days, she feels this is the ideal life. On bad days, she worries about getting tenure and getting everything done in a manner that matches her high expectations for herself.

This chapter explores the interface between work and family from the perspective of early-career faculty—women on the tenure track who are also mothers of young children. Specifically, we examine how faculty women negotiate the demands of earning tenure and the demands of motherhood, looking at junior faculty perceptions of work/family conflict and compatibility. We examine these perceptions to provide insight into academic life, in general, and for new faculty members as mothers, in particular. The respondents come from research universities, comprehensive/regional institutions, liberal arts colleges, and community colleges. Institutional type differences are explored in chapter 7; here we focus on the commonalities in the findings regardless of where people work.

The data for this chapter are based on findings from first-phase interviews we conducted with early-career faculty. All of the women were in tenure-track positions (still untenured or in some cases very recently tenured), in the first five years of their appointment, and all had children under the age of five.

Silver Linings and Clouds: Common Findings about the Dual Role of Professor and Mother

Analysis of the early-career data across institutions reveals four major themes and multiple subthemes. The data indicate commonalities among the women we have talked with regardless of institutional type, discipline, or number of children. We have labeled these findings "silver linings and clouds," given the prevalence with which the women interviewed talked simultaneously about the positives and negatives of academic work from their perspectives as mothers of young children. The label highlights the fact that academic work is fraught with contradictions. For example, faculty work tends to be autonomous (a silver lining)—a work condition that can lead to isolation and ambiguity of expectations (clouds). Within this study, participants grappled with all sides of a particular phenomenon encountered as an academic and as a mother. The emphasis here is on individual perspectives of how an academic job lends itself—or not—to the combination of work and family.

The themes that emerged are organized as follows: first, the joy of professional and personal roles; second, the greedy nature of academic and family life; third, the need to watch the clock; and fourth, how having children puts work into perspective.

The Joy of Professional and Personal Roles

In spite of the many challenges all faculty members face in the crunch for tenure, those interviewed find the academic profession quite satisfying. Faculty members are relatively free to pursue intellectual interests as both teachers and researchers without seeking permission or fearing reprisal.

These cornerstones of academic freedom and flexibility mark the profession (Schuster & Finkelstein 2006; Tierney & Bensimon 1996). The women in the study, despite whatever frustrations they feel about the struggles of balancing children and work and the pressure of tenure, find joy in both their professional and personal roles. The joy expressed by those in the study seems relatively absent from the prior academic literature on pretenure track faculty and represents a new finding worth highlighting.

The Joys of Academia

From a professional perspective, respondents talked about the love of scholarly exploration and of seeing students learn and grow, and about the boost to self-esteem that comes from having work recognized by colleagues in the field. The joys of teaching were exemplified by the following faculty member:

> Professionally, I find joy in making a good environment for students. I find joy in encouraging students to do their best and be their best, and I also find joy teaching students something that they see no use for and having the revelation of, "Well, maybe it's cool, maybe I can see this." I like watching students learn. I'm as proud as I can be in the classroom and doing things that enhance the environment of our students.

For others, joy comes from the research aspects of their job. For example, one study participant explained: "I really like the work itself, it is really fun. I like writing. I love going out and giving talks at meetings." Another explained that she liked "the joy of doing a research project and making meaning of people's words and trying to think about them in multiple ways and hoping that something that I have written has some value in terms of people rethinking how public schools work or how they don't in the sense of equity issues. That's the most exciting part of what I do."

Related to the scholarship component of the work, many faculty women noted their gratification from recognition they received from others. As one respondent stated, "I get joy from success, being recognized, and for helping others . . . to be known for what I do and to be successful. I get a tremendous charge at publishing and being respected." Similarly, another faculty member explained:

> I think if I have any self-esteem it comes from my job . . . that I've pursued this. I get so much pleasure out of it. At this conference that I just came from there are people who only know me in the professional capacity, so it's actually really nice because you do get a sense that it's a confirmation. I mean, we're all really insecure in academia. You love the confirmation that you're doing something good and are appreciated and all of that.

Interestingly, several of those in the study also noted that part of the joy of being an academic comes from being able to show your children that adults find pleasure in the work they do. Several noted that despite the pressure and stress of academia, being a faculty member actually makes them better mothers. A typical comment was, "Why it is so important for me to have this career in addition to having children is I want [my child] to see that doing this [having a job] can be a good thing. It comes from my background and my parents not being happy with their work. The idea that somebody can be happy with her work is important to me."

The Joys of Motherhood

The women in this study love being mothers and appreciate the time they spend with their children. They were almost glowing in their praise of their children and had a strong desire to spend time watching and helping their children grow. Choosing a typical comment from the interviews is difficult, because each mother expressed her love for her children in such passionate terms. The following quotations are representative of how faculty members talk about the joy of motherhood.

> Personally, my sources of joy are my kids and watching them achieve and do things and find new things and say funny things. When my oldest was three he was big into infinity and I thought that was so cool, and we had discussions about what infinity was and the fact that whenever he started learning, he learns all these new things. I love watching him grow up and learn new things, learn about the world.

Joy is easy. Just seeing these little kids grow up and spending time with them. I love being a parent more than I thought I ever would. Having these two little beings totally in love with me and totally dependent on me, and totally trusting of me and sharing with me their way of seeing the world, which is so different, because I never really liked kids that much and I thought well, I was worried maybe I wouldn't like it. Then you are stuck, but it has been great with both of them.

THE GREEDY NATURE OF ACADEMIC AND FAMILY LIFE

Motherhood and academic life are greedy institutions that call for total commitment and dedication of their participants (Coser 1974). The structure of academic life, especially for those in their pretenure years, has characteristics that can both encourage and inhibit women with small children. Among the most encouraging factors, for example, are the flexibility and autonomy afforded to faculty. Within limits, faculty members are free to work when they choose and to work on what they choose. Those limits, however, are important to heed. Indeed, while touting the flexibility of academic life and its helpfulness in raising a family, faculty members also noted the significant price one has to pay. The price comes in the form of a workload that never ends and the related problem of not having enough time in the day, combined with the ambiguities of tenure expectations and the expectations for working a "second shift" at home (Jacobs & Winslow 2004). These themes are discussed below.

Flexibility and Autonomy

The academic literature is almost completely devoid of positive sentiments about the life of pretenure faculty members. The women in our study, however, were quick to identify the flexibility and autonomy offered to tenure-track faculty members as helpful in allowing them to achieve some sort of balance between work and family. The freedom and flexibility of academic life tend to allow faculty members to set their own schedules and spend time with their children. This is not to suggest that the women in this study did not put in long hours on their academic work. Instead, they recognized the flexibility in their schedules and how they could organize their days, as indicated by the following comment:

> The schedule I have is really a great schedule for a mother, a working mother, because I only teach my two classes and the way our department works you do not have to be on campus unless you are teaching your classes or unless you have a meeting that you must attend. They expect that if you are not on campus that you are writing or doing research or you are doing a presentation of some sort. It is really a great schedule for me because I can pick my daughter up earlier than a lot of mothers can, not all days but a lot of days.

Several noted that prior knowledge of the flexibility was what attracted them to the profession in the first place. One, for example, referred to her father, who was a college professor. She explained: "My dad had been a college professor so I knew that the lifestyle was something that I thought would work with having kids. My dad was a very involved parent. He could be there when we needed him and he worked at home a lot." Another referenced her advisor, who utilized the flexibility of the profession to his advantage as a parent and professor. Others talked about work schedules that could fit around their family. Respondents talked about working when they felt creative, which for one professor meant at 4:00 in the morning and "juggling to fit it all in."

In addition to the appealing flexible schedule, faculty members also commented on the relative autonomy that faculty life entails. In particular, participants noted the academic freedom to pursue topics of interest and the fact that faculty work is not subject to the stricture of reporting to a boss. One respondent's comment stands as typical. She stated, "Really there is an awful lot of freedom. I could be doing what I like. It's true, a huge amount of independence."

Along with flexibility and autonomy, however, comes a simultaneous understanding about the responsibilities and pressures of doing the work necessary to achieve tenure. Freedom and responsibility go hand in hand. The following quotations are examples of study participants' understanding of the "cost" of freedom, coupled with their appreciation of the same.

It's a real privilege that higher education has for all of us, in general. No matter what you choose to do with your time as parents, you can work at night after the children go to bed, at the computer, or like I do on the weekends. It's a privilege . . . [but] it's not a privilege to work the long hours that we do and to have the stress that we do, so it's push-pull.

There's a lot about it I like. Flexibility is one of the very important things that you get in academia: flexibility of when you work, flexibility of what you're working on and it's good for a family. But, it's only good if you're going to get tenure and you feel like you're achieving what you want to achieve.

Academic Work Never Ends

Faculty members were quick to look beyond the flexibility and freedom and recognize the significant pressures to achieve tenure and to be successful in one's work life. Consistent with findings of other research on junior faculty (e.g., Boice 1992; Gappa et al 2007; Tierney & Bensimon 1996), the women in this study repeatedly asserted that there is considerable pressure to be productive and to work all the time (Jacobs & Winslow 2004). This is a reality for many of the women in the study, and it is a fact that causes a significant amount of stress in their lives. As one faculty member explained, "It is not like you have an eight-hour shift and when you finish your shift you are done; that's not the way it is done." Academic work is distinct in that it can be, quite literally, never-ending. There are always articles to read, papers to grade, syllabi to update, and proposals to write. In addition to facing an overwhelming quantity of work, many study participants commented on how the portable nature of academic work (much of it residing on an ever-present laptop) makes bringing the job home a regular occurrence. Some faculty members felt they had to handle their e-mail inboxes on Sundays to have any hope of being productive on Mondays. We also heard many comments about nights and early mornings spent working while families were sleeping.

In discussing workload, many referred to the illusion of flexibility as a barrier that stands in the way of many women completing all those tasks that are necessary to achieve tenure. For example, one study participant stated:

You have to put the effort in and be really competitive or you are not going to make it. Up front, in the first years, it is really important. You obviously have to spend time with your kids, but I also think you cannot be successful if you constantly take the position that I have to go to every school function, because sometimes you can't. You have to come to some compromise that you can live with where you spend time with your kids and they know that you love them and they like doing things with you. It is also very important that at very early ages to make it where your kids are very adaptable.

Never Enough Time

Part of having a workload that never ends is feeling there is just not enough time to accomplish all the tasks that need to be accomplished. Repeatedly, respondents noted that they felt that time was a precious and rare commodity. As one woman explained, "It just doesn't feel like there are enough hours in the day. Part of that's my own personal time management inabilities, but part of it is because there are so many things that I would want to do and it all takes so much time." Another stated, "The biggest thing for me is that I feel like I don't have time. I used to work so many more hours and I just don't have those hours any more. And, I'm constantly struggling to . . . I mean during those hours I feel I have so much to do. But I don't get the time to stop and think and do creative research, I'm just kind of up-keeping all the time."

Lack of time in the day often meant losing the personal maintenance activities that keep people sane. While some of the respondents mentioned that they personally felt shortchanged by the stresses of motherhood and academia, many seemed to express guilt and some hesitancy in stating their own personal needs. The longing for personal time—either for exercise or just time to think—was an important component in the lives of many of these women. Related to a lack of time is the guilt the women in the study felt about spending too little time with their children and too little time on their academic work, as succinctly captured in the following comment: "Ever since I had my son, I've felt like when I'm with him I should be working, when I'm not with him [working] I should be with him."

Ambiguity of Tenure Expectations

The freedom and flexibility of academic work are often mitigated by the ambiguity of tenure expectations. The process required for tenure, and precisely what and how much must be accomplished, are often ambiguous, unclear, or even unknown to junior faculty members, and this uncertainty created a significant amount of stress among the women in the study. One faculty member referred to the tenure process as a "black-hooded affair in the forest where you don't even know who is on the committee"; another described tenure as "an albatross around my neck," and a third described the process as "smoke and mirrors." These colorful comments are representative of the study participants' views about the tenure process.

Although the stresses associated with tenure were not unique to faculty members with children (Boice 1992; Gappa et al. 2007; Philipsen & Bostic 2010; Tierney & Bensimon 1996), the concern about having a gap in one's academic record due to taking time off to have a child is a unique concern for these women. A typical comment follows:

> You hear a lot on different people's views on what it takes to get tenure around here, and what they say is there can be no gaps. If that is the case, I already have a gap [because of having a child] and I am doomed. On the other hand, if people are actually more reasonable than they are reported to be, this [research] will escalate into a big enough project by the time my decision will come up in four years. . . . You can't dwell on it every day.

Tenure clocks are finite and can be unforgiving of gaps in research productivity, especially at institutions that are focused on research. Academic women, unlike women in most other professional fields, are faced with having to either avoid or explain places in their dossier where they have not produced at regular intervals. The trajectory of an academic career puts the greatest amount of pressure on a faculty member at the beginning of her career, and tenure-track junior faculty feel the constant pressure of "publish or perish." This is also a time period that coincides with the waning of the biological clock for women.

Working the Second Shift

For academic mothers, one of the most time-consuming aspects of their lives, and a source of significant personal stress, is the fact that many feel as though they work a second shift at home (Hochschild 1989). While progress has been made in the domestic realm of equity of labor for childcare and housework, the bulk of this work is still done by women, even when both spouses have careers (Drago 2007; Somerville 2000). In our study, we found that women continue to shoulder the primary responsibility for anticipating the needs of their children, which can be psychologically and physically consuming.

A majority of the women in this study were primarily responsible for taking care of the children and chores at home. Even though most of the women utilized daycare in some form, these women felt as though they were the one in the family who was expected to get the children ready in the morning, take them to daycare, pick them up, feed them, play with them, and put them to bed. One mother summed up her frustration well: "I bear the bulk of the parenting role. I do everything in the morning and when it is 10 A.M. I feel I have already lived a day before I have even gone to work." Another stated that although her husband works longer hours than she does, "he is really in the doghouse now. I would say it is 80 percent me and 20 percent him, and the 20 percent would be when I am traveling." These quotations represent the norm for the women in our study. While some of the women described their husbands as "enlightened," in that they did an equitable share as father and partner, the majority had spouses who were personally and professionally "supportive" but who were relatively uninvolved in the second shift, especially when their children were young.

THE NEED TO WATCH THE CLOCK

The women in this study carefully considered the timing of having children. Some had their children while they were in graduate school, some during postdoctoral work, and others waited until they were in a tenure-track position. A woman's decision about when to have a child was influenced strongly by the spoken and inferred advice of others. For many, their thoughts about when to have children were shaped by their graduate school experiences and by their advisors' expectations of them. As one professor explained, "I was never told [not to have a baby] personally, but we all understood that our advisor didn't put a high value on family." Others looked at the lives of their faculty advisors and concluded, "There is no way I want that life." These findings substantiate what others (Rice et al. 2000; Golde and Dore 2001; and, more recently, Mason et al. 2009) found in their studies about graduate students' reticence about seeking faculty positions given their perceptions about the consuming nature of faculty life.

Concern about tenure combined with age of the mother was a significant factor in deciding when to have a child. A typical comment, for example, came from a professor who stated, "I was turning thirty and I wasn't going to be one of these women who waits for tenure and then faces infertility.... There wasn't really going to be a better time." Another explained, "I kept putting it off until I felt like I couldn't put it off any longer because I am going to be too old to have kids." Others stated that they faced subtle, and not so subtle, encouragement to wait to have children until they had earned tenure. As one woman elaborated, "I can't tell you how many people I have known who got their notice of tenure and threw away their birth control pills. I saw that and I didn't want to do that.... If you're a woman in academia you're expected to have no kids, although you kind of are entitled to one. But ... if you have it before tenure, that's kind of pushing the envelope."

Similarly, the timing of childbirth to coincide with summer breaks was at least considered by most of the participants in this study—though many found timing of a due date to be beyond their control. As one woman who had her child in June explained, "I was very lucky with the timing.... What if you have a child in the middle of the semester? What do you do in that case?" In terms of timing, another faculty member explained, "I've heard stories of department chairs who will sort of call in all the young women [in the department] and say 'Now if you're thinking of getting pregnant try to time it so that it doesn't cut into the semester.'" In offering advice to others, several respondents expressed the idea that since there really is no good time, one should just do it when they feel comfortable. One faculty member elaborated: "I really am suspicious of the argument of 'Now is not a good time.' It will never be a good time in terms of society's understanding of what women are trying to do."

Having Children Puts Work into Perspective

Adding a child to their career added a perspective to life that, for most respondents, was absent prior to having a child. Academic work is consuming and for most of the women in the study, they were consumed, in terms of time and energy, by their responsibilities as professors and mothers. A child changed the way work got done and also changed their perspective on the relative importance of work in the big picture of life.

One of the most common sentiments expressed by study respondents was that having a child imposed priorities in their lives. For many of the women in the study, children were the number one priority. Repeatedly, study participants asserted that regardless of the consequences to their career, their children came first. Comments in this regard came in the form of advice to graduate students or others who might follow in the footsteps of these women. As one woman suggested, "A family is going to be the most important thing in your life and you can't let concerns about what others think determine that. I would say if you want to have a child, even if it means you are going to lose a particular career option, if that's what you want, go for it." Others personalized the issue of making their children the number one priority. For example, one professor stated: "No matter what, [my child] has to come first. And, you know, sometimes I have to make some hard decisions, and I manage it. . . . I think that my career is important, but my role as a mother comes first. Ultimately, that's what matters."

Having a Child Can Make You More Efficient

There is no question that having a child changes how faculty members accomplish their work. Interestingly, many of the respondents in this study claimed that having children made them more efficient and organized—a silver lining. This finding supports the more quantitative data found by Bellas and Toutkoushian (1999) that having a child does not contribute to a lack of research productivity. According to one faculty member, "Clearly having her [a child] was a major change in my lifestyle and how I dealt with things, and made my hours change significantly, for the good and bad. The good was I had to become much more efficient, the other side of it is that I live within my hours at work." In offering advice to others contemplating motherhood while on the tenure track, one of the respondents captured the nature of the efficiency expressed by others in the study. She explained: "First, I would say just back up and say it can be done if it is important enough for you and you prioritize your time well enough. You have to be good at utilizing your time effectively. It can be done [but] it's not going to be a nice steady road."

Similarly, having a child means that faculty members cannot engage in "workaholic" habits, as many describe doing prior to having children. For example, one woman explained that she now works forty hours a week because that is how much child care time she has available. She continues, "Compared to the number [of hours] I used to work, forty is nothing. You don't realize how much you were working until you are restricted." In fact, it was common for respondents to confess that before having children they used to work constantly, a phenomenon familiar to most academics (Schuster & Finkelstein 2006; Tierney & Bensimon 1996). One study participant put it this way, "I think if we [faculty members] didn't have kids we would be working all the time and we would be really burned out."

For some professors, having children changed the timing of when they got their work accomplished. As one explained:

> In the old days before [my child], I tended to procrastinate and just kind of not be good about sitting down regularly. I'd sort of telescope all my writing into longer periods here and there, as opposed to a half an hour when I could grab it. Now, it's two hours when [my child] is napping, that kind of thing. You have to reshuffle your whole way of doing work. Having a child is great in many ways for your research even though you assume it's bad. It makes you much more businesslike about when you're going to do it.

The Art of "Satisficing"

A common coping mechanism among the women we interviewed was recognizing that one cannot fulfill all of the responsibilities and expectations as well as one might if there were fewer roles to play. Satisficing is an economic term used to describe decisions that are "good enough" though not necessarily optimal (Simon 1981, 35). Satisficing typifies how women in the study got their work done given the limitations of time, energy, and resources. This phenomenon is not necessarily unique to women faculty with children, as all junior faculty, and especially those on the tenure track, are constantly faced with deliberations over quality versus quantity in teaching and research (Boice 1992; Tierney & Bensimon 1996). The findings from this study suggest, however, that these pressures are compounded for junior women faculty with children and that satisficing may be more prevalent for this group.

Along with the idea of satisficing comes the notion of not being able to be the best all the time—but being content with being good enough. Examples of satisficing and being good enough abound from the interviews. In most cases, the women expressed some discomfort with not being the best, as they had been high achievers up to this point in their lives. Nonetheless, they also recognized that some things are worth sacrificing for others. Not everyone compromised on the same things. For example, some compromised on the kinds of research projects they were going to accomplish, as one faculty member explained:

> I'm striking a balance but I'm realizing I have to adapt my visions of how I'll work. . . . My next big project was supposed to be, and I hope it still will be [someday], a book on a topic that would require a lot of travel to archives in Europe and really hard, difficult research topics, just very complicated topics. I've kind of shelved that for the time being. Because I feel like, with a small child, it's not the kind of topic I can pursue without travel and a lot of intensive just sitting in the library. I need a project where I can shut myself up after [my child] has gone to bed and work a few hours every night, but not have to rush out to libraries all over the place. So I've kind of come up with a different book topic for my next book. So maybe I won't contribute the greatest in the way that I wanted to. . . . But I think I'm willing to make that sacrifice.

Other women described compromising on the types of venues in which they were going to get published, the overall level of scholarship they were going to produce, and ultimately the level of "fame and fortune" that they were going to achieve. For example, one woman stated, "I would like my son to be my highest priority. . . . I try really hard to keep it balanced, and that's why I made this decision to crank out an average amount of research and not really excel." Another stated, "I think I do a good job, though I am not going the extra way to publish tons of papers, I am not going to be a star in the field because I do not have the time."

Others recommended satisficing when it comes to teaching and service responsibilities so that they would have time for other aspects of their job. For example, one woman explained that when it comes to service "you can't please everybody" and that sometimes "enough is just enough." Another stated, "I think it is very easy as a young assistant professor to want to spend a lot . . . of time on the teaching aspect of the job. But the research is so important for tenure and raises and promotion. . . . I love to talk to students but you really have to prioritize."

Summary of Findings from Early-Career Faculty

The overall findings from the early-career faculty in the study suggest that in spite of the challenges associated with the academic career and having a young child, it can be done, and, in many cases, done with joy and professional gratification. Yes, there are challenges associated with having a child, but for the most part these women were passionate about their careers *and* passionate about their children. While the academic job has its share of challenges, it was also considered by most of the women we interviewed to be compatible with having a family, given the flexibility.

Another finding from the early-career interviews was that institutional context shapes the overall experience—where faculty work and the mission of their institutions shape the daily experience of being an academic and a mother. In chapter 7 we will shift attention to institutional type differences, but next we turn to a discussion of the experiences of the mid-career faculty.

CHAPTER 5

*

Mid-Career Perspectives on Work and Family

Andrea is enjoying her life as an associate professor and the mother of two school-aged children. Life is still complicated, but the stress of the pretenure era and of having little babies who rely on her for everything seems to have dissipated to a large degree. The big stress in Andrea's life right now seems to be keeping track of everybody's schedule. Both of her children, who are in school full time now, are involved in a lot of after-school activities. Making sure that everyone is in the right place at the right time is a major part of her life. When is the soccer practice? What time does Susan, her daughter, have to be picked up from choir practice? Whose turn is it to go to the grocery store? What time will her husband be home? Is he available to help with the pick-up and drop-off of the kids? Negotiating these kinds of demands is time consuming—but very different than the demands placed on Andrea when the children were little. Those time demands were more focused on physical needs—breastfeeding, nap schedules, changing diapers, arranging daycare. Those things were difficult, but at least the children weren't so mobile.

On the home front, Andrea finds that her husband is able to and willing to help more than when the children were little. There are still some remnants of the second shift, but a lot of that has eased as the children have gotten older. One of the things that helps Andrea is that she now outsources some of her domestic duties—she hires someone to help clean the house every other week, she carpools with other parents, and sometimes she even hires a local college student to transport her kids from one activity to another. The other big personal difference now, as compared to the pretenure phase, is that she has more time to take care of herself. Andrea has started exercising again, a couple of times a week. She had given that up when the children were little and when the demands of the tenure track were particularly acute. She now belongs to a book club that meets once a month, and now that the children are more self-sufficient she has started to take back some of the personal time she had forsaken when they were little.

At work, things are also different than they were pretenure. Andrea finds work to be a bit more enjoyable now that she has passed the stress of the tenure decision. She notes that she still has post-tenure review and a goal of wanting to get promoted at some point, but with tenure, she has a different relationship to research. Absent the pressure of the tenure decision, she realizes how much she did some things because of the pressure and because she felt scared not to do them. Now she finds herself thinking about her work and wanting to do research because she has something to say and values her contribution to the field.

Andrea feels she is still getting over the stress of the tenure clock, but envisions herself eventually being promoted to full professor. Still, she feels a little hesitant about putting herself out there for that next step. There is a sense of fear and hesitation about making herself vulnerable again in the review process. She is officially eligible to go up for promotion next year and is starting to get herself ready, but she feels she needs to get more done to be prepared for promotion. Despite some fears about going up to the next level of full professor, Andrea is quite content in her current job. She cannot imagine moving somewhere else—in large part because it would involve uprooting her family and her husband, who is also employed in the area. On bad days, she feels a little stuck. On good days, she feels this is the kind of place where she could spend the rest of her career.

Andrea likes her work, especially the flexibility, and finds great pleasure in it. She finds her academic position is one that allows her to gain a sense of balance between work and family responsibilities. Balance is not a word Andrea used when she was pretenure and feeling the pressure to perform, but now that she is more established, she is comfortable describing her current state as balanced. Andrea regularly works more than forty hours a week but can structure her time in ways that allow her to do things with her kids and not have to sacrifice. She makes use of time in the morning before her kids get up to get ready for the day at work, and she can use time after dinner when her kids are doing homework to grade or edit papers. She acknowledges that there are times when the job is incredibly stressful, especially in the face of deadlines and when her kids' schedules conflict with hers, but she savors the freedoms of academic life. She is able to pursue her passions in research, have a say in the classes she teaches, and she feels able to be present as a parent. People complain all the time about faculty life, but she finds it a "good gig" for integrating professional and personal life.

We use Andrea's experience as a way to represent the overall findings of the mid-career faculty interviews from the second phase of the study. To be sure, not every person we interviewed found the level of equanimity that Andrea expresses, but overall, faculty women in the study, even those who have encountered major difficulties in their careers or personal lives, find that at this stage in their personal and professional lives, with more experience as both professors and parents, they are generally happy and settled in their multiple roles.

A major impetus for adopting a longitudinal perspective in this project was and is to more fully understand the career experiences of faculty women as they progress through academic life. We also thought it was important to see what changes took place as their children moved from infancy to school age. Careers and parenthood are not static, and it is important to recognize that the balance and integration between work and family is in a constant state of flux (Evans & Grant 2008).

MID-CAREER FACULTY WOMEN: LOOKING FORWARD, LOOKING BACK

There are several themes that we pursue in this chapter, including how parenting offers perspective on women's careers, how parenting concerns shift as families and careers evolve, how career foci shift as families evolve, thoughts on promotion to full professor, ideas about career development, burnout in the faculty role, and the role of mentoring and support in career development. Each of these is discussed below, with some dialogue about comparisons between early and mid-career stages. Many of the women we talked with in the mid-career interviews highlighted what had changed since their early career years; we see this as an important benefit of having longitudinal data.

Maintaining Perspective

In the face of the often stressful tenure process, the early-career faculty members in this study found that having children helped them maintain a sense of perspective and equanimity that they attributed to their dual roles of mother and professor. Work helps to buffer the challenges of family life, and family helps to buffer the realities of work life. This view was maintained by women later in their careers, as well, but was seen from a slightly different angle. Later in the career, maintaining perspective is about having realistic expectations about work and family. Based on their experience as parents and as professors, the mid-career faculty members were focused on realistic accomplishments within their jobs and their families (both overall and for any given day). They had enough experience to know what is possible and realistic to accomplish in terms of particular tasks. As one faculty member expressed it: "Our evenings are preoccupied with kid activities and homework; I just can't keep up the pace as I did earlier in my career and maintain balance at home." Such comments were typically accompanied by self-reassuring phrases such as "I'm doing the best I can."

Maintaining perspective for faculty members later in their career provided a way for them to keep realities about work "in check" and also to adopt a view that did not just involve work. Family is also part of making decisions. One faculty member expressed how having a child helps her make decisions this way: "I've come to the realization that when the kids are sick and my husband can't stay home, kids come first. . . . I don't do it often, so when I do it they [people I work with on campus] realize it's a major issue. It's not like I'm abusing the system or taking advantage of 'oh well, I have sick kids at home.'"

For mid-career faculty members, having a balanced and integrated view of their lives involves the adoption of what we call a "parenthood lens"—a filter that is used to examine and vet decisions about their careers and more generally about life. For example, the decision to change institutions and relocate is not just about the faculty member, but also about her family. This was also the case with considering administrative positions. The calculations in deciding whether to advance in administration includes ages and activities of children, work commitments of one's spouse, and individual commitments. To illustrate how the parenthood lens shapes decisions, one faculty member relayed her experience about not changing positions even though it would have meant a significant pay raise and career advancement:

> The only way to get a really good pay raise is to go somewhere else. I'm kind of stuck in that I've been here awhile and with salary compression, people that have been hired later, after me, that have less experience are either getting paid more or getting paid the same. I've had to sacrifice some career advancement and stay put until the family is raised. . . . I could be in a different position, or making more money or at a different university, possibly doing some more things if it wasn't for the family obligations.

The reluctance to uproot families, including kids and spouses with jobs, to advance their career, was a key theme for the mid-career faculty women. For some in the study, being established in a career and in a community was a source of security, happiness, and comfort, and a welcome change from what one faculty member referred to as her "early-career gypsy lifestyle." The early-career faculty members were in a state of flux and uncertainty, and talked a lot about potential job changes, whereas the faculty members at mid-career were more settled, in large part because of their family rather than because of their career, as indicated in the following remark: "I'm happy here. It seems weird to think of just staying in one place your whole life, but I don't see any reason to go somewhere else either. I like it here. It would have to be a really cool place to live or some major motivating thing to get me to move."

Most of the faculty women in the study had had a fairly transient lifestyle prior to moving into their faculty positions. They did their graduate work in different places from where they had been undergraduates, and often their college locales were distinct from where they grew up. They typically took their first jobs in communities some place different again. In the first interviews there was the sense that they would potentially move again, and we often heard people talk about not having lived in places very long. In the second interviews, on the other hand, several of the faculty women indicated they planned to stay put. The positive side of staying, as expressed by many, was developing connections on campus and in the community, and being content within their positions. The negative side to staying in a position manifested itself as feeling stuck, as expressed in these comments:

> I don't have much mobility. Right now I'm not leaving for a better job. I put up with a lot of academic stuff for my family's sake.
> I have been very dispassionate about my job but I can't do anything else or go anywhere else. I am stuck.
> I'm place-bound with husband and kids so they know I put up with a lot more abuse.
> I haven't looked around—90 percent of that is family related. I don't want to uproot my kids my family, my house.
> I'm here so I've made it work.
> I would rather manage something less than ideal for me and let my family be happy.

Not all the faculty members who felt stuck were necessarily unhappy about staying; it was more a matter of feeling that moving was not an easy option given family responsibilities. Once children grow older and more established in the community, many families find it becomes more difficult to move. It is clear from the above comments the sense of being stuck can be part of compromise, with people realizing that they are actually pretty happy in their positions and community, or it can be viewed negatively so that people feel they can't leave their positions because of being restricted by their family situations—children and dual careers. (Dual-career concerns are discussed in more depth in chapter 8.)

To summarize, having children offers perspective in terms of making life more balanced and less focused on work to the exclusion of all else. Career mobility (and lack thereof) was a theme throughout the mid-career interviews that reflected how people filtered career decisions from the perspective of their family (the parenthood lens). In general, mobility was inhibited by family. For the most part, the immobility turned out to be inconsequential, but for others not being able to move was troublesome, especially if they found themselves in difficult work situations or if they had to change their careers in ways that they did not want to, but felt they had to in order to accommodate their spouse's career.

Parent Concerns Shift

The primary focus of the early-career interviews was on how to manage work, family, and the tenure clock, with a secondary focus on institutional responses to faculty members with children and how to navigate the policy environment. Early-career faculty were concerned about parental leave, availability and quality of daycare, the ability to stop the tenure clock, and what the implications having a child would be for tenure. The focus of parenting for the early-career faculty was centered on meeting the needs of young children in light of getting established as an academic.

The focus in the follow-up interviews was more on the juggling act of managing family as kids got older and work responsibilities as careers matured. There was little or no mention of institutional policies for faculty at this stage, since the predominant policy discourse related to work and family centers around accommodating childbirth and work reentry, primarily the concerns of early-career faculty (Lester & Sallee 2009). Some campuses talk about "work life" broadly to encompass not just children but also elder care and general wellness, as a means to foster more integrated and balanced lives for faculty members (Philipsen & Bostic 2010). But even though many of the campuses in the study take a holistic view of work and family and think broadly about dependent care, the message the faculty received is that work/family policies for faculty at mid-career with school-aged children are not useful.

For the women in the study, the emphasis shifted from changing diapers to arranging car pools. As children get older, their involvement in activities and the development of their own lives required the study participants to think about not only their own daily schedule (at home and at work) but also the schedules of their children. When kids are young, one woman said, "it's demanding because of their physical needs, but they are immobile, now that they are older it's more demanding intellectually and emotionally." This faculty member went on to say: "Now that my kids are older they want me around all the time." The mid-career faculty members were as a whole more settled in their faculty positions, more established as parents, and more aware of the "juggling act" of their daily lives.

The mid-career interviews brought to light a shift in shared child care duties that shaped changes in parenting. One of the major findings from the first phase of the research is the amount of second-shift responsibilities women maintained, especially when it came to managing the care of their children. Spouses helped, but the women we interviewed felt the emotional labor of parenting and anticipating children's needs were their primary concerns. Now that the children were older, their spouses and partners were more involved in shared parenting, resulting in another parenting shift, as explained by the following comments:

> When they [children] are bigger it seems that men tend to do more with them then so I have fewer responsibilities. He'll take them both here and there and then I can be home working if I want to. I've got more free time.
>
> It has gotten easier and as the kids have gotten a little bit older it has gotten better. There is more equity between me and my husband. My husband also does the shopping and all the cooking and that makes a huge difference.
>
> Something clicked in my husband and its more 50–50. Their dad enjoys sports and activities versus caregiving.

The children themselves also participate more in family life. "My son now drives so he can help shuttle his sister. It really helps." Also, as children grow, they have more of a say in family life, which shapes how people think of their careers, as we heard with regard to geographic mobility. Faculty women also mentioned that with older children, and their schedules, it is difficult to travel as much for conferences and for conducting research. "I used to be more involved nationally, and that's good for my reputation, but I just can't do that anymore. I can't do it all." And another, with similar comments: "I feel bad about not getting more research done. I feel bad about working at home to take away from family. I can't be gone or absent all the time, my kids have too much going on."

What this meant for women faculty at the mid-career stage was an attention to how to manage family responsibilities while thinking about the myriad of opportunities available to established faculty members, including administration, promotion to full professor, and changes in responsibilities.

Work Focus Shifts

Not only did parenting shift but the focus within jobs shifted as well. Consistent with other research (e.g., Baldwin et al. 2005; Neumann 2009; Neumann & Terosky 2007), the mid-career interviews focused considerably on how people think differently about their jobs and how some of their roles had changed and shifted. In particular, we found that service and administrative duties began to take up additional faculty time. As they became more established, faculty members in the study were taking on increasing involvement in program, department, college, and university service and administrative responsibilities. As one faculty member remarked, "I've become a whole lot busier [since I got tenure]. When I was on the tenure track they sort of left me alone, but now that I'm tenured, the committee work has piled on." For faculty members early in their career, there was a focus on getting tenure which became a means to make decisions (for example, not taking on service in the interest of focusing on research). Once faculty members earned tenure, there was no longer a buffer with regard to service.

Involvement in service was not just a matter of time expenditure; it was also a matter of increased levels of influence and responsibility—a more active level of involvement in shared governance. Early mid-career faculty are an important resource to institutions because they are familiar with the tenure-track process and they are also experienced enough to know their institutions (Neumann 2009). One faculty member's experience resonates with what we heard throughout the interviews: "Now that I'm tenured and further along in my career I get to do 'fancy' service. The kind of service that you do when the dean calls and asks you to personally do things—it's hard to say 'no.'" Faculty members in the study were involved in fairly high levels of service throughout their campuses, and many responsibilities involved managing different aspects of program development.

The emphasis on service also meant faculty members thought about prioritizing their time differently. During the early career, with the emphasis on getting tenure, getting established in research universities, comprehensives, and at many of the liberal arts colleges meant a focus on research. For faculty at community colleges and more locally oriented, teaching-focused liberal arts colleges, proving themselves meant preparing class materials, many times for a fairly large number of classes and large numbers of students.

But no matter what the focus of their positions or campuses, getting established means "having to do it all to prove myself," as one faculty member said. Early in their career, faculty members in the study felt they had to contribute to teaching, research, and service in some way. As more established mid-career faculty, study participants felt they had more latitude in how to spend their time, and they had to be a lot "more savvy with time in regard to teaching, research, and service." They also felt that institutional demands to do more service meant having to forgo other aspects of their positions. As one faculty member said: "I've found I can do two of the three [teaching, research, and service] and do it well, but I can't do all three all the time and be effective." Another managed the demands this way: "Now that I'm established I get more say in the balance of teaching, research, and service." It's not that faculty women abandoned particular aspects of their positions, but they did prioritize with an eye on focus and excellence. In order to be successful and productive, faculty members expressed a need to find a balance between teaching, research, and service, and how much of each one could realistically handle while advancing in her career and maintaining a semblance of sanity in her life.

Given the fairly high levels of involvement in service or what we would call "quasi-administration" (Ward 2003), we were surprised by the limited number of faculty women who had administrative aspirations beyond the programmatic level, since they were already engaged in administrative work (even if it was labeled as service). In part, this was based on the participants' concern about how to manage family responsibilities, given the additional workload associated with administration and promotion. It will be interesting to see if these aspirations shift as program responsibilities increase and as children get older.

Promotion to Full Professor

One finding that was more pronounced for the mid-career faculty across institutional types was how they thought about career advancement and, in particular, getting promoted to full professor. In the second phase, the participants had been faculty members long enough to realize the limitations and nuances of their workplace, and for some this meant not wanting to be involved in the promotion process. As one participant said, "I don't have the time to deal with personalities and politics." Although some faculty women were planning for promotion, and, in some cases had already been promoted, it was certainly a more predominant theme to *not* be thinking about promotion. We were dismayed at the limited number of women who were preparing for promotion to full professor even though they were eligible (or nearly eligible) for advancement. The promotion process was viewed as a political exercise that had to be intentionally prepared for, maneuvered through, and/or avoided.

When we look at the data overall, we see three ways that mid-career faculty members think about promotion: no plans for promotion, plan on eventual promotion, and promotion as part of the career planning process. Following are interview excerpts that illustrate the different ways women in the study talk about promotion:

No Plans for Promotion
You go through an enormous amount of paperwork and everything
   to get promoted to full professor. It's not like once you are full
   professor you have more respect or something else that is not
   monetary. Why do it?
I didn't feel pressed to jump back into my research. . . . I just decided
   I wasn't going to do it and I didn't care.

You only need to squeak by [for tenure]. I was a little nervous but I
knew it wasn't a slam dunk, but I thought there was a pretty hot
chance. I am not working on research to get promoted.

I didn't want to expend energy and expend the effort [going up for
full]. I don't want to deal with the emotional cost.

I've said: "Nuts to all this. I'm not going to do it."

Plans for Eventual Promotion

I have never been one of those ambitious people who want to make
a name for myself. . . . For me, it has always been just sort of
having day-to-day goals, not long-range goals. You do what you
need to do to feel good that day. So for me I feel like I always
want to be moving forward so getting full professor is part of feeling
like I am moving forward. I realize that part of my pay increase
and promotion is tied to this research and I actually enjoy doing
it, and it's not too painful and so far I've been reasonably good at
it. . . . So I take a much more utilitarian approach to it. I don't have
these lofty goals.

I'm really a sort of ebb-and-flow worker. I have periods when I
am really productive and then I have periods when I am sort of
vegging out. . . . I am probably the mentally healthiest person in
this department, but I'm the least productive. When I do work
I'm actually very productive. I just don't like to work that much.
I don't work on nights or weekends. I definitely want to make full
professor, but it's going to be four or more years. I'm not going to
kill myself to do it.

Career Planning for Full Professor

I want to get this book out and I want to get promoted.

I do want to make the big push for full.

I'm still an associate trying to push for full.

I'm working on doing stuff to get to the next level.

I wrote a book so didn't hesitate to go up for full. I inspired other
women to go up.

People second-guess themselves about going up for full. I was ready.
I didn't want anything hanging over me. No more hoops.

So, yes, some women in the study plan to go up for full (or already have), and as soon as possible, but that is certainly not the norm. The comments above illustrate the range of sentiment expressed about promotion to full professor. Given the demographics of our sample, it is difficult to calculate what percentage of women fall into each of these categories because the women in the study are at different stages of mid-career, with some eligible for full professor when we interviewed them and others not yet ready. Regardless, we think it is important to point out the different mindsets faculty members have about the promotion process, given the emphasis on the faculty pipeline (and women's progression in it) as a way to remediate gender inequities at different career stages.

For some of the faculty women in the study, the promotion process was one that required planning and preparation. As one person said, "I'm regrouping to go up for full," which involved the need to jump-start her career to prepare for the process of promotion. Why the need to restart the career they are already in? In some instances professors had become focused on service, typically not a highly rewarded activity in the promotion and tenure process, once they were promoted to the associate level. Now that they had tenure and had engaged in some other activities, people felt the need to "get back to research so I can get full." The need to focus on research was a concern not just for faculty members at research universities but for those at the liberal arts colleges and comprehensives, as well. In the community colleges, the focus was more on compiling materials to show involvement in service and teaching effectiveness.

The promotion and tenure process for early-career faculty members operates on a fairly rigid timeline. For mid-career faculty, the timelines are largely internally directed, since there is typically little guidance and no timelines to get promoted to full professor. The elective nature of the promotion process contributed to a considerable range in desire to get promoted, as we have seen. For some faculty in the study, promotion was certainly looming and lurking, while for others it was not a pressing desire or concern.

With regard to promotion, there was also some sentiment that "it's just not worth it." As one faculty member stated succinctly, "I don't really care about full. I'm not into money. I'm not ego-driven. I'm delaying relative to my peers, but don't care." Another faculty member shared her observations of why people don't care about going up for full professor: "It's all about 'emotional economy' and women don't want to owe the institution if they are granted full professor." This same study participant went on to say, "If I take out of the economy, by getting full, I don't want to have to pay back." This faculty member makes an important point about how much a person needs to invest emotionally in order to become a full professor and to calculate to what extent it is worth it if the person has to "pay back." Perhaps this is, in part, based on people's experience with getting promoted to associate professor and finding a fairly sizeable service load awaiting them once they get tenure. By extension, it could be assumed that additional promotion would also mean additional service for the institution and, in fact, many campuses reserve particular service positions (such as chair of the faculty senate) for faculty who are full professors. Some faculty members in the study felt it was simply not worth it to progress professionally to just get tapped by the institution to do more.

On some campuses, promotion to full professor involves a fairly signifi-cant pay raise, whereas on others the raise is minimal. We were actually surprised at the number of people who didn't even know what going up for promotion involved (in terms of process) and did not know the financial benefit for doing so, either. On the basis of comments about the promotion process, the costs and benefits of promotion, and concerns about what it means to be a full professor from an institutional standpoint, it is clear that promotion to full professor was not foremost in the thinking of many—even most—women in the study, a conclusion we find disconcerting , given the role of women in higher education and their low representation as senior faculty members on most campuses. We also found it disconcerting because it has potential implications for maintaining faculty vitality and learning in addition to overall institutional well-being (Neuman 2009). Faculty need to stay vital at all stages for institutions to be functional.

Family responsibilities are part of how people think about the promotion process. A faculty member from a liberal arts college was very articulate in saying, "As a mom, I can do two things really well in my job, teaching and service, but to get promoted I need to excel in all areas. Right now I just can't do that." For another it was a matter of timing: "I need to plan for full and I'm postponing going up for full until my ducks are in a row. My decision is to focus on family now." For yet another, it's a matter of prioritizing time:

"People give up on teaching, research, or service because something has to give and it's usually not family. I can't do it all and I don't want to wish my life away about going up for full."

How are we to make sense of the "take it or leave it" posture toward the promotion and tenure process? On the one hand, it is certainly the choice of an individual faculty member to engage in the promotion process. Yet, at the same time, many of the findings point to issues people have with promotion that are related more to process than individual preparedness to become a full professor. The decision to not pursue promotion is only partially attributable to individual preparation; the widespread perceptions about the process as political, unfair, taxing, and not worth it are disconcerting. Generally speaking, mid-career faculty have been largely understudied (Neumann 2009), but we do know that mid-career associate professors, as a group, are often dissatisfied (Trower 2010), and we also know the longer a person is in rank as an associate professor the more likely one is to stay an associate professor (Baldwin & Blackburn 1981; O'Meara 2007). If faculty members remain associate professors for an extended period of time and do not progress in their careers, it is likely they are not contributing fully to their campus in ways that reflect the totality of the mission of the campus. This is not to suggest that these faculty members are not contributing fully in particular domains, but as faculty throughout our study indicate, to get full professor ranking in most institutional settings requires sustained involvement in teaching, research, *and* service, and not some subset of these areas. For campuses to carry out their missions they need committed mid-career faculty contributing in all areas and not just select ones.

For women, the lack of progression to full professor is also a matter of representation. Traditional thinking on college campuses has assumed that more women in the faculty pipeline would automatically mean more female senior professors and more female administrators (Kulis et al. 2002). One of the major findings from our research is that entrance into the pipeline does not necessarily lead to advancement and promotion. Athough the majority of the women in the study did achieve tenure, it is important to recognize that this milestone does not automatically pave the way for ongoing career advancement.

The range in the study with regard to attitudes toward promotion to full professor depended in part on when people received tenure. For those recently tenured, it was early to be thinking of the promotion to full professor. However, for those further along as associate professors, there was still limited discussion about going up for full professor. As one faculty member put it, "Right now I feel risk-aversive. I'm pretty settled with what I'm doing and not interested in stressful situations or having to deal with politics and conflict. . . . I like my teaching and I like my research. For now, that's enough." It will be interesting and important to continue with this cohort analysis to see how careers continue to advance as children get older and to see how faculty members maintain their personal and professional vitality.

Faculty Burnout

Increasing pressure to do more with fewer resources, and to more fully prove oneself professionally as part of the tenure and promotion process, was a reality for women in the study and had long-term professional consequences. The lack of desire to go up for full professor was, in part, related to the politics involved, but was also due to shifts in activity after tenure. There was the general perception that earning tenure was an all-consuming process that left people depleted and burned out. As one participant remarked, "I worked so hard and so tirelessly to get tenure and after I got it I took a breather and before I knew it several of my research projects ended." This same faculty member commented that to get full professor "in many ways means starting over. . . . I'm almost ready."

Once tenure was achieved, it was not uncommon for those in the study to shift their priorities from what it took to get tenure to other elements of the career, like advising, departmental and institutional service, curricular change, and teaching. Now that many of the women in the study are eligible to be considered for promotion to full professor, their multiple responsibilities need to be negotiated. At research universities, in particular, to be promoted to full professor means that faculty members need to maintain a research agenda in the midst of other responsibilities. One faculty member mused: "I've been asked to go into administration, but if I want to get promoted [to full professor] what I really need right now is another grant." She went on to talk about how she needed to "gather [her] forces" to get her work ready for the next stage of her research. Mid-career faculty are an institutional resource that often get tapped to do more research, teaching, and service (Neumann 2009), and finding a balance in these responsibilities *and* stay on track to be promoted can be challenging.

There was variation in how participants viewed burnout and productivity after tenure. Becoming tenured gives people the opportunity to think differently about their career and about their professional focus. We found that at mid-career, faculty members felt they had more say in how to spend their time. Anna Neumann, in her recent book (2009a) looking at early mid-career faculty, refers to this stage as involving new kinds of learning. Neumann found that early mid-career faculty members are "working hard to hold onto their scholarly learning and also to learn other new responsibilities that come their way at this career stage" (101). Refocusing their work and owning how they wanted to move into the next phase of their career was one way for faculty members to deal with the burnout many experience after tenure.

It is not uncommon for people, once established in a career, to have to revisit or renegotiate aspects of their career—to learn new things—just as they do when they are first becoming established. John Smart and Marvin Peterson (1997), building on Super's (1992) theory of career development, refer to this as "career recycling," where professionals (in this case, faculty members) return to characteristics of the early stage of their careers. Faculty women in the interviews experienced much of the same angst and concern about "gearing up" for the promotion process to full professor that they did about earning tenure.

Throughout our interviews we found that past behavior predicts the future. Faculty members who struggled with getting established, negotiating the tenure process, and achieving tenure continued to struggle with finding a balanced and integrated approach to teaching, research, and service that would prepare them for success with the promotion process to full professor. For the faculty members who had a balanced and integrated view of productivity ingrained in their work life, this work ethic continued and readily prepared them for success with the process of further promotion. The work ethic and perspective faculty members bring with them to their careers remained fairly steady from early to mid-career.

Moving into Administration

Although participants acknowledged that administrative positions offer increased prestige, opportunity of advancement, and potential pay increases, other aspects of administrative life (such as additional responsibilities, lack of day-to-day flexibility, a longer work calendar, dealing with politics, and a shift from collegial to supervisory interactions with fellow faculty members) outweighed those advantages, at least while their children were young or still at home. In general, faculty participants were very actively engaged in shared governance on their respective campuses. Under the guise and nomenclature of service, faculty members were involved in a full range of activities, including program coordinator, graduate studies coordinator, assistant chair, faculty senate chair, and various presidential initiatives. Although some of these duties fall under the typical rubric of what we in higher education think of as service (for example, committee work), some of the service duties had significant administrative responsibilities. As one faculty member commented, "You get paid, it's administration; you don't, it's service." When probed about their administrative aspirations, even those faculty members already involved in administration often did not see themselves with administrative futures. This was largely a matter of not wanting to deal with politics and "picky people," not considering the duties worth the trade-off in terms of cost and benefit, and not wanting to have the administrative route interfere with children and family life. We now turn our attention to an explanation of each of these areas.

Not wanting to deal with politics. The politics involved played a role in people not wanting to deal with difficult situations, and also produced a lack of clarity about certain rules and what is involved in particular administrative positions. On some campuses, particularly at community colleges and small liberal arts colleges, there is much blending of roles between faculty and administration, making it difficult to work with and deal with people who are simultaneously peers and supervisees, and making sticky political situations at times. There is a definite perception that dealing with people and politics are the most difficult part of administration. "I'm just staying here [as a faculty member]. I think at one point in my career I wanted to be in administration but seeing the personalities and the muck you have to deal with I don't think it is worth it. I need alone time to recharge, and administrators need to be here every day. I don't want to give up the flexibility."

Not worth the trade-off. People become faculty members because they love teaching, working with students, and/or their research. Faculty life becomes part of people's identity. The move into administration means moving in a distinctly different direction, so much so that some feel that "administration and research are in opposition to one another," as we heard from a faculty member in the study. People perceive that they can no longer excel in their traditional faculty roles if they move into administration. As one faculty member remarked, "I love teaching, moving into administration compromises that." Another faculty member who had already done a stint as chair talked about the blend of traditional faculty work and administration this way:

> For right now I am just investing myself in some new teaching methods. I went to a conference just this last weekend that was really energizing. I toy with becoming a dean, but to be honest I am not sure. When I was chair I think I did a good job and I like that mix—because you are still in the classroom and you also get a piece of administration. I would worry about being fully administrative—I would not want to give up the classroom.

Moving into administrative roles calls for changes in priorities with regard to time, and the faculty women in the study, in general, did not feel prepared to make the shift. Changing into an administrative position also means shifting identity from being a faculty member to being an administrator—a change one study participant referred to as "moving to the dark side." It is also a job variation that has significant implications for how one spends their time at work and time with their families (Jacobs & Winslow 2004).

Administration interferes with family. A major consideration for faculty members thinking about moving into administration is how the shift compromises time with children at home, especially in the summer. As one faculty member commented, "I was asked to apply for associate dean, but I didn't want to give up summer with my kids." And another: "When you become dean you give up your summers—and I love my summers at home. I'm really glad to have that flexibility and be home. I would not seriously consider it until my daughter was a senior in high school."

Some of the faculty members we talked with are planning on an administrative career in the future—a long-term goal—but not now with children at home: "I will [be chair] in twenty years, maybe when my kids are out of school. So, I know at some point I'll probably get into that administrative role. I don't think it is something I am jumping at because I became a faculty member to teach. At some point I want to do more administration, but not now." Another said:

> I would be interested in making the transition to administration as a long-term goal. I would say that my kids would be well into high school before I would make a shift like that because that is a longer commitment—twelve months versus ten months. Now is the time when I think I'm needed more when they are out of school for the summer, versus when they get a little older. I'm looking at a long-term goal, but I'm one of those people who like to plan.

People also did not want to compromise their flexibility—a clear job benefit of faculty life for working mothers. At mid-career, faculty women in the study frequently mentioned their autonomy and the flexibility they had with their schedules as more senior faculty. The flexibility is related to summers, as previously mentioned, but also is compromised by the additional meetings and work hours that require fuller days and sometimes evening obligations, which administration calls for. The demanding work schedule of administrators is a major deterrent for some:

> I am really doing a lot of administrative work—but I am officially classified as a faculty member. There are schools that have dean positions and I have been asked to apply. I don't want to leave my school and partly I don't know that I want to move into an official dean position because I have a young child at home. While I work very hard and very long hours, we have a lot of rights as faculty members. I can choose to leave at

3 P.M. and do my work at home should I wish to. . . . My understanding is that if you move into a more official dean position you are pretty much expected to be there from 8 to 5. I realized this spring that I do not want to have a job that does not allow me that kind of flexibility as far as time goes.

In short, "The challenge with administration is less flexibility."

Although the majority of the people in the study were not interested in administrative positions, there were some faculty women who were actively involved in service and administration and saw themselves building a career in an administrative direction. We think it is helpful to hear from these people and how they reconcile work and family and how they think about the transition to administration:

I would say I am clearly on an administrative track. I am doing a lot of statewide stuff and I sit on some committees with the chancellor's office. There are probably opportunities to go up to [the capital] if I wanted to, but I do not think I want to. I think I want to stay here. I probably even want to be a vice president of instruction, but not while my one child is as young as he is.

Participants also talked about the challenge of administration and the positives associated with the challenge, something they want to do at some point: "I want to move into administration—I like building things." Another faculty member talked about the benefit of trying something different and new: "I love teaching, but at some point I'd like to shift my career focus and move away from the classroom and do more administrative things."

Family was not the only consideration in thinking about next steps in the career, but it was a major consideration. Faculty members were not sure about how to manage their lives as an administrator, leaving one faculty member to ask, "How would I be an administrator and keep my family together?"

While participants, for the most part, were reticent about taking on senior administrative roles (such as dean or provost), they were active in service responsibilities that involved a fair amount of administration (such as program coordinator or director of graduate studies). Such roles built on experience and competence, but also challenged early mid-career faculty to maintain their research, especially in contexts that call for active research agendas. It is helpful to look at the research on mid-career faculty (e.g., Baldwin et al. 2005; Neumann 2009; Neumann & Terosky 2007), as well as what we found from our work that deliberately looks at the dynamics of work and family, to help build a narrative to explain the relationship between work, family, and academic career development in different career stages.

Mentoring and Support

One of the findings from the study was how mentoring and support systems changed over time. In the first phase of the study, there was talk about mentoring and the different programs available to mentor and support junior faculty during the tenure process. While there was a general sentiment that faculty succeeded "in spite of lack of support and not because of support" at the institutional level, there was also recognition that institutions attempted to help junior faculty succeed. It was common practice for campuses to have some combination of organized mentoring programs, new faculty workshops and orientations, and professional development activities focused on earning tenure. Early-career faculty members also benefited and talked a lot about the mentor relationships they had beyond campus and, in particular, their graduate school mentors and how these continued to play a part in the tenure process and faculty career development.

Once tenure was awarded, however, there was minimal talk about mentoring and support systems. Faculty women in the second interviews found mentoring about career issues generally unavailable and not something talked about on campus. There was a limited number of women in the second interviews who had met with any senior faculty and/or administrators, including their department chairs, about going up for promotion to full professor or moving into administration. Research on faculty careers illustrates the importance of ongoing support and mentorship throughout the career (Philipsen 2008). As one faculty member commented: "You have to have mentors . . . being on your own will just kill you." As mid-career faculty members, those interviewed were seen by their colleagues as established, and "people think you don't need help, but you still need help, you always need help." Although the mid-career women felt they could benefit from mentoring, there was limited opportunity to get this help.

The women in the study were still relatively early in their careers. Essentially these faculty members are "sandwiched" in the middle between junior and senior colleagues (Baldwin et al. 2005). Many of the study participants see themselves as mentors for their junior colleagues and as role models for graduate students and junior colleagues who wanted to have children and be successful academics. They also continued to need mentoring, but the form this takes may need to be different from what was provided to them in early career. Early-career mentoring in the academic context tends to focus on success with tenure; mid-career mentoring is more complex. Mentoring models for mid-career faculty need to encompass career advancement issues, concerns about work and family, and encourage administrative aspirations.

SUMMARY OF MID-CAREER FINDINGS

A longitudinal perspective on the topic of work and family is particularly important because time and experience change dynamics in families and careers. Neither career development nor family lives are static, and looking at the life course and all its nuances helps shed light on the academic career. Faculty women in the study, throughout their careers, do not so much seek balance between work and family as strive for more integrated views of work and family. The life-course perspective is particularly apt to help us understand how people go about their careers and go about their family lives. Previous research about faculty development (such as Baldwin & Blackburn 1981) failed to consider the role that family might play for faculty members in how they considered things like promotion to full professor or job changes. A life-course perspective recognizes the "web of interdependence" (Han & Moen 1999) that enmeshes people with children who also have careers. Given this interdependence, it makes sense that family consideration would be part of making decisions about things like moving into administration or changing jobs. The multiple spheres we live in as people shape one another and influence the actions we take within each domain.

As we discussed in the previous chapter, for early-career faculty there was considerable stress involved in finding balance and integration between work and family and the desire to succeed with the tenure process. Overall, we see considerable singularity of purpose for early-career faculty—they were concerned with how to manage getting tenure while having small children. The focus of faculty members at mid-career is not so singular. Yes, they are still concerned with how to manage work and family, but there are a lot more nuances to careers as they evolve—findings consistent with other research (Neumann 2009). There are many more choices that need to be addressed in the mid-career stage. Should I go into administration? Should I go up for full professor? What will happen to my time with students or research or advising if I become an administrator? To be certain, early-career faculty members were faced with some similar choices, but not nearly to the same extent. The focus on getting tenure helps narrow many of the choices junior faculty face as compared to when they become more established at mid-career.

The follow-up findings for mid-career faculty are heartening in that life, overall, is less stressful in terms of the physical challenges of young children. Faculty members talked of more time for self-care, time to pursue some outside interests, and time together as a family engaging in activities. We were also happy to learn that many institutions had become more progressive in terms of work and family policy. While it was not the focus of conversation with the mid-career faculty, they did mention that the policy environment with regard to work and family had evolved since they were earlier in their positions. Institutions, in general, have been responsive to work/family concerns and have created policies and regularized practices to make the combination less tenuous and more manageable (although the use of these policies needs to be regularized). The experiences of many of the women in the study provided an impetus for their campuses to create and/or update policies about work, family, and the tenure process.

Consistent with a life-course perspective, we also found that parenting and professing evolved simultaneously. People in the study were more comfortable in their roles as parents and had things a little more figured out than they did when they were new parents. They also had things a bit more in hand in their workplaces, since they were more established professionally. Unfortunately, we also found that the tenure process for some faculty members was one of depletion and professional burnout, leaving them feeling somewhat jaded about their productivity. Such a view compromised ongoing career development and the desire to engage in the process for promotion to full professor, and also to think with open minds about administration. We also found that mentoring and support systems are limited for mid-career faculty. Campuses pay little, if any, attention to ongoing career development for faculty members once they are tenured. This is something we will address more fully when we talk about policy. One thing we also found from talking to mid-career faculty is that context continues to matter. Campus context matters because it shapes tenure and promotion processes, how faculty members spend time, and how faculty members view their jobs and families. We also found that disciplinary context matters. How people approach their work, and in particular their research, is shaped not only by organizational context but also by disciplinary and departmental contexts—topics to which we now turn.

CHAPTER 6

The Role of Disciplinary
and Departmental Contexts

Throughout this book, as throughout the early and mid-career interviews, we were struck by the commonality of experience among the faculty women in the study regardless of where they worked and what discipline they were in. Academic mothers had more in common as a group than they had differences. That said, there are some issues that emerge from the data that require additional consideration and analysis. In particular, we want to address how different disciplines shape the faculty experience for women who are parents.

Knowing that disciplines are the "lifeblood" of an institution (Clark 1983), when we created the sample of women to be in the study we intentionally included women both from different institutional contexts and from different disciplinary backgrounds. The result was an initial sample that included 118 women—34 from the humanities, 21 from the social sciences, 30 from science, technology, engineering, and math (STEM) fields, and 33 from professional disciplines (such as education and business). When we analyzed the data at the early-career and mid-career stages, although we were struck by the commonality of experience across disciplines, a few disciplinary areas stood out with some particular distinctions for us to address as part of the overall picture of what it means to be a mother and an academic. There were limited differences between the early and mid-career stages, however, so we report findings about discipline across career stages.

Women in STEM Fields

Susan figured out that she was interested in science when she was an undergraduate. She worked in a chemistry lab with one of her undergraduate professors and liked the idea of discovering new things and running experiments. She also liked the communal nature of the lab itself—the range of undergraduates, graduate students, post-docs, and faculty all contributing to experiments. The lab was an exciting place to be, and Susan could see herself liking this kind of life. Susan pursued a doctorate degree right after college. She had gone to a strong undergraduate program and was admitted to a high-caliber research university. During graduate school, she worked as a graduate teaching assistant and also as a research assistant funded by federal grants. As is typical in many of the science fields, Susan met her husband in graduate school—they were in the same degree program—and they decided to marry and both pursue careers in science. After she earned her degree, Susan and her husband were fortunate to be hired as post-docs at a prestigious research university.

At this point, Susan and her husband decided that they ought to begin having children. There were certainly worries about how to manage the post-doc positions and the soft funding while having a child, but they realized they couldn't wait much longer if they wanted to have a family. There were no maternity leaves available for post-docs, but her supervisor was supportive of her being away from the lab for a little while. This supervisor had children who were now grown, and also had had a stay-at-home spouse to handle the day-to-day worries of parenthood. His daughter was a young professional, however, and this made him quite sympathetic to Susan and her concerns about balancing lab work with a new baby. There were enough other people in the lab to cover her absences—but Susan still felt guilty and felt the need to get back to work as quickly as possible.

There were not very many other women in her field, and few people to look to as role models for how to balance work and family; but between Susan, her husband, and a cadre of reliable babysitters, they figured out a way to make their lifestyle work with their research jobs. After about three years in her post-doc, she and her husband started looking for tenure-track appointments at research universities. As a fallback, Susan considered leaving higher education to go work in industry—she figured the hours would at least be a little more regular and that the pay might even be better outside of academia. Luck, talent, plus academic and social capital were on Susan's side, and she landed a job at a research university in her field. Her husband also luckily landed a job at a nearby teaching-oriented institution. In her new tenure-track position, Susan was given a generous start-up package that included laboratory facilities. She quickly earned a major grant and was able to fund graduate students and post-docs of her own. In relatively short order, Susan had established her own lab and her research trajectory, and was feeling pretty good about the expectations of her tenure-track position. Her first child was now four years old and she felt ready to have another child.

Like other women scientists she knew at different institutions, Susan tried to time her pregnancy with the academic calendar and was relatively successful in achieving this goal. The problem, however, was that her lab couldn't stop operating just because she wasn't available. There were funded projects that needed to be completed, students and lab employees who needed to keep going, and more grants to apply for to keep the "science machine" moving forward. Even though Susan was able to get a maternity leave from teaching, her lab work had to keep progressing. Susan figured out ways to make it work—she hired a few extra research technicians to cover some absences, and she attended meetings with her research team with her baby in tow. But she didn't feel as connected to the team as she had before the baby, and she felt she wasn't being as good a team player as she might normally have been. With the assistance of good day-care options, helpful in-laws, a supportive husband, and a full research team, Susan managed to make it work. She created what she and her husband considered to be "the new normal." Because of the collaborative nature of her research, there was hardly a dip in her productivity (as measured by published articles or even new grants) due to her parenthood status.

The machine kept going, and so did Susan. She earned tenure, and her work kept up apace. Falling behind didn't feel like an option, nor did stopping her work or relaxing the pace she had established early on. Pre- and post-tenure career success were tied together, and Susan was often hard pressed to see much difference in her work patterns before and after tenure—although she noticed an increase in service expectations once she earned tenure. By the time of the second interview, Susan was well on her way to being promoted to full professor. While her family life and responsibilities had changed pre- and post-tenure, her academic and research life remained largely static and productive.

One does not need to go far on a college campus or into contemporary readings about higher education to hear about the particular concerns related to women in STEM fields. The concern stems from the under-representation of women in these areas throughout the academic pipeline, and in particular in the faculty ranks. The representation varies by discipline within science fields. For example, in the biological sciences women have made great strides in all ranks, whereas in physics not so much (Rosser 2004). Even in areas like biology where women have made progress throughout the pipeline, there is still concern that the higher the rank and the more prestigious the position, the greater the representation of men (Etkowitz et al. 2000). Women today currently earn 41 percent of Ph.D.s in STEM fields, but make up only 28 percent of tenure-track faculty in those fields.

Women in STEM departments are often the "only one" in their fields, which can lead to isolation and ultimately concerns about attrition (Monosson 2008). The number of women in STEM fields declines at the transition point into graduate school and also with the transition into the workplace, leaving many concerned that there are few women in general, but also that there are few women to serve as role models and teachers for up-and-coming students (Hill et al. 2010). The number of women entering the pipeline has steadily increased; the advancement of these same women has not (Mavriplis et al. 2008). The lack of representation of women in STEM fields is attributed to the male culture of the disciplines, the historic absence of women in STEM fields, and the perceived incompatibility of what it takes to be serious about a STEM career and to have children (Etkowitz et al. 2000; Rosser 2004) Further, women in STEM fields often have options beyond academe that are not limited to full-time and tenure-track positions. There are a lot of ways to be a woman scientist, and the academy is just one domain of possibility (Monosson 2008). To be sure, not all women who work in STEM fields want to have children, but for those who do there is worry about the incompatibility between what is perceived as a greedy culture in science and the expectations of women in motherhood (Grant et.al. 2000).

In our research, we intentionally included women from different STEM-related disciplines, recognizing that it is likely to be different to be in environmental engineering than in wildlife biology. Although we did find some nuanced differences among women in STEM, the commonalities were more pronounced, and that is the focus here. The unique themes from the data analysis were the consequences of being the only one, the unique nature of lab research, and the strong identity of being a scientist. We now turn to a discussion of these findings.

The Only One

We heard repeatedly across the interviews from women in different STEM disciplines in different institutional settings about being the only women in their departments. While other research has pointed to the isolation created by being the only one (e.g., Etkowitz et al. 2000), this was not the primary focus of the interview findings. Instead the focus was on being the only one to be involved in particular campus initiatives. As one participant indicated, "I'm the only one [woman in my department], there is no place to hide." A biologist at a comprehensive college told us how she is constantly getting involved in presidential initiatives, the most recent one related to a cross-campus initiative to support interdisciplinary research. As the only woman in her area and the only person with grant-writing experience, she is regularly called upon to participate in this type of work. She shared with us the good and bad aspects of participation in such initiatives:

> I was encouraged to apply for the grant because the research needed matched my background. It ended up having strings attached, and I'm a

lot more involved than I want to be. I get release time from teaching, but it's still hard to manage everything. It's one thing to apply for a grant, it's another thing to get it. I'm at a regional university where a lot of people don't have much research. I feel like I'm expected to be involved in this type of research because I have grant experience and a background in biology that cuts across different areas. I like it and I'm glad to be recognized, but it is a lot of work and it definitely takes away from my family.

For this faculty member, being the only woman in her department, the only one with grant experience, and the only one willing to do interdisciplinary work have all led to increased opportunity, but also an increased workload.

Another faculty member, also a biologist, at a liberal arts college explained her involvement in grants to support undergraduate research. "I have a lot of students who want to work with me so I write grants for undergraduate research projects. They run all summer. I pretty much always have to be looking out for grants to support my research and to maintain my lab. I'm the only person doing work in my area so I need to keep it going." There are other aspects to being the only one, as well. One person commented about her involvement in service: "As the only woman, I feel like I have to be on committees." And another faculty member talked about the extra work that comes with being the only woman in her chemistry department and the only woman scientist in her college that has children. "As the only woman in my department who has children, every time we have a prospective female graduate student they always have me meet with them to let them know you can have a career and a family."

The consequences of being the only one cut across both early and mid-career faculty. Faculty members did not necessarily begrudge or lament the increased involvement, but they were very aware of the extra work that comes with being the only woman, the only scientist, the only mother, and the only one for people to turn to for a myriad of activities.

The Unique Nature of Lab Research

In the early-career findings, in particular, faculty women talked about how working in a lab created unique circumstances for faculty members, especially when getting established. Setting up a lab space is costly, time consuming, and necessary for particular kinds of research. As one early-career faculty member commented, "It's my lab. I needed to set it up. I'm in charge. I need to be worried 24/7." Faculty in the early and mid-career interviews talked about how the pressure to maintain lab spaces and positions for undergraduate and graduate research assistants as well as postdoctoral researchers added additional pressures to the job. "You can't just stop your lab. Even if you take a leave, the lab keeps going. It keeps going after you get tenure, too. It is always there, although as you move up you are less likely to be the person actually running the experiments. You are the person responsible for getting the grants to keep the lab going." Grants and research are the currency in science, more than in other disciplines (Etkowitz et al. 2000). Regardless of institutional type, faculty in STEM fields in our study had active involvement in grant writing.

Looking at our data over time, we noted that faculty involvement in lab research and grant funding contributed to greater continuity with research throughout the early and mid-career stages. In other disciplinary areas, we noted a definite ebb and flow to faculty research productivity, but as a group the STEM faculty maintained more continuity. We attribute this to the need to stay current, maintain labs through grant funding, and also the group orientation of lab spaces.

There are both pros and cons to working in "communal lab spaces," as one our respondents called them. The plus side was that when faculty took a maternity leave or had lulls in personal productivity due to having a baby or other family-related issues, the collaborative nature of research conducted in laboratories did not make those lulls evident. As one faculty member remarked, "I've had two leaves of absence associated with having my children and if you look at my productivity it's not evident. Yes, it was a lot of work and stress to keep the lab funded and going when I wasn't there, but I have a whole team to work with me." We also attributed the more collegial relationships among work groups to the communal nature of laboratories. As a group, the STEM faculty tended to do more socially with people in their departments. As one person told us, "You spend a lot of time with people in your lab."

A faculty member at a research university shared the negative side to all the "lab togetherness" by commenting: "My colleagues that don't have children stay at the lab late and go to the pub after to discuss work. I see this is part of what it takes to be successful. I can't do this with having a family. I choose not to." She went on to tell us that when she was a young scholar she felt the pressure to be more involved in the lab activities, during work and after, but now that she is more established she realizes she just can't be "gone or absent all the time from my family," and then out all night as well.

STEM Identity

Another distinction among the women in STEM fields in the study has to do with disciplinary identity. More so than in other disciplinary areas, women in STEM strongly identified with their fields (Monosson 2008). They refer to themselves as scientists and engineers more than as faculty members. The identity is also part of what gives them other options in terms of careers. This, in part, explains the leaky pipeline between graduate school and throughout the early academic career. Women in STEM fields, unlike other disciplines, tend to have options outside of academe that are attractive and often similar to the work they would do within the academic context (Monosson 2008). For faculty looking to balance work and family, sometimes options in industry are more attractive. The goal for many people is to do science, and they aren't always particular about where—this is different from many other fields. If, for example, you want to do research in Middle Eastern studies, there are not many options for doing so beyond the academy. In contrast, women in STEM fields have other options, and with higher education's "bad reputation" as a pressure cooker with low pay and an unending workload, these other options are often attractive (Mason 2009). The women we spoke to, for the most part, were committed to the academic setting, but having options in terms of other career settings did help them transcend some of the challenges of their campuses.

The concerns of women in science have not gone unheard. Recent changes in National Science Foundation (NSF) funding recognize the need not only to improve the pipeline for women in sciences but also to provide greater work-related flexibility to women in research careers. Specifically, NSF, the leading source of federal grants for many research fields, will now allow post-doc and early career researchers to delay or suspend their grants for up to one year in order to care for a newborn or newly adopted child or fulfill other family obligations. The new policy makes provisions for supplemental funds to pay for research technicians while principal investigators are on family leave. To help change culture, NSF promises to publicize their family-friendly opportunities and to allow review panelists to conduct virtual reviews rather than being asked to travel to a single location. The goal is to increase flexibility and reduce dependent-care needs. NSF also plans to use its leverage with institutions to advocate for institution-specific family-friendly policies as well as for dual-career hiring policies. While this policy change is only a first step, it does serve as a recognition of the culture of the scientific enterprise and provides incentives for institutions to consider making changes themselves to be more family friendly.

FACULTY IN THE HUMANITIES

Monica has always loved reading. She read constantly as a child and was thrilled to learn, when she went to college, that is was possible to major in literature and even fashion a career out of her passion. While in graduate school, Monica worked as a graduate teaching assistant. It was here that she figured out that not only did she love literature but she also had a passion for teaching undergraduates. Monica decided early on in her graduate work that a teaching-focused institution was the best fit for her. She also thought that a relatively noncompetitive tenure system would work best for her goals of raising a family and pursuing an academic career. She knew some women faculty members who had children, but most of their children were already grown up, and she didn't have many role models for how to make the academic career work with a young family.

Before she had even finished her dissertation, Monica began applying for jobs. She knew from being a student on a search committee that there were lots of qualified applicants and too few tenure-track positions available in her field. She knew there were nontenure-track options available, but she had her heart set on a tenure-track position. Her interest in teaching and her positive student evaluations, along with the prestige of her degree and advisor, led her to become a finalist in many search pools. It took almost two years, however, before she landed a tenure-track position. Her husband worked as a

K-12 teacher, so he was relatively flexible in terms of where they could live. He did secure a position in a nearby school district shortly after Monica was hired. Monica and Steve had decided to wait to have children until they were settled in their new jobs. They wanted to give Monica a chance to figure out the job requirements, to establish a pattern, and to begin working on her book—which seemed to be the main requirement for tenure at her striving regional comprehensive institution.

The teaching load was three classes a semester, and Monica, as the junior person in the department, was expected to teach a lot of the freshman-level writing classes. She was allowed one advanced literature class in her course rotation. Monica was a good teacher, having learned from her GTA experiences, but she was slightly ill-prepared for the grading expectations she faced in teaching beginning writing classes. There were so many papers to grade and so many grammatical problems to solve that it was sometimes overwhelming. This was clearly the part of the job that seemed to take the most time.

In year three of the tenure track, Monica had a baby girl. She used sick leave to cover the time she was away from classes, and her department chair let her teach one of the classes online, waived the requirement to teach a second class, and hired an adjunct to cover her third class for the time that she was unavailable (she took a six-week partial leave). One of the decisions that Monica had to make during her pretenure period was about the content of her book project. She had once been very interested in European literature, but the project she envisioned would mean spending a significant amount of time in some archives in France. Given her new family, that was not a feasible option. Instead, Monica decided on a literary analysis project that didn't involve travel. The project she was working on was not quite as compelling as the other, but it seemed much more feasible given her multiple roles. The teaching requirements also precluded extensive travel.

Monica and her husband managed their daily lives by taking turns watching the baby and doing household projects. Monica often woke herself up at 4 A.M. to work on her book, and would often grade papers after dinner or while her baby napped. There weren't really enough hours in the day to get everything done, but she managed to do the best she could—even if she cut a few corners. The good news about her work was that it could be done anywhere at any time—all she needed was her books and her computer. Monica's book project was a solitary one—and while it needed to get done, she had a fair amount of flexibility in terms of how it got done. By the time Monica went up for tenure, she was pretty exhausted. She had a little more seniority, so she didn't teach all of the freshman-level writing classes, but grading papers continued to be time-consuming and unending.

After getting tenure, Monica wasn't sure about what her next book project should be. She was a bit burned out from the last one—she had finished it, but did not feel it was necessarily worth the time and struggle she had invested. Although she earned tenure, she found that period so difficult and isolating that afterward she was just happy to focus on her teaching and on her service responsibilities. Once tenured, Monica was asked to help coordinate the institution's general education reform efforts—in return for a course release—and she found working on service projects for the institution to be fulfilling. She wasn't sure about ever going up for promotion to full professor, and she didn't see herself becoming an administrator—it would take too much time away from her family. The thought of finishing a second book seemed daunting and, frankly, she felt there was already a lot on her plate. Monica didn't know what the future held—she liked her job and felt content. Moving to another institution didn't seem feasible—but she wasn't really sure where she was going with this job either.

For faculty in disciplines associated with the humanities—languages, literature, philosophy, history—there were four aspects that stood out in the findings: the time-intensive nature of working with students on writing (this is especially true with large undergraduate sections of writing), the solitary nature of research, the focus on writing books as the currency for success, and the limited job market (Schuster & Finkelstein, 2006). The essays in Rachel Hile Bassett's book (2005) all represent stories of faculty who teach in the humanities and reflect some of the ideas we found in our work.

Working with Students on Writing

Faculty we talked to highlighted two aspects here. One was related to the very large sections of introductory writing classes. Early-career faculty members, who often are targeted to teach large undergraduate sections, talked about the extensive time involved in grading. The second aspect was related to teaching classes with a large writing emphasis and how student writing was not always up to par and required significant time and energy.

Talking about her large undergraduate composition courses, one faculty member observed, "If I don't stay up and grade after my kids go to bed, I just can't keep up." As part of the interviews, faculty members shared with us their daily schedules, and we noted in particular among those faculty who either taught composition classes or taught classes with large writing components that grading was a significant part of their day. This was exacerbated among faculty members having to do writing for their own research. A typical day for one faculty member: "I wake up very early to get my own writing done. My daughter is still in bed, and I write. It's me time. Time for my research. It's the only time I can get things done. I have to say with having a child this is harder to maintain because I'm tired. . . . At night after I get my daughter to bed, I need to grade. I have to stay up to keep up."

Solitary Nature of Research

The research that faculty in the humanities carry out tends to be solitary. This had both up- and downsides, according to the faculty we interviewed. The upside was that you could do it "anywhere, anytime" as one faculty member told us. She went on to say, "After I had a baby I actually changed the direction of my research because I used to have to do research with some fairly obscure archives that required a lot of travel. I'm still doing work in the same area, but I changed my focus so I could more readily take my work with me wherever I go." Some of the downsides of solitary research include loneliness and isolation, and also the lack of accountability. As one person commented, "If I don't get my work done, I have no one to blame except myself." Having children actually helped some faculty be more productive.

"I used to waste a lot of time, but now that I have a baby and I need to drop her off and pick up I need to be more focused with my research and writing. I piddle a lot less than I used to."

Within in our sample we interviewed two women from theater, where the research process is more focused around creative work, and in theater it is particularly related to productions. The direction and performance of theater is not a solitary pursuit and is more similar to the lab experience in its communal orientation. One of the theater faculty respondents indicated, "The theater is like a family to me. We work really closely together. It's nightly when we are in production. We learn how to work together and it helps." When talking about how this works with family, she went on to say, "I feel like my son has been raised by a committee in my department." The other person in theater observed that when a production is in process it is difficult to focus on much else, and this can conflict with family. As with the communal aspects of laboratory research, there are pros and cons to research endeavors that involve working with others or in more solitary settings.

Research as Books

Another element to research in the humanities is the focus on production of book-length manuscripts. Generally speaking, faculty members in the humanities talked about the need to publish books as opposed to articles or other shorter pieces. "In my department it's clear. If you want to get promoted and tenured or promoted to full professor you need to have at least one book for each promotion." The need to have a book published generated a lot of pressure for early-career scholars in particular. Faculty members in the mid-career interviews talked about having their book as their indication that they were ready to get promoted to full professor: "I got my book done, so I knew I was ready to be promoted to full, and I was, it's helped some of the people I work with get going too." In other disciplines, research can sometimes be quicker, but in the humanities the research process tends to be slow and deliberate, requiring a building process. People often took a long time to get their doctoral degrees, but now that they were on the faculty they felt the pressure to keep focused. Another challenge related to books is getting published. With the advances in technology, publishing in the humanities has changed significantly, leaving some faculty members finding it a challenge not only to complete a book but also to find a publisher.

Limited Job Options

The humanities fields are well known for their limited academic job opportunities, especially in recent years. Generally speaking, departments in these areas more readily hire adjunct and part-time instructors rather than tenure-track faculty (Schuster & Finkelstein 2006). Tenure-track positions are coveted, leading faculty members who have them to go any lengths to keep them. One faculty member in the study talked about this situation: "My husband got a job at [campus] that is five hours away. It's not ideal. We want our kids to be in schools here [where she works]. They are so much better. I also know that it is not easy to get a job in English. . . . I have this job and I intend to keep it."

In contrast, another faculty member who left her community college tenure-track position teaching English to accommodate a cross-country job for her husband said, "I woke up one day and wondered what I had done. . . . These positions are hard to come by and I couldn't believe I left one." After she had been out of the workforce for a year, she worried she would not be able to get back to working as a faculty member—a concern that is validated in research about faculty. One study about the academic profession (Schuster & Finkelstein 2006) confirms that it is difficult to reenter tenure-track positions once you leave one, and also that it is difficult to be in a part-time position and then transition to a full-time tenure-track position. This faculty member's concerns about reentry turned out to be warranted. When it was time to reenter, she was not able to find a position at a community college, due to a combination of few open positions and poor pay compared to what she made before she moved. After additional time at home, and recognizing the difficulty in finding a full-time position teaching at the postsecondary level, she opted for teaching Advanced Placement English at a local high school. "It's good; I was a hot ticket item. They definitely wanted me to come and work there." Her doctoral degree and her experience teaching at a community college helped her reenter the workforce teaching English, just not in the collegiate setting. "It's worth it because I have found I really love the job." Having a family and accommodating their needs in limited job markets meant for some faculty they had to be creative with finding positions both inside and beyond the academy.

Faculty in the Social Sciences

"I used to waste a lot of time," is how Margaret responded when we asked her about how things have changed now that she has children. When she was in graduate school in sociology, she was in a large program and there were a lot of students around. They were all mostly single and childless and pretty much worked all the time, although in retrospect Margaret recognized that not all of that time was productive. "I was at work a lot, but I also had a lot time where I accomplished very little." When she got her first faculty job, still childless and single, Margaret worked all the time. She was in her office pretty much every day from 8 A.M. to 7 P.M., and then would sometimes even go out to dinner and drinks with colleagues. Her early faculty life and her graduate school life were very similar. She was quite productive and felt she was off to a good start as a tenure-track professor at a research university (although, as she says, "not a really intense research university"). In her third year she met the man who would become her partner, got married, and had a child. Having a family suddenly changed how Margaret conducted her work. She could no longer spend all day at the office, and she suddenly had to be more efficient and productive with her time if she was going to get things done. Having a child was a huge shift in terms of how she used her time and how she related to people at work. She had a lot less time to "hang out," and she was in a department where people did a lot of things together. She was worried how this change would affect her colleagues' perspective of her. There were a lot of older faculty in her department who were waiting to retire, but they were also very strong in her department. There were also a couple of senior female faculty members who, she felt, had really paved the way for junior women, but they did so when they did not have children and were single. How would they react to her change in status?

As a junior faculty member, Margaret worried a lot about what people thought about her and her research. She was well aware that expectations had increased significantly over the past ten years, and the amount of research she was expected to do was a lot more than what her senior colleagues had to produce. She confided in us how odd it was to have people reviewing her materials even though they had not necessarily kept active in the field in terms of research. She was careful to say "we all get along," but there are some clear lines between late-career senior faculty and the junior faculty and recent associates. There were also some clear lines between senior women who seemed to sacrifice families and marriages for their jobs and the junior faculty who thought they could "have it all." They were all in the same department, but in many ways occupied very different worlds.

Throughout the past thirty years, opportunities for women in the social sciences have rapidly increased as many of these disciplines have become "feminized" (Spalter-Roth & Merola 2001; Kalleberg & Reskin 1995). Although all social science fields have seen increases in the numbers of women, the extent of change varies by field. Specifically, the numbers of women in psychology and sociology have rapidly increased, whereas in economics and political science the growth has not been as great.

Regardless of their entry into feminized fields and in spite of their success in many social science fields (Van Vooren & Spalter-Roth 2008), the advancement of women continues to be a challenge (DiFuccia et al. 2007; Kulis et al. 2002). Not all, but some of the lack of advancement is attributed to work and family challenges (Spalter-Roth & Merola 2001). In our research, we identified two main themes associated with working in the social sciences—working in critical-mass fields and the generational differences among faculty.

Critical Mass of Women

The numbers of women in fields like sociology and psychology have rapidly increased. What impact does this have on women with children? Does working in a feminized field make it easier to manage work and family? What we found from looking at the experiences of women in these fields is that many of the same challenges exist as they do in other fields. One phenomenon we did note with regard to more women was the presence of more babies. "In my department over the past couple of years we have had several babies." In one case this meant a greater reliance on family-friendly policies and having a network of people to call upon for help in navigating a leave, but in another department this meant that different faculty had cut different deals with their department chairs, leading to concern about fairness and equity. We noted in one instance, after talking to two faculty women in a social science department, that in spite of being very similarly situated—both were new and on the tenure track and had young children—they ended up with very different experiences using policy and interacting with their department chair about how to accommodate work and family. They had cut different deals with their chair, a woman. Having more women in a given setting does not automatically mean that the interactions necessary to foster healthy and productive working relationships of women will automatically develop.

Generational Differences

In conducting our research, we also noted how generational differences shape the experiences of women in the study. This was particularly pronounced when talking to the women with children who were in the study and also when talking to their colleagues. There may be new gender configurations within departments, but traditional gender norms still prevail. One senior female faculty member in a department with several female faculty members, two of whom recently had children, said: "I'm not really sure how you can have a serious career as a psychologist and also plan to have children. I'm just not sure it is possible. It takes a lot out of a person to try to have a family and to have a career. I'm not sure you can do both. I couldn't."

The self-referential mindset of "I did it (or didn't) and you should (or shouldn't) too" is a pervasive one in academe and part of the faculty mystique. This particular mindset was one we heard referenced regularly throughout the study in all disciplines, but in the social sciences we noticed it more among senior women. In many instances, senior women in departments remained childless to succeed, as did the person we just heard from, and their reactions and interactions with junior women who were taking a different path within their careers and in their personal lives were not always positive. Newer faculty cohorts tend to seek to "have it all" with regard to work and family, and unlike earlier cohorts of women faculty who saw having a family and having children as either/or propositions, faculty members today seek to have both/and with regard to a meaningful career and a family. Newer cohorts of faculty do not come into their jobs with self-sacrificing mindsets (Trower 2010), unlike faculty members from previous years. Such generational differences can cause rifts, as some women in our study noted. While generational rifts were and are present throughout the data, they were more pronounced in the social sciences, where there was a greater presence of woman than in other fields.

WOMEN IN PROFESSIONAL FIELDS

Penny came to the community college from a well-established career working in information technology for a large corporation. After she earned her master's degree in Management Information Systems she had considered staying in graduate school, but was offered a job she couldn't refuse in the corporate world. She worked there for five years and mostly loved it. While working, she took some additional classes to stay fresh and up-to-date in the field. She found she loved being in school, and she missed it. She continued to take classes and was toying with going back to complete her Ph.D. and also toying with the idea of a career change. When she was asked by a colleague if she was interested in teaching a class at the local community college, she jumped at the opportunity. For two years she worked full time and taught classes in the evenings and on periodic weekends. She loved teaching and definitely had the bug. When the opportunity came up to teach full time, she eagerly applied and got the job. This was good timing, because her company had gone through some recent changes and a merger that called for Penny to travel, and with two kids and a husband who was in law enforcement, and often on call, traveling for work was not feasible.

When we interviewed Penny the first time, she talked a lot about the comparisons between her work in the corporate world and her work in the community college. She loved the flexibility of being a professor and found that it was much easier to accommodate her schedule with her children. She arranged her teaching so she was done at 3 P.M. Tuesdays and Thursdays so she could meet her kids and take them to their afterschool activities, something she was never able to do while working her corporate job. The one thing she did not like about teaching was that she felt she had to work all the time to keep up with advances in technology. While working in technology and in the corporate sector, keeping up was a central part of her job. While teaching, however, keeping up and staying abreast of new technology and, in some instances, learning new technology, meant constantly have to revise her syllabi and constantly having to retool—activities that often do not fit into a full day of teaching. She referred to "having homework almost every night" so she would be ready the next day. She loves what she does, but also told us she feels like she works all the time to keep up.

At mid-career, Penny was a lot more established in her teaching career, and she had also recently returned to school to finally get her dissertation done. Her kids were older and that helped, because her son drives and is able to help with transportation for her daughter. Now that she is more established in her position, Penny feels a more central part of campus, and she is actively involved in working with students and also the coordinator for her area. Although she doesn't have administrative aspirations, as one of the few full-time faculty members in her unit, Penny ends up doing a lot of administrative work. She likes it and she thinks she is good at it, but she thinks this level of administration is enough. Now that her kids are older and she is more established, she finds she is more efficient with her time and doesn't work at night as much as she used to. She has a new dean who wants all the faculty members to have pretty set office hours that include a lot of face time in the office. On the one hand, she would prefer more freedom, but on the other hand she is working a lot less at home. She is able to keep work at work and home at home. She's also more connected in the field now than she was earlier in the career, so keeping her classes up-to-date has been easier. She feels she has a system down and feels that the integration of work and family "has definitely gotten easier as I've become more established as a faculty member."

As a group, the experiences of women in professional fields were unique along two dimensions—they were able to compare their work experiences in academe with experiences in other professional settings, and they faced challenges associated with staying current with trends in the profession. Faculty members in professional disciplines work in different areas ranging from nursing to business to education to information technology and other applied fields. To be sure, there are some distinctions across these fields, but in our analysis of the data we saw some commonalities among these groups, as well. We focus on these themes here, in particular, having experience in other settings that provides a means to compare work settings, and also the need to keep up on trends in the profession (in addition to trends in the discipline).

Comparative Perspectives of Work Settings

Unlike faculty members in other disciplines, women in professional fields had often worked in other types of organizations in addition to working in higher education. They brought the comparative occupational lens to their faculty position and could more easily compare the nature or work in academic and nonacademic settings. Many of the faculty members in these areas had previously worked in banks, hospitals, and K–12 schools, leaving them very grateful for the flexibility afforded by an academic job. As one faculty member told us, "I used to work as corporate trainer, and to attend a doctor's appointment or a school function meant taking leave. As a faculty member my teaching is done at 3 P.M., and most days I can get home to meet kids coming off the bus." The ability to compare the largely autonomous nature of academic work with the confines and strictures of the traditional American workplace left the women generally happy in their positions. Previous experiences in the corporate world or other professional settings helped the women in the study see how good it is to work in a flexible setting. We saw this same finding with the women at community colleges—many of whom who had worked in other settings—who had a different base of comparison from women at other institutional types (Merton & Rossi 1968).

Keeping Current with the Professional Fields

Another aspect of working in professional fields is staying current with trends in the field and maintaining connections with constituencies in the profession (Becher 1994). We heard from women teaching in business fields with a technology emphasis, in particular, how difficult it can be to manage the traditional faculty work load and to stay current with professional trends so as to teach them in the classroom. As one faculty member said, "I constantly need to keep up. I have to be aware of the latest technology to stay current with my teaching." We heard similar sentiment from faculty members in areas like nursing, where the clinical setting and keeping students current with clinical procedures requires the faculty member to stay current. The need to stay current was felt especially strongly by faculty members in professional fields who teach large sections of students and for those teaching in community colleges. In the community college setting, in particular, faculty members, and their supervisors, have found it crucial to stay current in the field so students would have a good experience and ultimately be more competitive for particular jobs. What this meant for many women in the study was staying up late and getting up early to prepare for class. As one person told us, "Every time I teach a class I essentially need to start from scratch if the class is to stay current. The field [technology] is changing so rapidly."

SUMMARY OF DISCIPLINARY FINDINGS

Disciplines have distinct cultures (Becher 1994). Disciplinary culture shapes faculty orientation. In disciplinary cultures like the humanities, where work is more individually oriented, we found that the women in the study were able to create work patterns that met their work and family needs. The individualized nature of the discipline transcends time and place with regard to research, and we heard of a lot of creative work arrangements that involved work hours when babies were sleeping. More than in other fields, we heard of late nights and early rising as times to read, write, and do creative work. This is in contrast to STEM fields, especially those that are lab based, where the women in the study had to worry about the work of the lab going on with or without them. The community orientation of the lab sciences made the women we talked to aware of their absences because the larger lab community relied on them for continuity. Times out to meet parenthood-related needs made these women feel their absences were obvious. The women in these environments also felt more compelled to maintain productivity and meet the norms of the profession more than the norms of their particular campuses. The focus on grants in the STEM disciplines also creates a different set of expectations—a finding consistent with Becher and Trowler's (2001) landmark work related to the disciplines. Maintaining funding streams, which in turn maintain labs, put additional stress on faculty members. For women with children, this was largely manifest in stress about not missing deadlines and timelines to maintain grant continuity and staying current for students.

Faculty members work and live in different layers of culture (Austin 1990)—the culture of the discipline, as we've discussed in this chapter, and individual cultural characteristics emanating from different backgrounds (such as gender and ethnicity) that has been the focus of our work from the inception. The culture of the institution, the focus of the next chapter, also plays a significant role in how people approach academic work, given the perspective of motherhood. Where faculty members work shapes how they approach their jobs as parents and as professors at early and mid-career stages.

CHAPTER 7

Institutional Type Differences

Generally speaking, research related to academic life, work, and family has failed to consider organizational perspectives. The vast majority of research on academics and motherhood is based on the experiences of faculty at research universities. But the experience of women faculty who combine work and family is likely to vary according to their work context. The design of this study was thus based on the premise that the type of institutions where faculty members work shapes the experience of academics who are also mothers (cf. Wolf-Wendel & Ward 2006). Accordingly, we included women from different types of institutions, including research universities, comprehensive/regional campuses, liberal arts colleges, and community colleges as a means to explore how work norms and expectations shape faculty life from the perspective of women with children.

In examining academic mothers in the different types of academic institution, we call upon Burton Clark's (1987) foundational research on the intersection between institutional diversity and academic life. His work describes the diversity of institutional types within the U.S. system of higher education and offers a glimpse of faculty life in different types of colleges and universities. According to Clark, "American academics are distributed in widely varied institutions as well as in different disciplines, in many kinds of universities, four-and two-year colleges as well as in numerous subjects. The structures and cultures of those diverse settings cry out for our attention; *they heavily shape academic life*" (Clark 1987, xxii, emphasis added). Clark's research influenced our approach to this study in terms of methodology, analysis, and presentation of the findings. From him we understand that the complexities of reconciling faculty life and motherhood cannot be decontextualized from the institutions in which faculty work. Not all institutions are the same, and factors like mission, location, and prestige may make the balance between work and family either more manageable or more precarious.

Robert Birnbaum's signature work, *How Colleges Work* (1988), also highlights the fact that the function and organizational approach of an institution shapes how different campus actors interact with and within particular contexts, and also how people expend their energy in the workplace. The organizational milieu also shapes how people make decisions about their work. For faculty women, this means deciding how to spend time on a daily basis (Research? Teaching? Service?) and, for academic mothers in particular, the organizational and institutional setting can shape decisions about families as well (When is a good time to have a baby? Should I take a leave? How many children should I have?). Organizational perspectives that emanate from the research of Clark and Birnbaum aid our understanding of the complexity of the faculty experience for women faculty as mothers in different types of institutions and help us to analyze what we found.

We were struck by the commonality of experience within each type of institutional context and, therefore, present the findings from the different types of institutions in two ways. One, we continue our use of vignettes as a means to introduce the reader to what it was like for the early and mid-career women within particular types of institutions. And, two, we use fewer, but longer, quotations in an attempt to capture the "typical" faculty experience, first at the early-career stage and then at mid-career.

Research Universities: Early-Career Faculty Perspectives

Jennifer's graduate school experience can be seen as fairly typical. She worked closely with her advisor, was a full-time student, presented papers, worked on grants, and pretty much spent the bulk of her time socializing herself to be a successful faculty member. Jennifer knew she wanted to have children at some point in her life, but as a graduate student she learned not to talk about it with faculty or others associated with her graduate program. She knew of one woman who had a baby while in the doctoral program, and everyone talked about her as if she was not serious about her studies. The word on the street was "Don't do it."

Jennifer was hired in what was considered one of the "best openings in the field." She noted, "I got the job and I love it, I really do." Jennifer thought her students were great and her work environment was very stimulating. She appreciated how nice it was to graduate from a top program and then to move into teaching in a top program. She had gotten married in her last year of graduate school and after two years on the job was feeling a bit more settled. She decided it was "now or never" if she wanted to have a baby. She was thirty-five and her husband was thirty-seven. As she noted, "we were not getting any younger."And as she said, "I got lucky because my baby wasn't due until May." Jennifer was happy that the arrival of her baby would not interfere with the academic year. She acutely felt that she was in "uncharted territory," being the first woman in her department to have a baby in twelve years. There were other faculty with children in the department, but their kids were all older. Jennifer noted that she did have a male junior colleague with a child, but his wife stayed home, so the pressure they felt was different. Jennifer felt she was a role model for her graduate students, but didn't feel that she had role models of her own to follow.

Jennifer didn't take any maternity leave. She noted that the campus maternity leave policy was pretty much nonexistent, and instead she was told to negotiate what she needed with her chair. The chair seemed as though he might be supportive, but Jennifer decided it would be safer and better for her career to stay away from talk about a leave. When her baby was one year old, Jennifer noted that she was "pretty much back in the swing of things." The biggest problem she felt was that she couldn't work all the time, as she used to, and she was taking on projects with a slightly different scope to make it all doable. She described herself as much more efficient with her time. Jennifer does a lot of work very early in the morning and at night after the baby goes to bed. She notes that she is "doing the best I can and that has to be good enough." Jennifer felt some anxiety about tenure when she started her job, but since having the baby she doesn't feel as concerned. She describes this as a "welcome relief, really."

Jennifer's productivity did slow down a bit with the birth of her baby, and she worried about how that might look on her dossier. She had just submitted a grant and an article, and had a paper accepted for a conference. She felt pretty good about things because although the tenure process seems ambiguous, it was clear about what was expected to earn tenure. Jennifer expressed her joy about being a parent and was beginning to think about having another baby. She indicated that she always wanted to have two kids but was worried that "two babies on the tenure track at this place is unheard of!"

This faculty member's experience was similar to that of many of the professors in the study, and frankly her (and others') equanimity about combining academic work and motherhood was a little surprising. Several publications, including Clark (1987), Tierney and Bensimon (1996), Finkelstein et al. (1998), and Fairweather (1996), portray a sense of what academic life is like for not-yet-tenured faculty at research universities. The press for research at these institutions overshadows other aspects of faculty work, namely, teaching and service (Ginther & Hayes 2003). In describing an outstanding academic at a research university, Clark articulates the centrality of research while "teaching trails along as a way of imparting the results of research and thereby bringing others up to the mark" (123). The literature on faculty at research universities is replete with negative messages about the tenure process, criticizing it for its ambiguity, unending demands, and seemingly impossible standards (e.g., Tierney & Bensimon, 1996). The findings from our study (as can be seen in the above vignette) reveal, in contrast, that one of the unanticipated benefits of having a child while on the tenure track at a research university is the joy a baby adds to life at a time in professional life that is typically fraught with stress and ambiguity. In short, having a baby while involved in the tenure process can add a welcome perspective to an otherwise consuming stage of the academic career.

The new perspective afforded by the presence of a baby manifests itself in two ways for women on the tenure track at research universities. First, the faculty member often has a new outlook on the academic career (that is, the baby becomes the most important thing in a person's life, placing the focus on, and worry about, work into perspective). Almost all faculty members we interviewed from research universities mentioned this new perspective, although it was particularly salient in the comments of faculty in top-tier programs at top-tier institutions where the pressure to produce, and to produce without interruption, is nothing short of acute. The second response encompasses the economic notion of "satisficing" we discussed previously, where the new parent does the best she can in all the various aspects of her life and career, recognizing that excellence in all areas may be out of reach, given conflicting demands. People do the best they can even while realizing it might not be the best or the optimal they could do.

Role modeling was another theme that emerged from the data analysis of women in research universities. A majority of the women interviewed lacked role models who led a life that included young children, so they found themselves in new territory when it came to managing work and family as a faculty member, especially a female faculty member. The other aspect of role modeling was that the women in our study saw themselves as role models for other new faculty and graduate students considering combining an academic job with parenthood. These two aspects are aptly described by the comments of two faculty members:

> You know in academia I don't have any [role models]. There are not a lot of people in my immediate circle who have kids . . . or their kids are older. Their kids are grown and I don't know how they got to where they are because I wasn't there when their kids were little.

> I can tell that I am watched and a role model to a lot of graduate and undergraduate students in the lab, especially when I was pregnant. I remember we were interviewing incoming graduate students and every one of the female graduate students talked to me about pregnancy. Many of them would like to have kids but they didn't know anybody who was great at managing both.

In short, tenure-track mothers at research universities found that they could navigate the challenges of combining motherhood with their academic careers, although the effort required personal commitment and endurance.

For many, balancing their work and family lives meant becoming more efficient in their work habits, and, in many cases, moderating their expectations for their productivity. These adjustments do not minimize the challenges tenure-track faculty face regarding ambiguous guidelines for tenure and the unending workloads that characterize academic life at research universities, but their new perspectives as mothers and academics allowed these women to accept these challenges with greater equanimity. Further, the data make clear that although the participants in the study found the combination of having a child and being on the tenure track doable, they tended to manage not because of institutional support but rather in spite of its absence.

Research Universities: Mid-Career Faculty Perspectives

Not much in terms of the academic work had changed for Bonnie since she got tenure. She describes it as "kind of a letdown. You get tenure one day and the next you still have to get back to work and keep on going." Bonnie was involved in so many projects that she notes it is easier to be productive and active as a scholar than it would be to let things go. Bonnie felt fairly integrated in the department and had taken on the role of graduate studies coordinator. She earned a course release for the coordination and enjoys working with graduate students. Bonnie expressed no further desire to pursue an administrative position. She noted that deans and department chairs "Work all the time! No thanks." Bonnie noticed that many administrators at her institutions either have grown children or don't seem to have to worry about scheduling and carpooling as much as she has to. Bonnie planned to give up the coordinator job eventually because she saw it as negatively affecting her research productivity. While eligible to go up for promotion in a year, Bonnie wasn't sure she was going to be ready and envisioned going up some time in the distant future. She noted that while there is some discussion of staying on track for promotion, there is quite a bit of variability across campus and no one has talked to her about it.

For Bonnie, the family part of her life seems easier than before. She notes that it is still hectic, but not so physically demanding. She recalled, "I was so tired when I talked to you last." Now, she tells us, she is busy with all the kids' activities. Although she notes that it is "fun to go to their games and participate in the school activities," she also explains there is a lot of planning and arranging that she has to do. Bonnie's husband is more involved now, which makes life easier for them as a family. Bonnie has no plans to leave her institution, noting that it would be hard to "relocate to a place where my kids would be happy, where my husband would have a job, and where we can afford a house." Bonnie sums up this period of her life by noting "life is good."

This faculty member's experience captures some of the findings that focus particularly on research university faculty. There are two themes we want to highlight that we found unique to the experience of the research university setting—research productivity and administrative aspirations. Although we addressed both of these issues in the common areas of concern, there were some unique aspects in the research university context that require additional consideration.

Research Productivity

Consistent with the mission of the research university, the primary dictate for faculty success is research. For faculty members to stay active in their field calls for active engagement in research, including grant development, data collection, advising and directing graduate students, and disseminating findings. Generally speaking, faculty members at research universities were active in research to achieve tenure and felt it was essential to get tenure and be promoted. Research productivity for faculty who maintained scholarly activity was ongoing, and just needed to be compiled and presented to get tenure (and then promotion to full professor). Some faculty members, however, had done "just enough research to get by" (i.e., satisficing) for tenure, and ongoing career advancement meant having to get research started again. As one faculty member commented: "I pretty much need to start over. I took a breather after tenure, got involved in other things, and now to get promoted I really need to restart my research agenda."

We thus noted a sharp contrast between two groups of people among research university faculty: those who maintained their research agendas and for whom promotion to full professor was a logical next step, and those who felt burned out by the tenure process and needed to jump start their research in order to seriously consider promotion to full professor.

Administrative Aspirations

Generally speaking, research university faculty had the least focus on moving into administration compared to faculty at other institutional types. For those in administration or taking on some administrative role, it was viewed as a way to balance research involvement. As one faculty member told us: "I filled in with administrative stuff instead of doing more research, which is a good temporary shift. It's a way of having these activities that count toward your annual evaluations and you are still doing things at a time when you are not able to do research." Involvement in administrative roles was also viewed as a way to expand work perspective, experience change, and "try on a new role" as one woman noted: "Since taking the administrative job, my work hours have actually eased off a lot because I was writing and thinking about things [all the time]. I miss the other part of my job and will go back to it soon. For now administrative work is a nice break."

Administration is a way to try something different, perhaps leading to taking a different path in the career. Faculty at research universities generally have research as a primary identity, and moving into administration is viewed as interference with the focus on research, as was expressed by one faculty member: "I will never be an administrator. I love research and you basically give that up. I hate paperwork and forms. I think if someone else was depending on me it would drive them crazy."

Although not every person interviewed at mid-career had maintained the same level of research productivity that they had needed to get themselves established and to get tenure, research continued to be their reference point for what it takes to succeed; their measures of success were now the promotion and tenure process and the respect of their colleagues. The focus on research generally precludes faculty members from wanting to pursue administrative careers. For research university faculty, there is a disconnect between the service orientation of administration and active involvement in research. Although a faculty member who decides to move into administration does not necessarily choose to be an administrator rather than a researcher, the daily realities of administration can make it difficult to do both and to do them well. In research university contexts, in particular, service tends to be undervalued and underappreciated. To advance in a research university context calls for involvement in research, yet faculty, and especially women, are called upon to be actively engaged in service, an activity that is necessary to keep the university running, but is not valued to the same extent as research (Neumann & Terosky 2007). This disjuncture is what Misra et al. (2011) call the "ivory ceiling of service work."

Involvement in service can help explain women's passive posture toward promotion to full professor—if people are spending additional time on service it could be at the expense of research, an activity required for promotion. Dealing with the tensions of service and other aspects of the faculty job was also something experienced by faculty at the comprehensive institutions, a subject to which we now turn.

COMPREHENSIVE COLLEGES AND UNIVERSITIES

Faculty work at comprehensive colleges and universities is characterized by an emphasis on teaching, with some level of expectation for research and service. Clark (1987) notes that comprehensive colleges are the "middle of the institutional hierarchy" (126) and that they can be difficult to characterize because the category includes former liberal arts colleges that have added more vocational and master's degree programs, as well as state colleges that are actively seeking to emulate their research university counterparts. Clark adds: "The academic job at comprehensive colleges is different from that at universities. Although influenced by university norms, conceptions of the ideal are pulled toward local realities" (127). Articles by Finnegan and Gamson (1996) and Henderson and Kane (1991) both conclude that faculty life at comprehensive colleges is shaped by the institution's concern with their historical teaching mission, combined with a desire to create and foster a culture of scholarship. This research also suggests that faculty life changes at these institutions as their missions drift. Striving becomes part of the culture of many comprehensive colleges, as these campuses seek to justify their placement and location in the academic hierarchy (O'Meara 2007).

It is this tension that characterizes faculty life at comprehensive colleges, especially at institutions whose missions are unclear or who aspire to attain higher status.

The women we interviewed from comprehensive institutions had the most diverse range of experiences. We confirmed the two distinct types of comprehensive college identified by Clark. The first we refer to as "striving comprehensives." These campuses are striving to adopt research cultures like those of research universities, the intent being to emulate institutions with the most status (Finnegan & Gamson 1996; Morphew 2002; O'Meara 2007). Berdahl (1985) calls this phenomenon academic drift, which is the "tendency of postsecondary institutions to copy the role and mission of the prestigious institutions" (303). We found that these campuses had missions that were in a state of flux and cultures with unclear work norms for faculty. The striving campuses were, in essence, caught between old expectations connected to teaching and new expectations guided by research norms. These campuses were often adding new doctoral degrees but did not have strongly established graduate programs in a broad base of disciplines.

The other type of comprehensives we identified as "regional comprehensives." True to their history, these campuses are tied to their communities, with their purpose to fulfill regional obligations for education, with a clear focus on teaching (Cohen & Brawer 2008). The emphasis of these institutions was on providing education at the undergraduate and master's levels.

We separate the analysis of this category according to the differentiations discussed here in order to give a more accurate representation of the data. In fact, the differences between these two types of comprehensive institutions represent the major theme of this section, as they strongly affected the institutional experiences of the women in our study.

Striving Comprehensives

Maggie was in her third year at Regional U and felt things were going "reasonably well." She indicated that she loved being a professor even more than she thought she would, but that the work was "really hard." When Maggie arrived at the institution she already had two children and was pregnant with her third. Her job came up late in the year and she wasn't really planning to apply, but because it was close to her family she decided to apply. She got the job and then, after only three weeks of being there she had her third child. While Maggie explained that she managed her first semester, she was also a little resentful that no one even suggested she take any time off. She hadn't yet earned any sick leave and didn't know what was available on campus in terms of maternity leave. No one said anything, so she didn't ask.

Maggie told us that she feels she has to work all the time—a feat that she describes as impossible to accomplish with three young children. She noted that in order to be successful at Regional U, "you have to do it all." She teaches three classes a semester and is in a small department, which means that she teaches different courses every semester. She notes, "I'm constantly working on new preps." Maggie is active in her research and has gotten things out for review. She has two major publications thus far. Maggie feels a press to get grant money, but doesn't feel she has the kind of support for research that she observed when she was in graduate school. She notes the lack of grant management personnel as well as a lack of graduate students to help carry out the work of the grant. Maggie also does a lot of service. Because she is new and young and connected to the field, she sees students constantly at her door seeking advice. She is working on building her program, too, which involves recruiting students, working on the Web site, and trying to update program materials. The workload is literally endless and it seems as if it keeps getting added to with nothing being taken away. Maggie likes her job, but feels she is still trying to figure out the balance between serving the university with so much to do and being a good mother with so much to do.

Maggie notes that the hardest part of her existence is not so much related to having kids as it is about the mixed messages she gets about tenure. She notes that last year two people were refused tenure because they had not done enough research. This was a first for her college. She adds, "the notion of publish or perish is alive and well." The general perception is that those faculty members who were denied tenure were used as test cases to let the other tenure-track faculty know that research really is important. This press for research stands in direct conflict with Maggie's teaching load and the lack of resources available for research. She notes, "Faculty here have to do everything. The faculty at the research university where I got my doctorate do, too, but we have to do it with double the teaching loads, no internal funding, no graduate assistants, and an incredibly mediocre library." Maggie explained that the mixed messages are compounded when you are a mother to young children because time is so limited and workloads at home and at work are never ending.

The missions of these striving comprehensive campuses are in a considerable state of flux, leaving faculty uncertain about what it takes to get tenure. They have had a shift in their mission: where teaching and advising was historically the focus of faculty work, they now strive to be more like research institutions, so faculty face increased expectations to participate in service and additional expectations to carry out research (including grant acquisition and management) (Jacobs & Winslow 2004). These latter expectations do not replace teaching and advising, they are in addition, creating what can seem like unmanageable workloads (O'Meara 2007). Striving comprehensives, in trying to "ratchet up" the scholarly productivity of their faculty, create additional pressures for the not-yet-tenured and for mothers of young children.

The theme of mixed messages about mission (and consequently tenure) and the impact this had on faculty time was the most pronounced finding for those faculty working in striving comprehensives. The experience expressed by the above faculty member makes clear that the upward mobility the campus desires is often at the expense of faculty and, in particular, those on the tenure track. For example, several professors described being expected to teach four or five courses a semester and publish several research articles a year. This pressure was exacerbated by the absence of a research culture and an institution where senior faculty had limited publication records so were not helpful or realistic in terms of setting expectations. The mothers of young children at these institutions described the demands on their time as intensive, and indicated that the only way to accomplish the tasks needed to earn tenure was to work significant hours in the evenings and on weekends. At these institutions, mothers of young children felt that both their jobs and their children called for a tireless commitment.

Regional Comprehensives

When Linda was in graduate school it seemed as if she had two choices if she wanted to be a professor. One, she could mimic what everyone around her was doing and try to get a post-doc so she could get a research university job or, two, think more about her whole life and how she could make a faculty job fit into it. She realized that just because other people were talking about post-docs and planning on careers intensive in research, it didn't mean that she had to. Linda finished up her dissertation mid-year, so she stayed on in the department and taught a couple of classes. This made her realize how much she loved teaching. She also had a positive experience as an undergraduate at a local state college and thought that working in a similar place would be good for her. She noted, "I was lucky this position came open; it's near my family and was also near to where I got my doctorate." Linda is confident that she will have a long and fruitful career at her institution. She notes that she barely thinks about tenure and doesn't have much reason to. She teaches four courses a semester and always gets good reviews. She presents regularly at conferences and has had a few papers published. She notes, "This seems fine to everyone around me so it's good for me!"

Linda always knew she wanted to have kids, and she didn't want her career to get in the way. She believed she could have both, and she wanted to have both. Linda was married in her last year of graduate school, and she waited to land a job before she had a baby. She had her first child over the summer between the first and second year in her position, and had the second a few years later. She notes that the second child was easier because she had more confidence in herself and "knew the ropes." Linda doesn't believe that having children interferes with her quest for tenure. This place is a good fit for her, and she believes it is a good fit for anyone who wants to have a baby early in their career.

Linda's experience makes clear that regional institutions are guided by a mission with a focus on teaching and service, with less of an emphasis on research. Women at these institutions seemed more at ease about the institution's expectations regarding tenure—"What matters is that you are a good teacher and that you are available to your department and your students when they need you." The mission of the campuses that we identify as regional comprehensives tends to be clearer than their striving counterparts, making them a more manageable place to work. Many of the women at the regional comprehensives described the expectations for tenure as not only reasonable but also as being in synch with the demands of motherhood. In fact, the choice to work at a regional comprehensive for some was the perception that they are good institutions for wanting to integrate work and family. This represents the major finding for faculty we interviewed from regional comprehensives.

Comprehensive Colleges and Universities: Mid-Career Faculty Perspectives

Rachel noted that getting tenure was a pretty big relief because the tenure-track years were so confusing. What was required for tenure, she noted, was constantly changing. Rachel's university had three provosts in five years, and every one of them had a different emphasis, leaving faculty to wonder what one really needed to get tenure: Teaching? Research? Service? Somehow Rachel managed to get tenure and believes that things are, for the most part, going pretty well. She adds, "I have to be honest, I'm ready for a change, but I just don't know how I can get it together to move." Rachel's kids are eleven and thirteen and actively involved in activities and sports. Her husband has a good job and likes living here. They are all actively involved in the community. She explained that she is postponing thinking about a move until her kids are older and out of the house. In the meantime, she has been trying to reestablish her research agenda and is really enjoying it.

Rachel told us that right after she got tenure she felt she couldn't say "no" to requests for teaching and service. She was pretty burned out, but she felt she owed the institution for giving her tenure, and felt bad about no one else stepping up, so she ended up doing her share and a little extra. As a result, Rachel felt overloaded with teaching and service. She explained that now, "I finally feel like I have some say in how I spend my time [although] I constantly get asked to do things by my chair and dean." She notes that she is taking time for herself and her research. She finished a book last year and is going up for promotion next year. She noted, "It feels good to finally have a sense of what I want to do instead of trying to please everyone else. It's a constant struggle because I'm constantly asked to do more and more and at first I did it, but now I'm taking better care of myself and my priorities at work and it's not easy."

We have discussed early-career comprehensive university faculty operating in two types of settings—those that are striving to be more like traditional research universities and those more locally and regionally focused. The mid-career faculty in comprehensive institutions did not talk as much about their campus context, and the distinctions between striving and regional comprehensives were barely recognizable. We suspect this is in part due to the tenure process. To earn tenure, faculty need to mirror institutional priorities, and those priorities were quite distinct for the two types of campus. Now that faculty had tenure, they were less focused on the mission of the campus in terms of promotion. They were also more established, making it easier to navigate existing terrains instead of constantly trying to learn the nuances. Although we still found there was a lack of clarity of mission at comprehensive colleges, more than in other institutional types, it did not have as much of an impact on mid-career faculty members as it did early in their careers, and was not emphasized so much in the follow-up interviews. The focus of the interviews with the mid-career faculty women at the comprehensive institutions was related to service and agency, shifting emphasis in work roles, and career development.

Service and Agency

The service activity of faculty at the comprehensive institutions had an interesting aspect, that of agency. Yes, faculty were actively involved in service and in many ways felt the involvement created limitations, especially with regard to time, but faculty also mentioned how involvement in service gave them opportunity to do what they wanted and to carry out priorities as they wanted. Service tends to be viewed negatively because it is undervalued (Ward 2003), but it is also an integral part of faculty life (Neumann & Terosky 2007). Service is also a way for the faculty in the study to exercise their passion and to participate in activities that are important and that call for change (Baez 2000). As one person said, "If I'm willing to step up and do it [service] I can often do whatever I want." This was not expressed as a way just to carry out personal agendas, but more as a way to exercise leadership. If faculty members were willing to step up, they were able to carry forward initiatives to improve their departments, programs, and even the campus as a whole. Another faculty member expressed it this way: "On the one hand they [department administrators] know I'm place bound so am likely to put up with a lot, but on the other hand I can demand to make things better. I try to make things better and have a fair amount of say in how things are done in my department."

There is a double-edged sword to faculty involvement in service, especially for women. While our findings suggest that faculty members enjoy certain aspects of service, they do so at the expense of emphasis on teaching and research (findings emphasized elsewhere: see, for example, Misra et al. 2011). In the comprehensive university setting, faculty members are more likely to be rewarded for a combination of teaching, research, and service; yet, faculty members at all types of institutions are disproportionately rewarded for research (Fairweather 1996). We found, and it is supported by recent research, that service for associate professors often inhibits research productivity and that "when faced with multiple demands, they [faculty] sacrificed research first" (Misra et al. 2011, 2). This finding may also be connected to what we found unique about career advancement among the comprehensive university faculty.

Stifled Career Advancement

The comprehensive university faculty members in the study, as a whole, were the least focused on promotion to full professor. This is not to nullify the experience of faculty that were on track to be promoted and either have or plan to engage in the promotion process as soon as they are eligible. But, we also found a general apathy about promotion to full professor, as illustrated by these faculty members:

> I'm not sure I want to be full professor. I would be eligible next year, but I'm not convinced my scholarship is good enough to get full professor and I honestly am not sure I want to put the packet together again. The title doesn't mean that much to me. There's a raise but I don't know if it's enough of a raise for the hassle of putting it [promotion dossier] together.

> I don't want to expend the energy to get full. It's not worth the effort. I don't want to deal with the emotional cost.

The attitude about full professorship was also one that was fairly permanent. Faculty members talked about not being interested in going up for promotion at this juncture in their career, but also not being interested in the future, either. There was a general sense of being satisfied in their current place.

Expectations

There is a certain irony we observe for faculty in the comprehensive setting. While they are, in general as a group, the most negative about their positions overall and talk about their positions in terms of frustration and being stuck, they are also very involved in service roles and some quasi-administrative roles. As a group, they are fairly committed to their campuses, and see them as good places to work for managing work and family. Faculty see themselves as part of the fabric of their campus, even though they find it a frustrating place to work. In part, the frustration stems from the mixed messages they perceive about what is valued. While mid-career faculty members feel freer to say "no" than they did earlier in their career, they also feel limited in some regards because they are the only ones able to do the service.

In essence, they are told what is required to be successful and to thrive (excellence in research), but the campus resources to be able to fulfill these requirements are limited, and the workloads related to teaching and service inhibit involvement in research. Comprehensives are multipurpose institutions with missions focused on meeting regional and local educational needs. The mission of the campuses is largely focused on teaching; research and service are also a part of the culture, but often in ways that are ill defined. The ambiguity of such environments is most acutely experienced by faculty who, in essence, are the members of the campus that enact the campus mission. Faculty members are not sure where to expend time and energy. More research? Focus on teaching? Managing service? At mid-career, this manifests itself differently from the early-career findings. When focused on tenure, the mixed messages and unclear and ambiguous work roles were very worrisome because people were at a loss for what to focus on to be successful with tenure. In the mid-career interviews, there is a certain resignation about working in an environment that lacks clarity, though it takes its toll. Service roles actually help people feel they have a say in how things run. Being a senior faculty member helps people decide how to spend their time, but people feel they "have" to do certain things because no one else will do them, and also if they are not engaged in research then service and teaching become the focus. It is this quandary related to work role expectations and realities that leaves the early- and mid-career comprehensive faculty members in the study frustrated in their positions.

LIBERAL ARTS COLLEGES: EARLY-CAREER
FACULTY PERSPECTIVES

Emily's college was founded on the premise of family. All the brochures talk about family and the family environment students will find when they come here. The campus is residential and the town is pretty small, so faculty members are expected to help create a community- and family-oriented atmosphere. This created a challenge for Emily when she had her first daughter, because it made her realize that as a faculty member she was supposed to be a mother to her students and then as a mother she needed to be a mother to her daughter. Emily found herself unprepared for how much these two notions of motherhood would clash.

Emily noted that she does a lot of advising, some of which verges on counseling. Faculty members are all involved as advisors in something, and are supposed to be available throughout the day to attend to students' needs. A major part of Emily's job, in addition to teaching, is working individually with students. Now that she is a mother and sees the needs of her own child, she feels she is better at this part of her job: she feels she has a lot more empathy than she did previously. However, she also has a lot less time, and finds the work with individual students draining.

The part of being a mother and a professor that she had not thought much about in advance was "face time." There are a lot of unwritten expectations for where faculty members are supposed to be. Faculty members are expected to be at all faculty meetings. They are also expected to attend all campuswide faculty functions, which seem to amount to about four a semester, and they are typically held from 4–6 P.M., which can be tricky with daycare. The part that Emily finds most difficult is the expectation that she attend student concerts and recitals, sporting events, and any evening speakers. Sometimes she feels as if her department chair keeps a list of who attends these events. It's not that she doesn't want to want to support students in their extracurricular activities, but as a parent she finds that when she needs to be on campus all day and then again for evenings it can be very taxing. She asked, "I'm still trying to figure out: How much is enough? I know teaching is important and will be the primary basis of my promotion and tenure case. I also know that I'm expected to remain active as a scholar. But this ambiguous service is so challenging, I think it's the hardest part of my job now that I'm a mother." She added, "I get the sense it can make or break you around here."

The interviews with women at liberal arts colleges reveal that family-oriented campus norms shaped the experience for women faculty with children. Liberal arts college faculty members are expected to take a very active role in student development and the creation of community on campus (Braskamp 2003; Braskamp et al. 2006). Residential liberal arts colleges call upon their faculty to contribute to the family feeling of the college, leaving women faculty to balance the demands of creating a family-like atmosphere for students with having to manage their own new families. The metaphor of family often used at liberal arts colleges had additional meaning for the women in the study since, as new parents, they were expected to act in a parental role not only for their own families but also for their students. One of the faculty members in the study went so far as to refer to herself as "the mother of her students . . . and the only mother they have ever had." For the women in the study, a decline in their level of participation at events after having a child was a cause for concern, but an important part of the teaching role for these professors was setting boundaries as a teacher, just as parents do for their children. The issues are stated clearly by this liberal arts faculty member:

> There are events that go on in the evenings—a list of things from sporting events, fine arts events, theater productions, recitals, to specific events for faculty. Faculty development seminars—those sorts of things that happen in the evenings and require you to come. . . . It is clear you should be there if you can. The other things are vague. The problem that I'm suggesting, the barrier, there is ambiguity of expectation there. It would fall under the notion that we're a part of this community and are to be part of our students' lives. . . . What does that mean exactly? Does that mean I go to one basketball game a year or one theater production? Or do I go to all the senior recitals for students who have been in my classes? What exactly?

The interviews illustrate this aspect of service, more prevalent at liberal arts institutions than at some of the other categories (Tierney & Bensimon 1996): the expectation that the professor be an active and involved member of the campus community, and the sense that participation in these events was monitored, in ambiguous ways. Because many of these campus and community events happen at night, they were more of a concern to mothers of young children than more typical service activities (such as committee meetings) that happen during the traditional workday.

Research on faculty work at liberal arts colleges is somewhat limited. Clark (1987) describes faculty at these colleges as focusing on teaching, while also engaging in some research (often with students) and considerable levels of institutional service. Baldwin (1990) adds that the most vital faculty at liberal arts colleges engage in more research and scholarly activities than would be expected at such an institution. Further, Ruscio (1987) discusses how faculty members at elite, nationally known liberal arts colleges have much in common with their research university counterparts. The difference, he notes, lies in the liberal arts college desire to justify research as an investment in students. Teaching and research at liberal arts colleges are integrated as a way to bolster the teaching, learning, and development of students. These themes from the literature play out in the lives of the women faculty we interviewed from liberal arts colleges.

Liberal Arts Colleges: Mid-Career Faculty Perspectives

Eliza noted that the hallmark of her job right now is that she is constantly being asked to do more and more service. She added that it felt as if her colleagues were just waiting for her to get tenure and once she did they tapped her to be more involved in service, and it hasn't stopped. Eliza liked being involved in certain campus initiatives, but notes "it just doesn't seem to let up." Teaching is a major priority on campus—really it's *the* priority. She adds, however, that "service just seems to 'eat my lunch' and I can't get away from it. I kid you not. 'I'm a service dog.'" Eliza notes that it is her research that has suffered. Research was never the focus of her work, and the reason she works at a small school that emphasizes teaching is so she didn't have to focus on research. But, at the same time, she notes that her research really fuels her. She adds, "I hope I can get back to it once things slow down. Not sure when that will be."

The thing about a small school that Eliza both loves and hates is that she is a very central part of the community. She works closely with the administration on several different initiatives and enjoys that aspect of her work. She is also very involved in helping run her department. The chair relies on her to provide insight and direction on things related directly to her major and her students. The department is small, and since she is the one with expertise she gets called on

to do a lot more than she would in a larger department. She notes, "I can't hide. There really is no one else to do certain things so I'm it."

Eliza notes that this is the best environment for raising kids. She lives close to campus, which helps her to be able to go back and forth, especially for night activities on campus. She tries to limit what she does beyond the regular work day so she can be more present for her family, but it's hard to maintain those boundaries. She notes that she is required to be "on call 24/7. I try really hard to be clear about the need for limited night responsibilities and the need to be with my family at night, but it doesn't always work that way." She recalls a colleague who moved further away from campus because she felt the place was strangling her. "Work all day and then come back at night and work some more and then get home and check e-mail." Eliza noted that her family life is easier now that her girls are older. They are a lot more independent in terms of after-school care and they are able to get themselves home. The big challenge now is juggling their activities and sports and music lessons with what Eliza needs. She and her husband try and share the shuttling and chauffeuring, but it seems to fall mostly on Eliza because she is the one with the flexible job, and her job is closer to home and the middle school. She adds, "I feel like I'm constantly running from one place to the next."

Eliza isn't sure what is next in terms of her career. She would like to get promoted to full professor at some point, but she has barely thought about it because she has been too swamped. She notes that she is not even sure what is expected or required. "I figure when the time is right I will put my materials together." Eliza has given a little thought to moving to get closer to her parents, but she can't really imagine moving. "It's partly inertia and I just don't feel like I have the energy to move and it's also related to being pretty involved on campus." She indicates that there is a comfort in knowing the campus and community and that she doesn't feel as though she can move her family at this point. They have grown up here and everyone knows them. She notes, "For now, I'm staying put, although I never thought I'd be here this long. I like working at a liberal arts college and was intentional to pick this type of campus, I just didn't think I would be at this particular campus this long."

The theme of service surfaces once again, but the liberal arts faculty women talk about service in a slightly different way. For the liberal arts college faculty in the study, the focus on service has to do with the mission of the campus. Liberal arts colleges often call upon the metaphors of family and community to define themselves, and faculty play a key role in creating such environments. Faculty are expected to play an active role in shared governance to help keep their campuses running smoothly (Tierney & Bensimon 1996), and they are also expected to play an active role in student life and development (Braskamp et al. 2006). The context and culture of the institution and the unique nature of the liberal arts campus clearly shape the experiences of the faculty in the study.

Service—Can't Hide

The gist of this finding is that faculty in the liberal arts college setting cannot make themselves invisible. The campus is small, departments are composed of a minimal number of people, and a person can't hide from their responsibilities, especially once they get established. As one person said: "I'm in a small department and you do a lot of administrative work no matter what. We are small and it creates more service." When commenting on their involvement in service and how it melds with other aspects of the position, faculty members had this to say:

> I'd like to remain a scholar, but the institution makes it hard. There is definitely a conflict between the parts of my job.

> In a liberal arts college you're so indebted, the institution is going to fall because there is nobody to pick up what you let go. It's definitely the downside to a small environment.

In small campus communities, we found that faculty members wear many hats, a phenomenon that requires teaching beyond individualized focused specializations and also greater involvement in service. The service role was particularly prevalent as the faculty members in the study evolved in their careers. There was an expectation that the longer you were on campus the more service you would take on. One liberal arts college faculty member declared that "to get full [professor rank] around here you definitely need to take on a major committee as chair." For women, in particular, service is a way to "build bridges" on campus (Misra et al. 2011). Small campuses rely on faculty to participate actively in shared governance and service, making it difficult at times to manage the personal and professional aspects of life and to reconcile the demands of teaching, research, and service.

Family Culture

The family metaphor is prevalent at small liberal arts colleges, and it is often what led women in the study to work at a liberal arts college. They chose to work in this setting because they thought it would be family-friendly. Students come to campus (and their parents, as well) expecting a close and connected environment that includes ready access to faculty and staff. For the small and locally based liberal arts college, the family culture implies that faculty members are available to "parent" their students. Such a stance implies that women faculty will revert to their traditional gender roles as mothers and be caring and nurturing to students, so that women will do "mother work" in the domain of service and also in the area of teaching (Tierney & Bensimon 1996).

In the more competitive and nationally based liberal arts colleges, the small environment also harkens to a family-oriented culture and meeting the needs of students who expect a high level of involvement with faculty. The two contexts use the family metaphor in different ways, and both have important implications for women. One implication is the traditional gender roles, and the expectations that female faculty will take on the "mother" role for their liberal arts college students. What is expected is not so much mothering in terms of meeting primary needs (although there is some of that); it's more in terms of always being available and attentive to student needs, ranging from extra help on a paper to attending their concerts and drama productions in the evenings. A second implication of these expectations is the clash between mothering one's own children and mothering students on campus. Historically, faculty members were not women, and it was male faculty and their wives who often took on the parenting role for students. When women first became faculty members, they did so unencumbered by spouse and children, leaving them presumably more at the ready to fulfill *in loco parentis* roles as mothers. In a contemporary context where male faculty often have working spouses and female faculty have their own children, the mothering role for students in a family-oriented context can be a challenging one for women, in particular. In the liberal arts college environment where students can feel entitled to faculty time, it can impinge upon time faculty members spend with their own family. Faculty talk about the impact of the liberal arts family culture in this way:

> The campus has a very absorbing culture. I moved away from campus because I got too absorbed.

> There is definitely a conflict between having an intellectual life, a personal life, and an institutional perspective.

> They want us to be a mother to our students, but I also need to be a mother to my own children. It's consuming sometimes.

> We have a lot of students who feel very entitled to faculty time. They pay a lot of money to go to school here and they want me to be available all the time. I barely got tenure here because once I had kids of my own I couldn't be available to the students on campus all the time.

The same culture that attracts faculty to the liberal arts college—a small and inclusive atmosphere—is also one where it is difficult to manage different aspects of the job and of life, especially family.

COMMUNITY COLLEGES: EARLY-CAREER FACULTY PERSPECTIVES

Michelle was in her third year of working full time at the community college. She loves her job, finding it very interesting and challenging. She particularly enjoys the opportunity to translate what she did in the corporate world into the classroom. Teaching full time is much more challenging than she expected. Throughout the past couple of years, she has had several new preps and finds herself constantly rethinking and changing the content and methods of her classes. Michelle was an adjunct for three years before she started teaching full time and initially she only taught one course. Now that her teaching is a full-time job, it seems teaching takes a lot more time than she initially thought it would.

Michelle used to work as a corporate trainer for a large system of banks, and she enjoyed that job when she did it, but now that she works at the community college she notes: "There is simply no comparison. The community college setting is much easier to combine with my family life than work in the corporate world." In her corporate job, she had to be at work every day all day (and then some) and there was no flexibility. Michelle has two kids, ages three and six, and if they were sick or needed to go to the doctor it was a constant struggle to find time. She now doesn't work fewer hours per se, but her work is framed differently. As a community college professor, Michelle notes that she has a lot more flexibility than she did in the corporate world. "That's definitely the major difference and that difference means a lot to me as a mother."

Between office hours and teaching, Michelle is at work every day from 9 A.M. to 3 P.M. When she has a lot of grading to do and when she is teaching a new concept or a particularly difficult one, she works at home after the kids go to bed, and occasionally on the weekends to catch up. She typically teaches five classes a semester, but has it worked out so that on Monday, Wednesday, and Friday she teaches three sections of the same class and on Tuesday and Thursday she teaches two sections of a different class. She notes that it is a lot more challenging when she has new classes to prepare for or when she feels as though she needs to revamp her syllabus to keep things fresh. She takes her teaching role very seriously and it takes a lot of time, but the demand comes in spurts and she has a lot of control over how she spends her time.

There is an expectation in Michelle's department that faculty members be readily available to do advising for students and to be able to address general and specific questions about the department and its classes. Michelle holds office hours between classes and also after. Assuming it's not a heavy day for student traffic, Michelle is able to get most of her class prep and grading done throughout the day. There are not many full-time faculty in her department, so she does have to do some quasi-administrative stuff. About once or twice a month she has extra meetings to attend. She notes that she can usually fit in her work between 9 and 3, so her younger son doesn't have to be in daycare a full day, and she is home when her older son gets home from school.

Michelle's experiences and perspectives are representative of the stories we heard from the faculty members we interviewed at community colleges. In short, early-career women faculty at community colleges who have young children were a fairly contented group of individuals. Because most of the women we interviewed had worked in other professional contexts, as teachers in the K–12 setting or in industry, for example, they understood that academic life offered far more flexibility than was available in other professional realms. This understanding was what led many of them to pursue full-time work at the community college. It also made most of the women appreciate their work situation. This finding stands in contrast to the experiences of faculty in other institutional contexts, where most of their professional experiences were in academic settings, leaving less room for comparison. The community college women were distinct, as well, in that about half of them did not have a terminal degree (although most mentioned plans to pursue a doctorate), thus limiting them to teaching in the community college setting, a decision that, for the most part, made them happy. Even the tenure-track mothers with doctorates, however, were satisfied with the community college setting. The community college faculty members we interviewed were committed to their role as community college teachers. One professor commented that from the outside looking in, community college teaching seemed as if it would mean less work than her industry job, but "the reality is that it's a lot of hard work." She elaborated:

> I think a lot of people don't look at the actual time that an instructor puts into a course because courses out there are not already pre-done; you have to develop them. And then you have to redevelop them, and redevelop them, so you are constantly making changes to your course and then the nature of the discipline that I'm in [computer science] by the time you get a course just the way you like it something is totally different because the software has changed.

The community college faculty members were fairly consistent in their sentiment that teaching was compatible with raising a family, and that the job was fairly finite in terms of time—days, for the most part, were predictable, and work was mostly confined to regular hours. In some disciplines, however, the work extended outside the work day. Faculty who taught composition faced unending papers to grade, which simply had to be done on nights and weekends. Those in computer science and other technology-related areas, like the professor above, found that they had to constantly change and update their curriculum, which also meant that work infringed more on home life.

Combining work and family was a point of empathy between the community college faculty we interviewed and their students, as many of the students were returning to school while managing their multiple roles (work, family, school), as well. Faculty members noted that their roles as mothers helped them to have patience in working with the less academically able students with whom they interacted, and helped them to relate better to their older students who had children. "My students oftentimes have children and so they really like that [knowing I have children]; they feel a connection to me when I make those kinds of connections with them." Those interviewed saw considerable overlap between their lives as mothers and their lives as community college professors.

The community college faculty members with doctoral degrees in this study made the conscious decision to teach at a community college because they didn't want to deal with the pressure to "publish or perish" and believed that the community college focus on teaching would be more compatible with their decision to raise a family. As one faculty member said, "I just decided I could either be a good mom or a good teacher or good at research but I wasn't going to be good at all three. . . . I realized I didn't want to be in a lab all the time." These women felt that although they liked research, it was teaching that was most enjoyable. Like many of the faculty in the study, a passion for teaching is what led them to teach at a community college, a finding that is substantiated elsewhere in research related to community college labor markets (Townsend & Twombly 2007).

The teaching load at community colleges is quite high, typically five classes a semester, and professors are expected to be available for office hours. Most found themselves able to grade their papers and prepare for class during their office hours. Few of these women took their work home with them, except grading, and all of the respondents commented about how the flexibility of the job attracted them to pursue this line of work. The pressure for these women, like many other mothers who also work outside the home, is finding time to do everything that they want to do. Despite this stress, however, most of these women expressed happiness with their career choice and how it intersected positively with motherhood. According to Clark, the ideal professor at a community college is student-centered, caring, "loves the subject . . . and is able to convey his [sic] enthusiasm to other people . . . somebody who always keeps current with new developments" (127). Cohen and Brawer (2008) add that teaching is the primary responsibility of faculty in this sector and is the basis on which faculty are hired and promoted. Faculty work is shaped by heavy teaching loads of introductory courses and the need to serve a diverse, often underprepared student body (Twombly & Townsend 2008).

COMMUNITY COLLEGES: MID-CAREER FACULTY PERSPECTIVES

Karen is at a point in her career where she can take a deep breath and finally say "I'm content. I feel pretty balanced when it comes to maintaining my work life and my family life." Karen chose to teach at a community college because she loves to teach and because she didn't want to get caught up in the drama of maintaining a research agenda. She saw her advisors go crazy trying to manage writing books and teaching when she was in graduate school, and she knew she didn't want that life style. She also knew she always wanted children and she saw that a teaching career was more compatible than a research career with having children and with the type of life she wanted to live. She notes, "I've been here for eight years and it's been a good choice for me. I feel like a valued member of the campus community, and now that I'm more established on campus I feel like I get a lot of say in what goes on around here." Karen has been able to coordinate her schedule to have her classes on Monday, Wednesday, and Friday, which she sees as great in terms of keeping her schedule coordinated with her kids' schedule. She also teaches an online course. She thought that was going to be really helpful in terms of managing work and family, but it's turned out to take a lot of time, and her unit director doesn't take into account how much time she is on the computer with her online students at home. Her director wants to see faculty on campus thirty-five hours a week, but since she is teaching on line, Karen wonders how that works. "I'm still trying to figure out that part."

The biggest challenge for Karen right now is figuring how to manage all the responsibilities she has on campus. She feels as if she has the teaching part down, but as one of only two full-time faculty members in her area, she is trying to figure out how to manage all the other things her director asks her to do. Karen notes that if she doesn't "keep on guard I'd be on every committee on campus and I don't have time for that. I'm trying to figure out how to say 'no' and what I can say 'no' to."

Karen describes her campus as pretty family friendly. Among the full-time faculty members, there is a cluster of faculty who have children, and "people are pretty understanding if you have to stay home to take care of sick kids." There aren't a lot of collegewide family-oriented policies, but people seem to figure it out in their departments. The faculty union and the faculty senate have both discussed changing policies related to work and family, but it's a back-burner issue. There are so many adjuncts on campus that all the full-time faculty are just glad to have jobs. Karen notices that in the past couple of years the faculty women are reticent about asking for too much, and family-friendly policies are on the list of things they don't seem to want to ask for. Plus, she notes, people seem to get what they need so they don't need to change much in terms of policy.

Karen concludes that "Overall, life is good. As faculty, we all tend to complain our fair share, but I'd have to say this is a good place to work for someone that wants to be a professor and a parent."

The mid-career faculty members in the study from the community college setting share many of the same concerns and joys as faculty in liberal arts colleges, research universities, and comprehensive universities.

There are three themes we want to highlight with regard to the distinct characteristics of the community college context and how it shapes faculty life at mid-career: the time faculty members are expected to be on campus, the impact of online teaching on faculty life, and the unique policy environment.

Face Time

The community college faculty members in the study talked more than faculty members in other contexts about the time they are expected to spend on campus. On most of the campuses in the study, faculty members have specific guidelines about when they are supposed to be on campus. One of the unique characteristics of a community college is that while the faculty job is flexible, as it is on other campuses, it is also one that often requires faculty to work a certain number of hours a week, which are often clearly stated in union contracts.

The main task for faculty at community colleges is teaching (along with accompanying grading and office hours). There is flexibility in terms of setting teaching schedules, especially for mid-career faculty, yet the reality is that courses need to be covered, and unless one teaches online that means being on campus when classes are offered. Many community colleges set minimum numbers of hours where faculty members have to be available for students. "My contract says a full-time faculty member works thirty-five hours. . . . I don't know a lot of people who work thirty-five hours a week, most work forty or so." Some community colleges are quite strict about those thirty-five hours; faculty must be on campus and present between certain hours of the day. And as one faculty member told us: "My director checks. I'm expected to be here all day, and if she stops by to see me in my office and I'm not there, I hear about it." There was variability in terms of how contract requirements were stated and implemented. Like the faculty member we just heard from, some campus environments were very strict, while in some other environments the time was still required, but how faculty members met the time obligations was individually negotiated. Regardless, community college faculty members still see their jobs as flexible, and touted the benefits of the flexible schedule. Some typical comments include the following:

I do have some say in my choice of schedule selection and what classes I teach and what they are. Just having the flexibility has made working so much more doable. I think if I had an 8 to 5 job, I'm not sure that I would be willing to do that while my kids were in school.

I have the opportunity as a faculty member to work x amount of days during the year and have all that other time and the flexibility that I have with my kids and my family.

I always tell people that I have the best job in the world—with or without kids—but especially with kids because I have more flexibility. I am able to create the schedule that fits for me. I've done a lot of things in my life, and this I the best gig ever.

Online Teaching

Another issue that seemed to be somewhat different for the community college faculty was the role of teaching online classes. While there were a handful of faculty members in all campus settings that talked about online teaching, it was most prevalent as a topic of discussion for the community college faculty. Many community colleges have moved to online formats, and the faculty members that we interviewed who are using this mode of teaching give it mixed reviews in terms of the ability work out a balance between work and family. On the one hand, the online format allows faculty flexibility in the teaching realm, and they do not necessarily need to be on campus when they are teaching. Online teaching offers considerable flexibility, which works well for people trying to spend time with their family. At the same time, however, faculty note that they have to respond to e-mails and monitor the class all the time, which can compromise flexibility and make faculty feel like they are working all the time. Online students can expect their professors of online classes to be available whenever the student is available—and that can create a 24-hour "on call" status. In addition, one of the difficulties with online classes is that some institutions have not yet moved away from the require-ments that faculty still have to maintain "face time" or contact hours on campus: faculty members are therefore teaching online classes but are also expected to be present on campus during traditional daylight office hours. As one faculty member said: "We are still figuring out how online classes factor into required hours on campus. If I meet with students in my online class at night, how does that count toward my time expectations on campus?"

In summary, while online classes create considerable flexibility, they also create ambiguity in terms of time spent on campus versus working with students virtually.

Unique Policy Environment

The other issue that is distinct about the community college setting is the lack of formal policies to assist in work/family domains. While this is not an acute issue for faculty members at mid-career—in large part because they generally are not asking for any accommodations or policy assistance—it seems that the policy environment intended to help newer full-time faculty with family-related issues has not improved much over time (in particular, since the first interviews). Breast feeding is still an important dilemma at community colleges, exacerbated by the lack of private offices with doors for faculty in more open office settings (something more common at community colleges than in other settings). Parental leave and access to child care were also not front-burner issues for faculty women in the study, although some mentioned that these are major issues for their students.

Why the apathy toward family-oriented policies? Some of the faculty women in the study cited the unions as not caring about this issue as much as other issues, and that given a full slate of concerns, work/family policies were not foremost. Others noted that because of the growing presence of part-time and adjunct faculty, the full-time faculty don't ask for much assistance because they feel lucky to just be working full time. For others, the lack of policy stems from the nature of the work—teaching—which requires faculty to be present and therefore accommodations more difficult to manage. Faculty members don't think about differential loads, for example, as a way to compensate for time off from teaching. With the focus on teaching, there are fewer ways to modify workplace duties to accommodate having a child compared to other environments where faculty participate in research-related activities that can often be the focus for faculty while they are away from campus to take care of family concerns.

For the mid-career faculty, there was not the personal focus on policy, as there was when we talked to early-career faculty members. The topic of work/family policy came up largely because of the faculty member's involvement in service on their faculty senate or as representatives/liaisons between their unit and the campus. As one faculty member remarked, "I'm on the senate and we've talked about work and family policies, but we just don't seem to get very far. People think what we have is pretty good and it doesn't need to be changed."

Key Findings about Academic Motherhood and Institutional Type

One of the primary goals of our research is to prompt faculty members themselves, as well as those who conduct research related to faculty, to consider the role that context plays in faculty life, especially the lives of faculty members with children. Our research demonstrates that institutional type does make a difference for tenure-track faculty members who have young children. Like Clark, we found that the type of campus where a person works strongly shapes the nature of academic work. With regard to motherhood, we found that the merger of motherhood and faculty life creates a commonality of experience, especially when bounded by institutional context.

Faculty life for mothers is not experienced uniformly across institutional types. At research universities, faculty in the study perceive that their institutions are not very supportive in terms of policy and role modeling, especially for early-career faculty, but for the most part the roles of mother and professor were reconcilable, in part because the expectations for tenure and advancement, while sometimes substantial, were clear—publish your research, and tenure and promotion are likely. For faculty in research universities, the main problem at the mid-career juncture is how to maintain active research agendas in light of other aspects of the job.

Faculty members at the comprehensive colleges, more than those at the other institutional types, did not view their jobs in any uniform way; the level of prestige to which the campus aspired largely dictated the differences. This was a particularly pronounced for early-career faculty. For faculty women at campuses that are upwardly mobile (campuses that we call striving comprehensives), combining work and family could be very difficult, given never-ending demands to be all things to all people. Indeed, the tenure demands at these institutions seemed more intense than even at the research universities, as individuals were given mixed messages about what it takes to succeed, and most concluded that they needed to be equally productive in terms of teaching, research, and service. Faculty members at the regional comprehensives, in contrast, found focus on teaching and service to prevail over research, thus creating greater clarity in their tenure requirements. This sense of focused mission made it easier for women faculty to balance the demands of work and children.

For mid-career faculty, some of the distinctions (and the ensuing concerns) between striving and regional comprehensives dissipated, leaving them more focused on how to do it all in spite of the campus context. For mid-career faculty at comprehensive colleges, the focus is on maintaining career vitality in light of multiple, and often ambiguous, demands, as well as how to balance involvement in service that helps faculty contribute to campus change, but also maintain service loads that don't impede the ability to do the work they need to for promotion to full professor.

The liberal arts college faculty members in the study were in a unique situation to help fulfill the family-friendly ideal for their students while, at the same time, fulfilling their own family obligations, although the ambiguous nature of service on liberal arts campuses left faculty wondering: How much? What kind? This was an important finding, as the literature on faculty life more typically describes ambiguous expectations for research, not service. At mid-career, liberal arts college faculty members were also focused on how to maintain manageable service loads when they are often one of few faculty members in a particular specialty area.

The community college faculty members in the study were largely content with their jobs. In comparison to work in other sectors, faculty life at a community college was quite conducive to raising a family. The mid-career faculty women pointed out some of the challenges of being one of the few full-time faculty in their units and how challenging that can be in terms of student advising and service. These mid-career community college faculty members also focused on how to negotiate campus cultures that require specific times on campus, especially in light of increases in online teaching and in policy environments that were not particularly family friendly. Nonetheless, the mission of teaching and working with students that guides the function of community college setting did help provide direction to faculty work at both early and mid-career. The commitment to teaching at the community colleges led faculty to pursue careers in this type of institution, as they believed that it was feasible to be successful at work and at home at early- and mid-career stages.

So, what is it about having a baby and working at different types of institutions that is important and warrants further discussion? A macroscopic view of the findings points to two major concerns: first, time (and lack thereof) and its impact on the "ideal worker" norms that shape what it means to be a good mother and good professor at different institutional types, and second, how the ideal worker norms shape women faculty member's choices. These issues serve as the focal point of the following discussion.

Finite Time and Ideal Worker Norms

Motherhood provides a valuable lens to examine academic work at different types of institutions because, on the basis of time alone, faculty members who are mothers tend to have less time available to deal with the ambiguity in their environment than their colleagues without children (Winslow & Jacobs 2004). The entrance of a child into a faculty member's life instantly changes priorities and also creates a new lens from which to view work. A majority of the women in this study, before having babies, were what Williams (2000b) refers to as "ideal workers"; in essence, they were married to their work, leaving them fairly uncritical consumers of their environments—they worked hard (that is, all the time) and did what they needed to do to succeed. Early in their careers, and prior to having children, many of these women had bought into the "career mystique" of being a faculty member, and they were committed to their careers to the exclusion of other interests (Moen & Roehling 2005).

Barbara Lovitts (2001), in her study of graduate students, found that those who persist to graduation are socialized to adopt ideal worker norms, realizing that this is what is expected to be successful in academic life. It is often the birth of a first child that calls these norms into question. New mothers no longer have the time or energy to devote themselves entirely to their work. And the entrance of a baby offers a new perspective from which to examine the academic work environment and question its unclear standards and potentially unrealistic expectations. It is also not unusual when a woman has a baby to have her gender become salient to how people view women and how women view their work (Ridgeway & Correll 2004).

Institutions of higher education are greedy organizations that demand total commitment from their participants (Coser 1974). Not only is academe greedy but one could argue that the institution of motherhood is also greedy. Babies (and teenagers!) are, of course, greedy for their mother's attention, and the cries of the baby are often louder than even the ticks of the tenure clock, and more urgent as well. Further, the argument that motherhood is greedy stems from the traditional cultural mandate that women owe their primary allegiance to their families (Coser 1974; Drago 2007). We found that for most of the women we interviewed, traditional norms about parenting and housework still guide and shape what goes on in the home, as the vast majority of women in the study did the bulk of the child care (such as transporting children to and from daycare, buying clothing, arranging appointments) and housekeeping, even when both spouses were working. Thus, most of the women in the study, especially in early career and when their children were young, found themselves attempting to respond to two greedy institutions—motherhood and faculty life—which led to considerable conflict about where and how to spend limited amounts of time. The greediness persists as careers and families evolve, but we found a greater distribution of labor among partners for those in the study that had partners. As children got older, we found that the male partners became more involved with child care responsibilities.

In all institutional types, work expectations were high, and often increasing (Jacobs & Winslow 2004). At research universities, the pull on one's time comes from seemingly unending research expectations. At liberal arts colleges, the pull is toward being a great teacher and being available to your students at all hours as a way to create a family-like atmosphere on campus. The pull of striving comprehensives comes from multiple directions simultaneously—with heavy teaching loads, high service expectations, and substantial research demands, combined with few role models to demonstrate the feasibility of achieving these expectations. More regionally oriented comprehensive colleges and community colleges demand high-quality teaching, and lots of it, but these latter two institutional types seem to be a bit more reasonable about worker expectations; perhaps their focused emphasis on teaching is just clearer about what it takes to be a good worker in those two institutional contexts.

The case of faculty at community colleges was particularly interesting in light of worker norms and time limitations, as many of the faculty we interviewed at these institutions said they had previously worked in environments that were even greedier than academic settings and with considerably less flexibility. The community college faculty members, in general, seemed more content about their situations, and were generally more positive about the ability to successfully combine work and family compared to faculty at the other institutional types. One way to look at this is from the perspective of what Merton and Rossi (1968) term reference group theory. This theory suggests that individuals view their lives in relation to a comparison group. For community college faculty, academia is compared favorably to prior work experiences (in corporations, the military, or K–12 education, for example). Faculty members employed in other institutional types, however, often lack experience with other reference groups and, therefore, compare their experiences either to graduate school or to those of other faculty at their institutions. This comparison to other academics, especially their male colleagues, may enhance women's perceptions that academic life is difficult to manage in tandem with family life.

Ideal Workers Norms and Choice

Women faculty and doctoral students may face difficult decisions as they plan their academic careers in relation to their personal lives. These decisions are likely to include concerns about where to work (geographically and with regard to institutional type), how to manage personal relationships and dual careers, and may include choices about having a family. Research on doctoral students planning academic careers suggests that they face significant stress and worry, given the perception that academic life precludes personal preferences about where to work and how to live one's life (Golde & Dore 2001). Citing these concerns, some have opted out of pursuing an academic career (Golde & Dore 2001; Rice et al. 2000) or have turned to alternatives within the academic career (such as part-time or adjunct teaching) or alternatives in the academic setting (such as student services or program administration) (Wolfinger et a1.2009).

Given the folk wisdom that guides many women's decisions about where to work in light of their lifestyle choices (among them motherhood), organizational perspectives are a logical framework. Although anecdotal, there is evidence to suggest that women faculty who openly acknowledge wanting to pursue a tenure-track position and motherhood are encouraged to do so at lower-tier institutions (Wilson 2001). This has the potential to steer talented women away from pursuing faculty careers at top-tier institutions on the implicit assumption that the roles of scholar and mother are incompatible.

We found that the female faculty in the study made choices about where to work based on their perceptions of workplaces and how they fit not only with their personal visions of how they want to be an academic (more focused on research or more focused on teaching) but also on their vision of how different institutional types inhibit or foster the integration of work and family. While, on the one hand, thoughtfulness about where to work is smart decision making, it also contributes to gender stratification in the academic labor force (Ceci & Williams 2011; Schuster & Finkelstein 2006). The choices women make about where to work are, in part, constrained by perceptions about particular environments and how they fit with being a mother. If women perceive that a liberal arts college is more family-friendly than a research university, and opt to work in the former to accommodate their desire to have children, in the long term this stands to have ill effects on research universities and the labor market as a whole. Women are often faced with limiting and constrained choices based on gender role expectations that extend to what it means to be a good mother and what it means to be a good professor (Drago 2007). An organizational perspective of faculty life and motherhood helps clarify the nuances of places to work for women faculty who strive to succeed professionally, as faculty, and personally, as parents.

CHAPTER 8

Social Capital and Dual Careers

As discussed in chapters 6 and 7, the academic profession as experienced by women with children is shaped by the cultures and expectations of particular disciplines and institutions. There is another important layer that shapes how individuals experience their academic positions—that of their marital status and social class. Based on a review of the literature and our own research and experience, we knew that being part of a dual-career couple influences how women pursue their academic jobs and also how they approach having children and family involvement. We also found from our research that the ways women pursue their professional and personal paths were related to social class and family background. In this chapter, we look at these two characteristics—social class and marital status—as a way to give fuller consideration to the findings from our data.

SOCIAL CLASS AND BACKGROUND

In gathering demographic information from the women as we interviewed them for the study, we became aware of people's backgrounds, including where they were from, their educational histories, and their parents' professions. Although all the women, as advanced degree holders, had some social and professional capital (O'Meara & Campbell 2011), we noticed a difference in how people responded to particular questions and situations based on their inherited class capital. This aspect of the data was not an initial finding; it was something that emerged from looking at the data over time and across all institutions and disciplines. In particular, the women in the study whose parents (typically their fathers) had Ph.D.s and had been academics or researchers in nonacademic settings were more keenly aware of the nuances of the academic profession, which in turn influenced how the women reacted to particular situations. They also had their parents to rely on for advice. The accumulated cultural capital these women brought with them helped them to understand and use "educated language," and provided significant familiarity with the culture of academics that had been accumulated through their family upbringing (Bourdieau 1977). These women had clearly accumulated advantages as a function of having an intimate knowledge of academic life (Clark & Corcoran 1986; Valian 2005).

The academic system relies significantly on cultural capital and accumulated knowledge. It is *assumed* that faculty members bring knowledge about what is needed to succeed, or at least that they will have the sponsorship necessary to teach them what they need. The expectation is that this will have been achieved by socialization throughout graduate school and the early career (Ward & Bensimon, 2002). But more fundamental than graduate school socialization are the advantages of women with academic parents, who have built-in mechanisms of mentorship and sponsorship. They have observed firsthand, through family interactions, how academic life works. To be sure, many of these models of how academic life operates are no longer relevant in their own lives (or at least they need to be adapted) because the way the women in the study were navigating academic life deviated significantly from how their parents did it, but they still had an awareness of the academy and its nuances. For example, one of the women in the study compared her own academic life with that of her father: "My dad was a professor and when I was little my mom stayed at home. . . . My dad worked at the office, would come home for dinner, and then at the end of the day he often went back to campus." Although she was not able to employ the same ideal academic worker habits due to having her own family and being in a dual-career couple, she did learn from observing her father that the academic job called for a high level of commitment. She also learned from him how he interacted with students ("students often came to our house"). She adopted her own version of those academic norms. "When my son goes to bed at night I grade papers and get ready for the next day."

She learned from her father that being an academic is not a traditional nine to five job. She also has her father to rely on to provide input and advice on how to find her way in the academic terrain (something she often calls on), certainly an advantage when navigating the uncertain waters of the academic career.

Choices and Options

As we have talked about throughout this study, choice is a theme that permeates the findings. People make choices about when to have a baby, where to work, whether to take parental leave, whether to stop the tenure clock, and even about leaving their academic positions. We observe that many of these choices are related to the capital—economic, professional, and cultural—that people bring with them to their positions. Generally speaking, those with financial means, either inherited or from their spouses, that went beyond reliance on their own salaries, had a greater sense of possibility and agency. They felt freer to state their needs, and they also felt freer in their positions in general. As one person put it, "If I don't make it here [a top-tier research university] I have a lot of places I can go." She did not worry about earning tenure or how having a baby would be perceived by her colleagues. "I always knew I wanted to have a baby so I just did. It's none of their business." We would argue that her chutzpah is not just a function of her own self-esteem but is also partly a function of being a woman who comes from a highly educated family (her father has a Ph.D., also from a top tier institution), has significant financial means, and an educational background that includes graduate education in a top-tier program in her field. She does have a lot of choices when it comes to her position and her personal life, and she feels free to exercise them.

People also accumulated professional capital while in their jobs. Active involvement in particular kinds of service ("fancy service," as one person called it) or productivity through their research afforded people more choices. "Productivity gives me latitude and flexibility in my position," one woman said. Women in the study who either had distinct research programs, had been particularly successful with grants, or who were highly sought after out of graduate school and heavily recruited into their positions brought with them a strong sense of agency to their positions. In general, we noted, these women were not as concerned about what other people thought of their choices. That is, they felt freer to make choices that met their own personal and professional needs, as compared to making choices that would meet the needs or expectations of their colleagues or department chairs. Having capital gave people a sense of agency.

We also noted that a lack of capital diminished people's sense of agency. Throughout the analysis of the data, we observed that people who felt stuck in their positions had a sense of limited choices that stemmed from their lack of capital—both economic and cultural. Primarily as a function of diminished mobility tied to their spouse's career and to meeting the needs of the family, women who felt they could not leave their positions felt they had less choice and had to "make do" or "make the best of the situation." We also noted with curiosity that some of these women had spouses with positions that, while tied to the community, were not particularly positions of power or significant capital (such as working in criminal justice). This relates to some of the observations we made about people's orientations to their position.

Cosmopolitans and Locals

Clark's (1987) conceptualization of faculty as cosmopolitans (with a national or international professional orientation and disposition) or locals (an orientation more geared toward the institution) was helpful to us as we made sense of some of the findings from our data. We made connections between people who had greater cultural capital and a cosmopolitan orientation and between those with less capital and a local orientation. We also made some of these connections on the basis of institutional type (as did Clark 1987). Many of the women in the community colleges and the comprehensive institutions, for example, had a more local orientation. In general, these women were from the geographic area of their institution, and taking their faculty positions was, in part, based on the location. Generally, they did not make a significant geographic move to take the job. Their orientation was geared toward their community and their institution. The women who had a local orientation had one benefit in their favor, which was that many of them lived near to relatives who could assist them with child care and other family-related tasks. Having parents or in-laws or relatives nearby was an enormous help to many of the women in the study who stayed in communities in which they had roots.

This stands in contrast to women who had a more cosmopolitan and disciplinary orientation to their careers. These women were more likely to be engaged in national and international projects and to be identified more with their field than with their institution. These women were often isolated from extended family and could not rely on relatives to assist them with family-related concerns, problems, and issues.

DUAL-CAREER COUPLES

Although the marital status of women faculty is not a direct focus of this study, the majority of women in the study were partnered. Marital status is an important consideration, because their status as single or partnered influenced the choices people made as an academic and a parent—a finding we heard repeatedly from our data. A significant proportion of today's current and aspiring academics are in dual-career partnerships. However, female faculty members as a whole are more likely than their male colleagues to be single—15 percent compared to 8 percent (Ferber & Loeb 1997). A more recent study found that in the science fields, women were three times more likely to be single without children than were men (25 percent for women compared to 9 percent for men) (Gouldenet al. 2009). Of faculty who are married, 72 percent have spouses who are working professionals (Schiebinger et al. 2008). Academic couples (where one academic is married to or partnered with another academic) make up 36 percent of the American professoriate, with women more likely to be married to other academics than men (Astin & Milem 1997; Schienbingeret al. 2008).

There is some interesting research about dual-career couples that we thought might be helpful to provide some foundation to the topic. Being married to an academic is typically associated with greater research productivity than being single or being married to a nonacademic. These results seem to hold true for both men and women (Astin & Davis 1985; Astin & Milem 1997; Bellas 1992; Bellas & Toutkoushian 1999; Long 1990; Long & Fox 1995; Ward & Grant 1996). Studies of faculty productivity center on publications, since this is what is often pointed to as the primary predictor of success as a faculty member (Jarvis 1992). Although publication tends to be more important at research universities than at other types of institutions, Fairweather (1996) found that faculty members are disproportionately rewarded for research regardless of institutional type. It is important to note that research results comparing the scholarly productivity of men and women, without regard to marital or family status, find that women are less productive than their male counterparts (Astin & Davis 1985; Creamer 1998; Finkelstein 1987; Fox 1985; Moore & Sagaria 1991; Zuckerman 1987). Taking into account marital status serves to exacerbate the gender differences in research productivity, with married women producing less research than married men (Astin & Davis 1985; Astin & Milem 1997; Bellas 1992; Bellas & Toutkoushian 1999; Long 1990; Long & Fox 1995; Ward & Grant 1996).

Research on the productivity effects of being married to an academic assumes that both members of the couple can find academic work. Given the historical tendency for women's careers to be considered secondary to their husband's (in terms of both salary and importance) (Williams 2001), in a dual-career situation it is highly likely that women will limit their job search geographically, take a less-than-ideal position, or once hired in a faculty position decide not to pursue other employment opportunities (a factor associated with higher compensation) (Bielby & Bielby 1992; Ferber & Kordick 1978; Schiebinger et al. 2008). Although there is some evidence that women are more likely than men to sacrifice their careers to their partners' needs, it is also true that both members of a dual-career couple face concerns about finding rewarding work in geographic proximity to one another. Some research indicates that fears of not finding work for both members of a dual-career academic couple deters some doctoral students enough that they decide to pursue career paths outside the academy (Golde & Dore 2001; Rice et al. 2000).

Dual-career academic couples are an interesting concern for colleges and universities. The research suggests that as long as both members of a couple find work, they may be productive members of the academic community. These results are in opposition to the widespread belief that hiring a "trailing" spouse means that an institution has abandoned its quest for hiring the most qualified faculty member available. Although this is a possibility, research suggests that when institutions employ rigorous hiring procedures in considering an accompanying partner, only very qualified partners will be granted tenure-track positions (Schiebinger et al. 2008;

Wolf-Wendel et al. 2000a, 2000b). Institutions that try to accommodate the needs of dual-career couples are not necessarily "selling their souls to the devil," but instead are using responsive hiring practices in an effort to maintain qualified faculties.

Many of the findings we have discussed throughout this book are related to family circumstances and also related to being part of a dual-career couple. We now turn to a discussion of some of the nuances of these findings. Based on the interviews, we found that who one is married to or partnered with makes a big difference in terms of how women academics are able to balance and integrate work and family. Aside from the few individuals in our sample who were single parents, there were three different models of how women interacted with the partners in their lives. These included woman as primary breadwinner, woman as secondary breadwinner, and women who were members of dual-career academic couples. Some observations from each of these arrangements are presented below. As we have elsewhere in the book, we use vignettes as a means to highlight typical configurations as well as data from the interviews.

Mother as Primary Breadwinner

Charlene was new to a tenure-track position at a liberal arts college when she and her husband Tim decided to have a child. Tim had a degree in social work, but he wasn't excited about his job and he jumped at the chance to quit his job and stay home with their baby. While finances would be tight with only one income, Charlene and Tim figured that this might be an economically feasible idea because at least they would not have to pay for daycare. Charlene felt good about the arrangement—having Tim stay home and take care of the baby and be in charge of the domestic duties made her feel less guilty for spending so much time at work. Tim also enjoyed the arrangement; it felt good to be able to spend so much time with his daughter. In many ways, Charlene and Tim's family looked like a traditional family, albeit with the gender roles reversed. Charlene worked in the public sphere and brought home the funds necessary for the family to survive, and Tim took on the private-sphere responsibilities—taking care of their daughter, running errands, keeping the house clean, cooking dinner. The arrangement worked really well for both of them and only created a few tension points for the family—most notably having to continually explain to Tim's mother why Tim had decided to stay home (she didn't like the idea of her son not working and was not shy about expressing her discomfort with the arrangement). Charlene spent as much time as she could with her husband and daughter—but also felt free to commit herself fully to her job. She and Tim did share domestic duties, but the bulk of those in-the-house jobs fell to Tim. When their daughter turned five and began kindergarten and Charlene had earned tenure, Tim got a part-time position doing counseling at a local mental health center. He still did the bulk of the family's domestic duties, although much of the carpooling was shared. Their daily lives continued to be quite workable for both. Having the additional income was helpful, but the couple still looked upon Charlene as the primary breadwinner and Tim as the primary caregiver.

Although it would be unfair to describe Charlene and Tim's arrangement as typical among the women we interviewed, it was a pattern that surfaced a few times in our sample. In a handful of cases, the woman we interviewed was the primary breadwinner in the family. In these cases, the academic mother had a stay-at-home spouse or a partner in a position that was very flexible (such as artist, freelance, consultant) or a spouse who agreed to forgo work in order to take care of the children at least until they were in school. As with Charlene's case, it was not uncommon for couples in this situation to play out reverse gender norms, with the woman taking responsibility for the public sphere while her partner held primary responsibility for the private sphere. This arrangement had some costs to the couple, in that they had to live on a single income, and often this led to quite a frugal existence. In addition, some of these couples explained that it was difficult sometimes to explain the family's choices and arrangements to others. Parents, in-laws, teachers, friends, and colleagues often didn't understand these reversed gender norms and placed pressure on the couple to explain their choices. Queries about the arrangement were common, they felt, but not unpleasant.

There were benefits to this arrangement, as well. Most notably, there was much less conflict between work and family with this arrangement than was the case for women whose husbands worked full time. The women with these relationships experienced much less stress in their lives and seemed better able to handle work and family than women in dual-career households, perhaps because, despite the gender reversal, these families were actually quite traditional. The fathers served as the stay-at-home partner who took on the second shift, leaving the mother to concentrate on her career, and they could even embody, if they so chose, the ideal worker norms. Women in our sample were quick to praise their relationship and their family choices as being largely responsible for their sense of contentment. For example, a professor at a research university noted: "I probably should have said this first, my husband, as you know, that would be the thing that's able to make it all happen. If I didn't have that husband, you know, if I had married an academic, or teacher, high-ambition, financial guy, I don't know that I'd even have kids, you know, so he's first and foremost why it actually works." Another woman in this situation agreed, stating that her stay-at-home husband was "the only way I could be doing what I'm doing." Although these stay-at-home partners were not the norm, they presented an option that had some merit and made life on the tenure track and throughout the career manageable.

Mother as Secondary Breadwinner

Brenda worked as a professor at a regional comprehensive university. She met and married her husband Steve while she was in graduate school. Steve held a corporate job and worked very traditional hours—from 8 to 6 on most days. Steve traveled a lot for his job, often being gone for four or five days at a time. His job had structure, and he earned a lot of money. When Brenda and Steve decided to have children, Brenda knew it was going to be her responsibility to do much of the child care and housework. Their roles had always been pretty gendered—Steve mowed the lawn and took out the trash, but he wasn't home much and he came from a quite traditional family, so he saw many of the household duties as belonging to Brenda. Besides, he knew he didn't have the flexibility with his job to help out as much as he might have wanted. Steve was proud of his wife's position as a professor and wanted her to be successful, but he also didn't fully understand her position and what he saw was the flexibility and autonomy of her job, making it possible for her both to work as a professor and work the second shift at home. Brenda, however, felt the pinch of having to do two jobs full time—take care of her children and be a professor. Time and sleep were precious commodities for Brenda, neither of which were in ample supply.

This scenario represents the second grouping of couples in our study, those in which the woman's career as an academic was the secondary position in the family. This group includes spouses/partners who are in professional positions (such as lawyers, bankers, medical professionals, business owners) as well as those in blue-collar positions (such as police officers, construction workers, welders). What we found is that when the father is in the primary breadwinner, the mother's career ends up being devalued, and the woman ends up doing more of the second-shift work than her husband, regardless of the status of her partner's position. A lot of this comes as a result of the flexibility of the academic career compared to the husband's career, which is typically more rigidly scheduled. When the father's job involves a lot of traveling or time spent in the office or doing shift work that is not flexible, it is the woman who ends up picking up the slack in terms of managing child care, arranging schedules, cleaning the house, running errands, and cooking. Even in those situations where the father wanted to play a larger role, the woman ended up doing a lot of the heavy lifting. As one woman explained, "Since my husband's job is so structured and he has greater earning power, I don't want to make too many demands on his time when there's some conflict."

Traditional gender roles were most commonly followed in these relationships and, in fact, the more "gendered" the father's career (that is, a traditional male role like police office or attorney), the more the woman had to do in terms of home life. One faculty member explained that because her husband's job "is so inflexible it creates more parenting stress on me." She estimated that she carried 90 percent of the parenting responsibilities. There were some differences in the early career compared to the mid-career period for couples in this type of arrangement. Specifically, in the early-career period, child care was the primary responsibility of the mother. In the mid-career period, one of the primary roles of mothers was to organize everyone's schedules and figure out who needed to be where and when. Further, as the primary breadwinner in the family, it was often the father's job that determined where the couple lived and the extent to which the mother was able to commit herself to her academic career, especially if mobility was required for the father to advance. In some cases, the mother expressed the belief that her position was viewed more as a hobby than a career. Women in these relationships often felt place bound—some even expressing the feeling of being "stuck" and unable to advance their careers (at their own institutions or elsewhere). This led to some frustration at the mid-career level.

Dual-Career Academic Couples

Jessica and Evan met in graduate school. They were in the same program and had similar interests. They couldn't help it—they fell in love and decided to get married. The problem, of course, was going to be trying to find a place that would hire them both so that they could be together and both pursue their dreams of becoming tenure-track professors. While in graduate school, Jessica and Evan had heard horror stories of couples who could never find work in the same geographic region. They had friends in their field in which the wife worked in New York and the husband worked in Kansas City, and the two had to commute between the two cities just to see each other every other week. They also had friends in which half of the couple worked in an adjunct position while the other half was in a tenure-track job. Half of the couple wasn't fulfilled by her job, which left both of them constantly looking for positions that would be more satisfying for both. That wasn't the kind of life they wanted—they wanted both of them to have tenure-track positions in institutions in the same geographic region. Both applied for jobs and agreed that if one of them got an offer they would request a spousal accommodation for the other. Jessica was the first to be offered a position, and she raised the idea of having the institution hire Evan too—a package deal. The institution, a large research university in the Midwest, did have a dual-career couple hiring policy—but didn't have the funds available to offer Evan a tenure-track position. They offered a temporary, adjunct position to Evan, with the promise of trying to get something more permanent in the future. As the job market was tight, Evan agreed to give it a try. He moved with Jessica to the Midwest and worked hard in his tenuous position. He liked the teaching, but because he was an adjunct he had no time for conducting research and realized quickly that he was not going to be competitive for a research university position. Fortunately, a position opened up at another college in the area, and Evan started on the tenure track there. Evan's institution wasn't a research university, but it was a good position, and it allowed Evan and Jessica to live together and both pursue their passions. Once both were securely in their positions, they decided it was time to have a child, and agreed that they would share the responsibilities of parenthood and taking care of the household. Both positions were flexible, and both Jessica and Evan were committed to being co-caregivers. They were also both committed to attaining success in their academic careers.

It is not uncommon for academics to meet their spouses and partners in graduate school, and also not uncommon for both these individuals to want to pursue academic careers and family life, and actually get to live in the same city. Academic institutions have slowly come to recognize the needs of dual-career academic couples and to understand that accommodating them could translate into positive recruitment and retention decisions (Didion 1996; Schiebinger et al. 2008). A survey of chief academic officers in the mid 1990s showed that 44 percent of academic institutions provided some form of job assistance for spouses. An additional 12 percent of institutions indicated that they were planning on implementing a job assistance policy for spouses (Raabe 1997). Similarly, a survey of the chief academic officers of institutions belonging to the American Association of Colleges and Universities (AACU) found that although only 24 percent of respondents said that they have a dual-career couple hiring policy, only 15 percent of respondents stated that they would "do nothing" to assist spouses or partners find employment (Wolf-Wendel et al. 2000a). The majority of respondents indicated that they would help the spouse or partners of an initial hire on an informal, ad hoc basis. These studies of chief academic officers both concluded that research universities are the most likely of institutional types to have a dual-career couple policy. Responses to the surveys suggest that compared with many smaller institutions, research universities are more likely to help dual-career couples because they have more resources and have more flexibility in creating positions, both academic and administrative. A recent study by Schiebinger, Davies Henderson, and Gilmartin (2008) confirmed these findings.

Beyond the obvious problem of finding two academic careers in the same locale, a very significant hurdle, there were other issues that were unique to dual-career academic couples as they attempted to juggle work and family. In particular, when both the mother and father were faculty members, the father did not have the latitude to devalue the mother's career or mistake flexibility and autonomy for freedom to not work. As a result, dual-career academic couples engaged in a lot more tag-team parenting and sharing of family responsibilities. We heard many stories of mothers handing off their children to the fathers after he finished a class, and then arranging to pick up the child again when the father needed to be at a meeting. In a situation in which both members of the couple were under pressure to earn tenure, there was a greater sense of the day lasting twenty-four hours. Certainly, when couples were in the same career, they both understood the pressure that the other was under and attempted to facilitate the success of their partner as both a parent and a working professional. As in the cases when the father worked outside academia, women in dual-career academic couples also felt somewhat stuck at their institution, especially at the mid-career level. As one faculty member told us:

Getting remarried pretty much sealed the fate that we would probably stay here because when you have two people with tenure you can't just pack up and leave. When I made the decision to marry and be an academic and when I made the decision to have joint custody and a good relationship with my ex, I pretty much doomed myself. I pretty much locked myself into staying here. It would be a very difficult move. . . . But, since I like it here and I am happy, it is not like I think it is such a bad thing.

Clearly being part of a dual-career academic couple, in addition to being in a situation that involves divorce and custody (and tenure!), limits mobility. Another aspect of being a dual-career couple is figuring out how to be mobile and accommodate both jobs. An underlying decision is about whose job will take precedence. These issues arose both when the couple were both academics as well as when the spouse or partner was in a nonacademic position.

Career development as a faculty member is shaped by many different dimensions. As women have made progress in the academic market place, it is easy to look at them as faculty members independent of personal factors. To be sure, family background and marital status have salience for both men and women, but on the basis of societal expectations and gendered dispositions, we found in our research that the women we interviewed and their choices about academic life and parenthood were influenced by their family history and also by the interaction they have with their spouses. Historically, the tradition was for the woman to be the trailing spouse or to not be working at all, thus making it easier for her husband to be mobile and advance in his career—topics we cover in the next chapter when we talk about women working in positions alternate to the tenure track. For the women in our study, we found that being part of a couple had a major influence on how people perceived their positions and how open they felt to change and professional development opportunities. We also found that the choices people feel free to make (or not) are very much shaped by the sense of confidence and agency them bring with them to the job, on the basis of both their family history and the family and marital circumstances that shape their life.

————

Before moving on, it is worth looking briefly at the findings in this chapter relative to the role of family and capital through the lens of feminist theory. There is no denying that the choices described in this chapter are strongly influenced by traditional gendered patterns associated with family. And, while capital (economic, social, and cultural) gives these women some degree of personal agency and freedom to make choices, post-structural feminism suggests that these choices are nonetheless constrained by gendered norms and expectations (Ball 2002). In other words, women are not, in many circumstances, making "free choices," as their options and choices are constrained by their gendered roles within the family as a spouse and as a mother. Recall chapter 3, when we wrote that women from lower socioeconomic groups typically do not have the luxury to think about work and family as an either/or proposition and do not have the political, social, or economic power to be included in the discourse of work and family because not to work is not an option. Worrying about the extent to which the workplace is family friendly or not is a luxury afforded only to those with a certain socioeconomic status. Other women need to work in order to survive, and will do so even if their workplaces are not family friendly. Women from higher socioeconomic backgrounds (such as professors), especially those who have inherited capital as a result of their family background and resources, have a greater sense of choice and agency. As such, even within the professional class of women who are faculty, inherited capital makes the playing field uneven. Capital matters in terms of affording women more or less freedom of choice.

The issues related to dual-career couples also should be viewed from a poststructural feminist lens. There is an assumption that women are not the primary breadwinner and thus are subject to the professional needs of their husbands, who presumably make more money. Although there were examples of women in our study who found themselves to be "the trailing spouse," what is interesting is that they were not always the spouse who made the least amount of money. There were women we interviewed who felt and behaved like trailing spouses even when their professional positions would have arguably provided more capital to the family than their husband's (for example, a woman who is a professor with a husband who is a police officer or a woman who is a professor when her husband is a K–12 teacher). Women, whether primary breadwinners or secondary bread-winners, were making choices that reinforced traditional gender norms. From a liberal feminist perspective, the goal is to create equal opportunity for women in an effort to level the playing field and allow individuals to have options and make free choices. A poststructural feminist lens, however, suggests that we should recognize that the field is not even, and that choices made are shaped by gendered constraints that reify rather than problematize traditional gender roles (Allen 2011). In the next chapter we talk more about the choices—some forced, some chosen, all constrained—that the women in the study made with regard to their positions.

CHAPTER 9

Leaving the Tenure Track

What about people who did not get tenure? What about those who left the tenure track? Did people leave academia all together? Although it is hard to identify the specific number of women who did not get tenure, or who are no longer on the tenure track due to attrition between the early- and mid-career phases of the study, we are able to comment on the experiences of those faculty that we interviewed in the mid-career phase of the study who were no longer on the tenure track, either voluntarily or involuntarily. It is on these women and their experiences that we now focus. We do so by first looking at some existing research and perspectives about women leaving the workforce and then moving on to the stories of the women in our study who left their initial tenure-track positions.

"Opting out" is a term used "to describe the decision of married women to voluntarily quit professional careers and remain out of the labor force for a relatively extended period of time (beyond the duration of parental leave) during which they are engaged in family caregiving, primarily motherhood, to the exclusion of paid employment" (Stone et al. 2010, 1). These women "opt out" and "head home," in the words of Lisa Belkin, who coined the term in a 2003 *New York Times Magazine* article. In the case of academic women, as we found in our research, the choice to opt out generally does not take women entirely out of the workforce, but may be underlying decisions to work part time, or to work in nontenure-track positions, or to work in less prestigious institutions. While some may frame decisions about how and in what context to pursue an academic career and to subsequently opt out of it as a matter of personal agency, the decisions can also be viewed as being problematic because they signify that the tenure track is not an acceptable domain for women with children (Stone 2007). One reason women leave the work force is the perceived incompatibility of work as a professor and life as a mother.

Opting out is important to our work, as well as the work of other family researchers, because it highlights people leaving the workforce who have made significant investments in their education and professional status. Typically those with professional careers, the focus of the "opt-out revolution" (Belkin 2003), are those with educational backgrounds that merit professional status (such as engineers, professors, economists). Such movement out of the workforce or out of the mainstream workplace by this group of people can leave one to question: Why leave the workforce when so much is invested? Leaving the workforce to take care of children reinforces traditional gender norms and perpetuates separate-sphere thinking that puts women at home and men at work. Further, if these women leave the workforce, given their background and access to resources, what implications does this have for women who do not have access to such resources (Stone 2007)?

In our study, opting out took different forms. The first group we analyze include women who involuntarily opted out of the tenure track as a result of not getting tenure. The second group opted out of the tenure track to be full-time parents. The third group opted out of the tenure track to move into a different type of academic position, most often a nontenure-track position. We discuss each one of these situations separately.

INVOLUNTARY OPTING OUT

"What's the worst thing that can happen? Not get tenure?" We heard variations on this refrain in several of the early-career interviews. We found that the looming question of tenure (and not getting it) was something that most had grappled with as early-career faculty members. Although most women in the study never had to face their "worst case scenario," there were some who did, and we want to honor their experiences in this chapter. We also note that we did not craft a vignette for this experience, as it was not a typical experience and the specifics of how and why it happened varied greatly from person to person.

There were four women in the mid-career phase of our study who were denied tenure sometime before we interviewed them the second time. Two of them began at very prestigious research universities and ended up at different research universities, where they eventually earned tenure. A third one started out at a research university and after being denied tenure took a position at a selective liberal arts institution and eventually earned tenure there. The fourth one started at a regional comprehensive institution and ended up in a full-time position at a community college. Resilient is the word that we would use to describe these women. Of course, the negative decision was difficult for them to take, especially at the time, but in retrospect they all seemed reconciled to the situation and most of them felt there was a better fit for them at their new institutions than at their prior institutions. There is not much published research on what happens to people after they are denied tenure, so it is difficult to establish a comparison between faculty in our study and others who have experienced similar situations. Given how potentially awful this decision could be, we think the women who experienced it managed a very difficult decision with a lot of grace and dignity. From their perspective, having children helped them adopt a holistic perspective.

One woman recounted the following story about not getting tenure and how her family helped her put the job loss in perspective. She initially was denied tenure at a major research university and then went on to get tenure at another research university.

> It [going through tenure the second time] was more emotional because I'd been through that once unsuccessfully; although there are lots of ways I could have justified [not getting tenure]—nobody is getting tenured, there were fourteen people in a row who either left the third year or didn't get tenure in my department. I didn't have to feel like I was a failure, but it was traumatic. You have to move. I think tenure wasn't as scary the second time. I think my record was better, of course, and also I just realized that life goes on, and I didn't think we'd be happy here [at her new institution], and we love it here. I kind of realized that even if we had to leave, we make friends, we integrate in the community easily, and our kids are resilient. I think I didn't feel like it would be the end of the world if I didn't get it. It wasn't as scary, having been through that.

Probably I felt better about my, you know, I had more of a national reputation in terms of some of my publications and stuff. . . . If you don't
get tenure it's not the end of the world. There's research showing that
people are just as happy five years after not getting tenure as five years
after getting tenure. You've got to live in a place where you're going to
be happy. I figure I'm happy with my family. I get enough satisfaction
with that, that wherever we are I'm going to be happy. If it's here or
somewhere else, it's going to be ok.

For this woman, not earning tenure at her first academic job was certainly
a challenging time in her life, as it is for anyone who loses a job. When we
asked her to what extent having a family played into her not getting tenure,
she mused: "I was really close to getting tenure at [her first institution] and
maybe if I didn't have a baby I would have had more articles. I don't know.
I do know that having a baby was a good thing, when I got home at the
end of the day and I was totally stressed, I had this baby who wanted and
needed me so I couldn't focus too much on my job. It [having a baby] was
a good thing." Having a child helped her put her job loss in perspective
and helped buffer her from the grim realities of her workplace when she
did not get tenure.

Her job loss experience also highlights a life-course perspective which
sees that things happen throughout life (such as birth, sickness, death)
and things happen throughout the career (such as new jobs, losing jobs,
promotions). Events in the private domain shape the public sphere, and
vice versa. Historically, academic career development and socialization
models have ignored the impact of having a child and other life events
on the career (Ward & Bensimon 2002). Using a life-course perspective
to analyze instances of people not getting tenure offers a more holistic
view of the career and a more holistic view of being a mother. There is an
interdependence between different aspects of lives and careers (Han & Moen
1999), and to ignore the interdependence of these realities shortchanges the
faculty experience.

The story of another individual illustrates how she handled not getting
tenure. She started out as a foreign language professor at a research university. She indicates that she "didn't come up for tenure because I didn't finish
my book and there wasn't any point to it. I knew I wouldn't get it." So she

left before going up for tenure. Her husband was a tenured professor at a local institution, so she wasn't really mobile. However, she applied for and was hired into an adjunct position at a local community college that subsequently turned into a full-time position. Although she likes teaching at the community college, she admits that it is "hard thinking about status. It's the thing you stick on. It sticks in your throat. . . . 'Failure' is an awful word. Did you fail at something or did you get really lucky? Or did you fail at it because some part of you really didn't want to succeed at it and do better, or because you just couldn't do it? It's hard to work through those things."

Interestingly, her new faculty position at the community college pays better and is less stressful than her tenure-track position. She also believes that the new position gave her back her creativity. In retrospect, she claims "I'm enormously happy. It is the best thing that happened to me—losing that job, not getting tenure." She adds, "I wouldn't have picked this—I had to be forced into it." One of the things she laments is that she wasn't informed about community colleges as an option while she was in graduate school. In terms of thinking about her failure, she says: "Maybe I just didn't plan right. Maybe I did something wrong. Either I earned my failure or I earned my frustration for not having planned it out right. I didn't get the blueprint. I think really, on the whole, in many ways, I'm better off now than I would have been with an easier kind of success." While "failure" is not something that anybody wants, it was a reality for some of the women in this study, and tenure denial made them step back and evaluate their priorities and their choices about careers and work. In fact, most of these women say that they ended up with jobs that are better suited to them than their original positions.

People fear being an academic because of concern about tenure and the prospect of not getting it. Female faculty members also sometimes fear having children because it might impinge on career progress, especially on the tenure track. We know from prior literature that people even go so far as not pursuing academic jobs for fear they won't succeed (that is, not get tenure) (Golde & Dore 2001). Some people decide to not have children for fear it will mean a negative tenure outcome. What we found from talking to women with children who did not get tenure is that yes, it was a challenging situation, especially at the time, but with some distance and perspective they were able to look back on the situation and recognize that it was not the worst thing that could have happened. And having a family was part of what helped. For these people, not getting tenure forced job changes that ultimately turned out to be good ones.

OPTING OUT AND HEADING HOME

Although they were limited in number, there were a few women in our study who opted out of the workforce in the interest of staying home with their children and managing their households full time. Opting out describes the decisions women make to leave the paid workforce of their own volition as a means of taking care of their families full time (Stone, Kohler, & Ackerly Hernandez, 2010). In the second-phase interviews we interviewed only two women who had completely left the workforce to be full-time mothers. It is possible there are additional women who also opted to stay home, because between the early-career interviews and the mid-career interviews there were ten women for whom we were not able to find any contact information.

Although we interviewed only two woman who completely opted out, we thought it important to mention their experience, given the traditional and gendered ideals about women leaving the workforce once they have children, and also given conversations in the literature and the popular press about women opting out of the workforce to "head home" and take care of their children (Belkin 2003). In both instances, the women we talked to who opted out completely did so to accommodate their husband's positions. One woman left an academic position at a major research university to accommodate her husband's job opportunity in a different state. His new position was expected to be very demanding (he was becoming a chief surgeon at a major medical teaching hospital), and the woman in our study opted to stay home as a means to accommodate his difficult hours. Her husband's new position came with a significant pay increase, making it feasible to manage on just one income. The other woman who opted out did so to help further her partner's political career. He was elected into a fairly high state government position, and she did not think it would be feasible to maintain both her career and his. In the interest of supporting her husband, she opted out of paid employment. This situation leads us to think about leaving the workforce not only to manage work and family but also to accommodate traditional ideas about what a political figure's spouse does to support the career of her husband.

OPTING OUT (AND OFF) OF THE TENURE TRACK

More common than not earning tenure or opting out of the workforce completely to manage family needs was opting out of a full-time tenure-track appointment and choosing a different work arrangement to help meet family needs. Within our sample at mid-career, twelve women who we interviewed had left their initial tenure-track positions either for jobs outside academia or for other academic positions. There are two dimensions to what we found about women leaving tenure-track positions to accommodate family needs:. one had to do with accommodating dual-career issues, and the other had to do with meeting the needs of family and children.

Opting Out for Dual Careers

We heard from a faculty member of her decision to leave her tenure-track position at a research university to move with her husband to be part of the family business.

> We've moved a lot for my job. It took me awhile to have my two sons, so I was a little later coming to motherhood than I planned. I really enjoy being a mother, so when my husband had the opportunity to work with his brother to take over the family business, I was open to making a change. We had to move two hours north from [my university] so we had to move and I had to leave my job. Initially I stayed at home, but now I'm working part time teaching. . . . It works for us and I don't really want more.

This story was one we heard in different versions of from several women who had left their tenure-track or tenured positions. These women had opted into different types of jobs as a way to accommodate their family needs, including dual-career issues. From a gendered and feminist perspective, we see that it is more likely to be women than men who make these accommodations, something we find troubling. But we found that women felt they had chosen their path, and for the most part were happy with their decisions. From the perspective of personal agency, these women felt they had made good choices to accommodate the needs of the family. They had come to the realization that there is more than one path to being a successful academic (Monosson 2008). The very idea that there is only one way to be an academic (on the tenure track, full time) is itself an idea that has been dictated by an academic workplace that privileges one set of faculty (tenure-track and tenured) over all others (such as adjuncts, instructors, and part-time faculty).

For the most part, the women who opted to leave their initial jobs to follow their husbands felt fine about their decisions. As one faculty member who had left a tenure-track position at a liberal arts college in order to accommodate her husband's position and in order to stop commuting to accommodate two tenure-track positions told us: "I left the tenure track, in part, because of my husband's relocation. I wanted to be a more involved parent and have us as a family all in the same town. So I left my position so I could be at a research university and have our family together."

To accommodate her spouse, she is now in a nontenure-track position, but finds the "tradeoff is worth it. I'm happier at this institution and it's great for us all be in the same place." Another faculty member left her job teaching at a community college when her husband was offered a job on the east coast. She recalls saying: "Let's start a new adventure in our life. . . . I thought maybe this would be a good time for a career change for me. I had been teaching for a number of years. I'm getting tired of it. I don't know exactly what I want to do, but this might be a good time to start looking at that." Eventually, she admits that after the first year the angst about not having a job went up: "Oh my God. I'm out of the workforce for a year now, and will it be tough for me to get my foot back in the door? I interviewed at a few community colleges in the area but they were a long distance from my house, they didn't pay well, and I didn't get a good feeling from them. So, I took a second year off and I wasn't sure exactly what else I might like to do." Eventually she saw a job opening to teach English at the local high school. "They definitely wanted me to come work there. The salary looked good and the great thing was that I would have all the same holidays with the kids and only a five-minute commute." She added: "In low moods I think to myself, 'Okay you failed at what you set out to accomplish.' But in healthier moods, I think 'I found my niche. I found what works for me. And, that balance of family is just extremely important to me.'"

Not all of the women who made the decision to follow their husbands for their positions were happy with the outcome. One woman, in particular, stands out as being quite unhappy with how her life had turned out. She quit a tenure-track job to move with her husband to another city, where he was on the tenure track. She was hired as an adjunct at a research university. Her description of her life was less than rosy. In her words:

> I hope to get the hell out. I am forty-five and I'm a visiting assistant professor and it isn't going up from here. My whole life was geared toward becoming an academic and now I am screwed. We are exhausted, stressed, and horrified, but the baby is very happy. Being an academic means you move away from your family and then you are screwed again. I've got to get out. My life has been geared into being an academic and now it's just not working out. This isn't going to have a happy ending.

While certainly not the sentiment expressed by everyone, moving for your spouse involves trade-offs that don't always translate into happiness. As can be seen from this last example, when you have two people who are both driven in their careers and have aspirations that cannot be realized due to dual-career concerns and the primacy of the man's job, some level of unease, unhappiness, and dissatisfaction is bound to exist.

Though it was rare, there were a few cases where the women in our study decided it was their turn to pursue their dream career, perhaps at the expense of their spouse/partner. Such was the case with one faculty member who started out as a tenure-track assistant professor at a regional comprehensive college in Florida. She left her position to move to Europe to be with her husband while he was doing his dissertation fieldwork. Since her children were very young, she felt it was an "obvious choice to leave my job and to go to Europe and stay home with the kids." The problem was that she didn't like being a stay-at-home mother. She went on to tell us: "I was resentful and I was grouchy. I started feeling like a babysitter rather than a mother. I suddenly felt like I had absolutely no sense of anything academic anymore. I started to feel like I was vanishing."

When the couple returned from Europe (with school-age children), the woman was offered a tenure-track position at a liberal arts college. Excitedly, she explained, "I was so enthusiastic to be back and be awake again." Her husband was offered a tenure-track position in a different state, so the two faced a dilemma. They decided that they would live apart to accommodate both partners having tenure-track jobs. She told us her story:

> He is going to go to [another state] and I'm going to stay here with the kids. The kids are in good schools but also I've just put my career on hold for a long time and every single year that we have moved it has been for his career and it has never once been for mine. We're at the point right now where we both feel like we like where we live. . . . I've got kind of my dream job here so it was a really agonizing decision for us, but we decided that he is going to commute home on weekends. I think what has happened is that I've reached a point where I've decided that the next move I make needs to be mutually beneficial. If we continue to move and I continue to just be this adjuncting fiend then this is not going to make for a happy wife and a happy mother.

She concluded her story by stating:

> If you asked me ten years ago what I thought my life would look like I definitely would not have thought of this. I would have thought a Ph.D. and I would have thought that I would have been married and had kids. . . . I don't think I would have ever imagined moving every year of our marriage for his career. Certainly I never ever would have thought that I would say "Husband, you go live in another state so that I can keep my job." But yeah, I like my job.

In this example, the woman opted out of a tenure-track position (the one she was in when we initially interviewed her) to accommodate her spouse's job move. She then opted back into a different tenure-track position to accommodate her desire for professional fulfillment. She wanted a tenure-track position, just as her spouse did.

As we discussed in the last chapter, dual-career issues led people to make job changes or think about their job in new and different ways. Being part of a dual-career couple is complicated. The traditional model of one person at home made life easier to accommodate faculty careers and what are sometimes quite limited job options. For the most part, throughout our data we find that people make it work, but we also found that for the majority of the women in the study, it was they who made the concession rather than their partner. These findings relate to those of Bielby and Bielby (1992), who wrote about women leaving for their husbands' careers, but also having to stay put for his career, as well. Clearly prior research, like our own, indicates that a woman's career mobility is adversely affected by her commitments to family and her relationships to her spouse and children.

Opting Out for Family

We also found that people opted out of their positions to more generally meet the needs of their families, not just dual careers. One woman we interviewed in the early-career phase was working in a tenure-track position at a liberal arts college. Her husband worked as a high school teacher in a town about forty-five minutes away from her work and from their home. "Life was hectic with me teaching all day and with my husband having to commute to work. I ended up doing the majority of parenting because my husband was gone much of the day." Although she was well on her way to earning tenure, she opted out of the tenure track and opted into a full-time job teaching at the same high school as her husband as a way to better meet their overall family needs. In the new arrangement she told us, "We are all on the same schedule and life is so much easier." She finds the job to be very similar to her last one, and she plans to "get back to research soon." Although not a requirement in her high school teaching position, she has the latitude to engage in research if she wants to. She found that working in the high school setting helps meet her family needs, and she also was still actively engaged in her profession, just in a different setting.

In the workforce, in general and historically, the idea was that either you worked or you did not. Not always, but often, the "either/or" of work or no work for women accompanied having children. Women worked until they were married and/or had children and then left the workforce to support traditional gender roles of homemaking. In the academic sphere, this tradition is perpetuated in the sense of being a legitimate academic: to have legitimacy you either work a full-time tenure-track position, or you do not have a full-time position and therefore lack legitimacy (Monosson 2008). Although the majority of the contemporary academic workforce is composed of contingent faculty, most of whom work part time and all without the job security of tenure (Kezar & Sam 2010), the traditional and "ideal" academic is one who is on the tenure track. For women this has created a quandary—either meet ideal academic norms or lack legitimacy. This also creates a quandary, as we've emphasized throughout this book, for women who have children and want to approach their academic life in alternative ways. To be sure, the majority of the women in this study manage both family and tenure-track or tenured positions by co-opting academic and motherhood norms in ways that allowed them to "have it all." A small number of the women we interviewed, however, chose to approach work differently, and in the interest of managing and integrating work and family they did so by leaving their full-time tenure-track positions to work in part-time positions—both within and beyond the academy. These women maintain a professional persona, but do so in ways that help them to more easily manage their private and public spheres.

Analyzing Choices

From a feminist perspective, choices about leaving tenure-track positions are ones that are made within a larger milieu of cultural and traditional expectations of what it means to be a woman in the workplace and what it means to be a mother in society (Somerville 2000). Choice is an interesting concept because it is one that women (and men) should feel free to exercise. However, what we found throughout our research is that a lot of the choices women make, especially career choices to accommodate family needs, are made within the confines of traditional academic and family norms that are dictated by gendered roles. The nature of these choices also absolved colleges and universities from doing much to create change. If women choose to opt out of tenure-track positions, it's easy for institutions to wash their hands of responsibility, citing individual choice.

When we step back and look at our data through the lens of choice, including opting out (even when the choice is imposed on people, such as when not getting tenure) and choosing to work in different settings, we see the need to look at the findings from a feminist perspective. If we just look at the data from a superficial standpoint, it is too easy to continue to look at women as the cause of their own circumstances. "Good choices" get juxtaposed with "bad choices," and personal agency becomes primary. That is, if a woman opts to work in a liberal arts college, gets tenure, and is successful, she's made a good choice. And, in contrast, if she chooses to work in a research university where she eventually does not get tenure because she had three kids while on the tenure track, then she has made some bad choices. The reality is that most, if not all choices, a woman makes are shaped by the history and traditions that guide the American family. And, for women that means maintaining the household and taking care of children (Somerville 2000). Yes, personal agency plays a role in the choices women make, but still those choices are filtered through the lens of women's traditional roles at some level, whether that be superficial or deeply rooted. There are no free choices for women. In the data analysis, we see that women are making choices relative to their disciplines, their spouse, their family background, and their family needs. We are not saying that as a result the choices women make are "bad choices"; instead what we are saying is that as long as work and family and faculty career development discourse focus on women as actors and agents of their own fate, as a majority of policy and research does (Somerville 2000), then women will continue to make either good or bad choices and the people and institutions that surround women will continue to be absolved of their role.

Opting out suggests that, given competing options, women *choose* to leave the workforce. There are push-and-pull factors associated with the choice to leave work. For some it is the pull to be at home with children, but for many professionals it is the push to leave a workforce that is not very friendly to families that leads to that choice to opt out (Herr & Wolfram 2009; Stone 2007). For example, Blair-Loy (2005) found that women financial executives often leave the workforce not so much for the pull of motherhood as because of the push out of a workforce that favors complete devotion and ideal workers. Similar findings exist related to the tenure-track academic workforce. Mason and Goulden's (2004) work suggests that women with children opt out of tenure-line positions at greater rates than their male counterparts due to the perceived clash in culture between work and family in academia.

Opting out can have deleterious effects on women and on workplaces. For women who have fought so hard to enter the workforce and who have worked hard to find a place in the workforce, opting out can mean personal defeat. For organizations, women opting out can mean losing quality members of the workforce and institutional apathy toward workplace change. Opting out also perpetuates the notion that women are likely to leave their careers once they have children and thus may not be worth investments of time and resources.

On the one hand, opting out is the ultimate exercise of choice, agency, and free will for women with financial means; yet, on the other hand, it perpetuates workplace norms that are based on traditional gender roles. Further, choice is limited to those who have access to it, and "choices in the ways of living are an outcome of lifting of the material and cultural conditions of non-choice" (Somerville 2000, 239). The discourse surrounding opting out (and the choice to opt out) is important to our research in that it often shapes how women approach their work and their commitment to the academic workplace. We found examples in our work of people opting out of the academic workforce altogether, and those who opted out of traditional full-time and tenure-track positions, but opted in to other types of positions that they saw more compatible with having a family. The ways that women opt out are not all the same, and we see nuances of these decisions and choices in the stories of some of the women that we interviewed. Opting out is also a narrative prevalent in the literature on work and family in academia. Indeed, the extent to which choices are truly free or constrained and influenced by existing structures are important considerations as the academy seeks to be of high quality by recruiting and creating a more diverse faculty.

We next focus on institutional policies as they relate to fostering the choices of their faculty in dealing with the issues of work and family.

CHAPTER 10

⟋⟍

Policy Perspectives

Sarah got pregnant in her third year on the tenure track at a comprehensive state university. After trying to get pregnant for two years, she was ecstatic. She told a few colleagues she was pregnant and everyone was happy for her. One of her friends, a colleague in another department, asked her what she was going to do when she had the baby in terms of time off and daycare and, frankly, Sarah had not considered taking a leave. She didn't know what policies were available, no one mentioned taking a leave, and she just figured she would work it out with her husband and family. She didn't want to be a burden to the department because everyone was already overloaded. One faculty member was on sabbatical and the department had a vacancy to fill, so she couldn't fathom how there would be any leave available even if there was a policy. She was due in April and would only have one month left in the semester, so she didn't think leave was a big deal. She asked a colleague to teach classes for her for the first couple of weeks after her due date and she figured she'd be back to work before the end of the semester. Her mother was going to come from out of town to help take care of the baby and her husband planned to take a couple of weeks off to help as well. She would spend the summer mostly with her baby, but she figured she would get some work done, too, because as a tenure-track faculty member she felt it was important "not to skip a beat." She felt she was doing fine in terms of teaching and research in her tenure-track appointment, but she also felt it was very important to maintain productivity. She didn't want anyone to look at her dossier and see any lags.

When we talked to Sarah in the first interview, a year after she had her baby, she was totally fine with not having taken leave. Everything worked out. She figured the policies wouldn't have helped her because she was new and she didn't want to call attention to herself anyway. Her mother loved the opportunity to help her and spend time with the new baby. When we talked to her eight years later and she reflected back on not taking leave (for the first baby or when she had her second baby in the year when she went up for tenure) she told us: "I was stupid; I should have just asked and taken the leave. I had a colleague who just had a baby and she worked with our chair to take on some curriculum revision projects in lieu of teaching for the second half of the semester when she had her baby. I should have asked for something in terms of leave. Somehow it seems different now than when I had my baby. We have the university's Commission for Women talking about these [work and family policy] issues and people seem more open to taking leaves. It's become more the norm. Frankly, when I was pregnant and considered taking a leave, I was scared. I didn't want anyone to think I couldn't handle it. Like I said, I was stupid; I should have taken the leave. I trust myself more now, when I was on the tenure track I felt too vulnerable to ask for much."

Sarah's experience with work and family policy is unfortunately very common among early-career faculty. As new faculty members on the tenure track, assistant professors are reticent to ask for much, and asking for leave seems unduly burdensome for faculty colleagues, especially in small departments when everyone is already working hard. The lore of the tenure track is "full steam ahead" so people, especially when they are early in their careers and uncertain about so many things, are timid and unsure of what accommodation is available and how to ask for it. Department chairs, even well-meaning ones, often wait to be asked by the faculty member who is pregnant to determine an appropriate accommodation. They don't want to be intrusive. They figure that if the faculty member needs help, she'll ask for it.

Conversations and research about work and family, as we have highlighted throughout this book, take place on many levels. There has been considerable attention to the effects of work and family on faculty members; there are personal accounts and reflections on how having children shapes the career, and there is also information and discussion about policy. The policy conversation within work and family circles has a couple of different angles. One is a description of the types of policies that campuses have (or should have) to facilitate the integration of work and family (e.g., Hollenshead et al. 2005). There has also been discussion about people's disposition to use the policies and about facilitators and deterrents of policy use (e.g., Drago et al. 2006; O'Meara & Campbell, 2011). In this chapter we call upon these sources of information, as well as findings from our research, to highlight the policy arena related to work and family for faculty.

The intent of this chapter is first to describe typical policies used to assist women faculty in balancing work and family. These descriptions are based on published literature as well as on a content analysis of the policies in place at the institutions where we conducted our research. Where helpful, we include quotes from our interviews, primarily from early-career faculty but also from faculty members later in their career, as well as interviews from the chairs and colleagues of selected women in the study. Our intention is to learn about policy utilization not only from those who used the policy but also from those who surround the women in the workplace, to illustrate multiple perspectives on the use of policies. Next, the chapter uses data from the faculty and chair interviews to describe how the policies are perceived and utilized. The chapter also addresses some of the policy nuances on different types of campuses, highlighting the general climate toward policy usage in various institutional contexts. Finally, we look at the overall policy context through some of the theoretical lenses discussed earlier in the book.

TYPICAL WORK/FAMILY POLICIES

Several studies have been conducted that look at the kind of policies that have been implemented to assist faculty members in balancing work and family. Most of these policies focus on pretenure faculty members rather than on their mid-career colleagues. In our research, although we asked about policy utilization in both the early and mid-career interviews, it was more of a focus in the early-career discussions. This makes sense, because the majority of the policies that exist are focused on having a child (which most of the women in our study did early in their career) and on accommodation to address delays in the tenure clock—another early-career phenomenon. It is during the pretenure period that faculty members are most likely to experience work/family conflict, and also experience the physical demands of having a baby. Mid-career faculty members talked about policy primarily with regard to how policy environments have changed, and also retrospectively in terms of what they wish they had done with regard to taking advantage of policies.

As part of looking at the policies at the campuses in the study, we also looked at research of other campuses. A survey of chief academic officers at research universities in the mid-1990s concluded that 84 percent of institutions provided unpaid maternity leave; 74 percent provided paid maternity leave; 47 percent had on-campus child-care facilities; 21 percent offered financial assistance for child care; 36 percent offered accommodative scheduling to meet family needs; and 29 percent offered expansion of time for tenure for family-related reasons (Raabe 1997). A more recent survey of 256 colleges and universities indicates that research universities were the most likely of the various institutional types to have family-friendly policies (Sullivan et al. 2004). The most common policies were those without direct financial costs to the institution. For example, 79 percent of research universities offered institution-wide tenure stop-clock policies, and 52 percent provided unpaid leaves. The 2004 study also found that policies that cost more were less common. Specifically, fewer than 20 percent of institutions in the study offered paid leave for dependent care, 28 percent of research universities offered modified duty policies for faculty (i.e., course releases), 25 percent offered reduced appointments for either extraordinary or ordinary circumstances, and approximately 20 percent allowed tenure-track faculty members to have part-time appointments or to job share. Additional findings from a national study of parental leave in higher education found that private institutions are more likely to have leave policies than public ones (Yoest 2004).

The findings from our data mirror the policy-related findings of these other studies. The four most common policies were unpaid leave, as provided through the Family Medical Leave Act, the use of sick leave, the use of modi-fied duty policies, and tenure stop-clock policies. Each is explained below.

Family Medical Leave Act (FMLA): Unpaid Leave

In 1993, the federal government passed the Family and Medical Leave Act (FMLA), established to protect those having families and those with significant family responsibilities that could inhibit an employee's ability to work. Organizations with fifty or more employees, as well as all public agencies, are bound by law to provide up to a total of twelve work weeks of unpaid leave during any twelve-month period for one or more of the following reasons:

- birth and care of the newborn child of the employee;
- placement with the employee of a son or daughter for adoption or foster care;
- care for an immediate family member (spouse, child, or parent) with a serious health condition; or
- medical leave when the employee is unable to work because of a serious health issue (U.S. Department of Labor, 2010).

The vast majority of colleges and universities are bound by FMLA. This has had both negative and positive consequences for faculty members combining work and family. The legislation is positive in that it safeguards faculty members from losing their job and their insurance coverage when they take a leave for family reasons. It is also positive in that FMLA forces all covered institutions to consider issues associated with family leave—an issue that prior to 1993 was invisible on many campuses. It is negative, however, in that some campuses do nothing else but offer FMLA provisions to new parents, which means a grant of unpaid leave. It is negative, as well, in that the presence of FMLA can exonerate institutions from doing more to help faculty members negotiate the combination of work and family.

A content analysis of the policy documents in our study shows that most campuses mention FMLA and what it offers to employees needing family leave. Among our sample, this was the minimal provision offered and was the focal point of most institutional policies. Our research also shows that although the FMLA legislation has done great things to put the need for work and family policies on the conscience of contemporary society, it has also absolved institutions of their responsibility to adapt these policies to the unique needs of faculty (for example, covering a fifteen-week semester). However, we also found that some campuses were not even in full compliance with FMLA. Campus policies and FMLA language tend to exist on campuses simultaneously, but there is limited translation between the two. For example, it is common for campuses to have language that allows for a six-week unpaid leave in the event of the birth of a child, whereas FMLA allows for twelve weeks. This leaves faculty members to ask, how much leave am I entitled to? The length of leave allowed in FMLA is also problematic, as it does not coincide with a typical semester length—thus requiring someone (either the faculty member or a departmental representative) to figure out how to deliver entire courses. Clearly, the findings from our study suggest that FMLA alone is not enough.

Sick Leave or Disability Leave

Although no campuses in our study offered paid parental leave per se, many of the policies mentioned that faculty members could use sick leave (or vacation days, when available) to cover a leave period. On some campuses, faculty members on parental leave could apply for short-term disability. Since few new faculty members are able to afford a semester without pay, in most circumstances when a faculty member wants to take a paid leave she must use sick leave. This assumes that faculty members have accrued sufficient sick leave, which for new faculty members may not be the case. It also assumes that pregnancy is a sickness, equating pregnancy and childbirth with pathology. Further, asking faculty members to use sick leave creates a dilemma if and when a faculty member or a family member actually becomes ill—as their sick leave will surely be depleted. Finally, there is the tricky question of how to count sick leave for faculty—does one compute it on the basis of a forty-hour week, of the hours missed per class or office hours, or by some other means? Typically, colleges and universities do not provide clear guidance for how faculty members should count how much sick leave they need to take.

It is not uncommon for academic employers to provide pregnancy disability leave or sick leave on terms that are less generous than those available for other kinds of medical leave. For example, female faculty members who are using sick leave for maternity reasons are often told that they must find people to teach their courses before they can take sick leave. This practice is illegal under the Pregnancy Discrimination Act, unless professors who take medical leave for other reasons, for example a heart attack, are also required to find their own replacements, or to trade off other faculty benefits in order to take leave—which is unlikely to happen. Another example comes in considering the availability of pooled sick leaves that are donated by colleagues for chronic illnesses, which are not available to those wishing to use sick leave for maternity purposes. The same terms and conditions for leaves taken for other medical reasons should be applied to leaves taken for pregnancy and childbirth. Unfortunately, all of these things are concerns that a faculty member must negotiate on her own behalf with the department/school or college, which has responsibility for policy implementation and funding.

Modified Duty Policies

These policies allow faculty members, under specific conditions such as the care of family members or personal disability, to have temporary (e.g., a semester/quarter/term) relief from or reduction of some duties without loss of pay. For example, this might include partial or full relief from teaching, service, or research. Each modified duty arrangement is individually tailored by the provost, dean, or department chair, and is typically negotiated by the faculty member seeking the accommodation. These types of policies allow faculty members with new children (by birth or adoption) to request a modified workload and flexible schedule (typically within a year after the child enters the home). Modifications vary significantly. An example would be a faculty member who has a child in September and therefore negotiates to teach one course instead of two, limits involvement in service obligations, and maintains involvement in research but forgoes involvement in conferences. Modified duty might also call for faculty to serve in some type of administrative capacity or to engage in a project for the department in lieu of other types of work obligations. Such options keep the faculty members on campus and active in their work, albeit in a limited way. Typically the department/school (or college) is responsible for arranging for coverage of direct teaching responsibilities for the period of modified duties.

Modified duties are not the same as a leave of absence. Faculty members with modified duties status will generally be relieved of teaching but will be expected to be fully employed by fulfilling their other professional responsibilities that can be scheduled around the child's needs, such as preparation of research proposals, papers, and course materials; supervision of graduate student research; and academic service. Typically, during the period of modified duties, faculty members are expected to remain available to their colleagues and students, including continuing to be responsible for tasks for which the faculty member is uniquely qualified, such as advising doctoral candidates. Modified duties can provide a "win-win" situation for faculty and the institutions where they work. This approach recognizes the rhythms of the faculty career, where some times in the career are more productive than others. The difficulty of such policies is that they are typically negotiated by the faculty member and require a strong degree of agency and creativity on her part. Since there isn't a single model for modified duties, either the faculty member or the chair has to figure out the specifics; this creates a lot of variance in how such accommodations are made, even in the same department. This is further exacerbated by the fact that the department has to cover the expense of hiring an adjunct or cover the class in some other manner.

Tenure Stop-Clock Policies

Tenure stop-clock policies allow tenure-track faculty members to take a temporary pause (usually one calendar year) from their tenure track, usually after the birth or adoption of a child. "Stop-the-clock" policies at some universities also allow the clock to stop for other reasons, including health problems, eldercare concerns, and so on. In most cases, a centralized decision maker, such as a provost or dean, determines eligibility for the stop clock. At the end of the stop-the-clock period, the tenure clock resumes with the same number of years left to tenure review as when the clock paused. Some institutions limit the number of times the clock can be stopped—typically once or twice during the tenure probationary period. Some policies are "opt in" policies, meaning the faculty member needs to request that the clock stop. Other policies are "opt out" which means that new parents automatically have the clock stopped unless they request otherwise. The benefit of an opt-out policy is that it sends the message that the institution expects faculty to use the policies that are made available to them. Opt-out policies also avoid situations in which faculty members feel uncomfortable asking their chairs for permission to use the policy. It is important to note that there is not supposed to be a penalty for extra time at tenure review if this policy is invoked. However, when tenure review committee members expect "an extra year's worth of research" for each year the tenure clock is stopped, this is not stopping the tenure clock—it is lengthening the clock—which is a very different kind of policy that penalizes faculty rather than assisting them.

The most progressive institutions in our study included provisions for stopping the tenure clock for faculty who give birth to or adopt an infant. Interestingly, policies related to stopping the tenure clock existed in all faculty handbooks of the campuses we studied. However, stopping the tenure clock was not always mentioned in connection to having a child. It was more typically presented as an option in the event someone has to use it for sickness rather than for childbirth. Campuses with more progressive policies mentioned stopping the tenure clock as part of the parental leave policy and also provided specifics of how this actually works (e.g., tenure clock stops for same amount of leave). The potential for stopping the tenure clock is a strongly recommended policy component of the AAUP 2001 *Statement of Principles on Family Responsibilities and Academic Work*.

THE ROLE OF INSTITUTIONAL-LEVEL POLICIES

Content analysis reveals that institutional policies to support faculty members as parents are widely available, to varying degrees. In our interviews, however, we learned that managing work and family occurred in spite of the institutional policy environment, not because of it. This is not to suggest that campuses do not need to maintain and evolve in the policy domain; instead it means that existing policies, and perhaps more important, existing policy culture, do not support the use of policies with regard to birth and infant child care. The data from the study make it clear that policy use was viewed as an individual issue more than an institutional concern. Most of the women we interviewed were left to negotiate their own solutions without much assistance from institutional colleagues—a situation that needs to be addressed to advance conversations about work and family for faculty on college campuses and to shift the concern and burden about policy usage from the individual woman to the institution.

We also learned that there are three types of campus policy environments: first, institutions that either had no policies or such limited policies as not to be useful; second, campuses that had policies but faculty were fearful of using them; and third, campuses where policies had been implemented (in most instances recently) and were being used by only a limited number of people. Most official work/family policies are created centrally, typically at the provost level with guidance from human resource personnel. On one campus, the president had just implemented an automatic tenure clock stop for everyone who takes a maternity leave (although this was not yet actually included in the policy documentation), and on another campus it was the provost who had been particularly supportive and creative in spousal accommodation and policies for women as mothers, resulting in an "environment that is actually pretty good."

The institutional context sets the policy stage. The focal point for the women in the study regarding policy was at the department level. It was departmental context, not the institution-wide context, that was most influential in a faculty member's ability to manage both work and family demands. Indeed, even though most policies are established at the institutional level, they are utilized (or not) at the department level.

We now turn to findings from our data about faculty perspectives on the use of policies, which are largely drawn from the early-career interviews.

LACK OF AWARENESS OF POLICIES

Data analysis of the interviews reveals that many of the women in the study did not even know what policies were available to them. Many stated that information about policies was not communicated to them, and since no one mentioned the existence of maternity-related policies, they assumed they didn't exist. As one respondent in the early-career phase of the study indicated, "I was the first person in my department at [campus] to have a child in nineteen years . . . and that is why there was such an open interpretation of the maternity leave policy." It was not uncommon to hear participants in the study explain, "I didn't even know the regulations for maternity leave and how much time you get, or how that works." If people aren't aware that policies exist, it is hard to expect them to use them.

The lack of awareness occurs on all sides. The majority of the faculty we interviewed early in their careers either had a vague awareness of some type of policy availability—"I think we have a policy that allows people to take some time off, but it's sick time and I don't have any," or they did not know about policies and, as one faculty member told us, "I just assume that there isn't anything I'll be able to use [in terms of policy] so I didn't even ask." We were also surprised that department chairs were not particularly informed about how faculty could use the policies. Chairs know policies are available, but they also know that using policy requires working with individual faculty. We found that unless asked by their faculty members, with few exceptions, chairs were not very forthcoming in letting them know about policies they could use to accommodate childbirth. The onus was on faculty to ask about policy availability and utilization. Such a position requires a fair amount of agency on behalf of the faculty member, a finding to which we now turn.

PERSONAL AGENCY

An important finding in our study across institutional types is that faculty members felt they had to negotiate their own solutions to maternity-related needs. In short, it was up to the women having the child to arrange with their unit head to take a leave, cover their classes, stop the tenure clock, or receive related accommodations. Generally speaking, the responsibility for negotiating work and family was by policy placed on the faculty member herself, and there was the general perception that campuses were not particularly helpful to women faculty having children.

For faculty members with a strong sense of agency—the sense that they could choose their best course of action regardless of institutional pressures—this arrangement worked, leaving them satisfied with their choices. But other faculty members, especially those reflecting back on their opting in or out of taking leaves, felt they made choices in a very constrained environment. Yes, they used their agency to choose to take leave or not, but this choice was one that left them questioning their options. KerryAnn O'Meara and Corbin Campbell (2011) describe agency with regard to work and family decisions as "the feeling that the individual has the power to make decisions that are best for his or her balance of personal and professional lives" (448). The findings of our study indicate that although the early-career faculty members did feel some sense of agency in either taking leave or not taking leave, these choices were not free choices in that faculty felt their environments and their projections about the future dictated whether it was safe to take a leave or stop the tenure clock. It was clear from our data as well as from an analysis of existing literature that institutions need to continue to develop policies that are relevant and user friendly.

Agency was also exercised to a certain extent by faculty members who felt as though they could create their own solutions. Faculty women in the study went to great lengths to figure out how to cover their work duties, whether they took leave or not. Although faculty members should, of course, bear some responsibility for negotiating solutions to their concerns, not-yet-tenured faculty are in a vulnerable position to make such arrangements. They are worried about how they will be perceived by their senior colleagues, and they need guidance through the process of negotiating the use and application of family-related policies. This problem is exacerbated by the fact that many policies are quite vague, and women, often new to an institution and certainly lacking power, have to decipher the rules, many unwritten, as they figure out the nuances of maternity leave and tenure-clock policies and how their use ultimately intersects with the tenure decision.

Our interview transcripts are replete with examples of individual women going to great lengths to make arrangements to cover for them when they took leave associated with having a child. In many instances, chairs were the last to know about the solutions being created. The typical response we heard in this regard is, "I had everything worked out and then talked to my chair about what I planned to do." The faculty members we talked with took extensive measures to create solutions so that they did not appear too "needy" or needing too much "help." They also endeavored to miss as little work as possible. This leads us to conclude that faculty members are making choices about work and family leave policies in very constrained environments—work settings that are dictated by ideal worker norms, which suggest that taking a leave or stopping the tenure clock signals a deviation from ideal work norms and could jeopardize career success in greedy work environments.

We found from talking to department chairs that they, in general, want to be helpful. They are open and willing to provide whatever accommodation they think is reasonable. However, the chairs we spoke with maintained a reactive stance. As one chair told us: "I'm open to giving faculty what they need, but I wait to see what is requested. I don't want to assume people need help if they don't ask." Although it is incumbent on the faculty member to be forthright about what they need in terms of accommodation, if chairs maintain a reactive stance and if faculty members do not make a specific policy request, or if they feel they need to navigate the request on their own, faculty can end up not using policies either because they don't know what's available or don't know what is acceptable to use or ask for from their chair. Traditional academic workplace norms can inhibit faculty from feeling as though they can make the request to use policies without fear of reprisal.

Fear and Bias Avoidance

There is considerable research to demonstrate that postsecondary work/family policies tend to be underutilized by faculty (Drago & Colbeck 2003; Finkel et al. 1994; Hochschild 1997; Raabe 1997; Ward & Wolf-Wendel 2004a; Yoest 2004). Many policies are still too new to know if they can be used without hurting one's chances of earning tenure, leaving the use of such policies a risky proposition. Further, there is research to suggest that faculty, and especially women faculty members, go to great lengths to avoid being seen as "in need of assistance" while on the tenure track, which in extreme cases prevents some women from having a child. Women faculty members who have children often avoid using available policies for fear of reprisal—a behavior identified as bias avoidance (Drago et al. 2005). Based on their survey of faculty at a research university, Finkel et al. (1994) found similar results. A majority of faculty members, regardless of gender, rank, and family status, supported the idea of paid leave for women faculty for childbirth and for newborn care, and supported unpaid leave for ongoing infant care. A majority of faculty members also supported stopping the tenure clock in these circumstances. Interestingly, however, these same faculty members reported that taking such a leave would hurt them professionally and, as a consequence, of those surveyed who had children (almost 50 percent), only a small percentage took all of their allowable leave.

Our findings support these conclusions. The mere presence of a policy does not mean that faculty will feel free to use the available options (nor does it mean that they know the policies are available). How this is manifested varies by campus, but the presence of fear and concern about policy usage was common across faculty members in the study. Only a handful of women in our study used available maternity leave policies and tenure stop-clock policies when they had their children. For these women, the use of these policies was a mixed blessing. On the one hand, women found "turning back the tenure clock definitely made a difference"; on the other hand, there was concern that utilizing the policy "would make me look less serious" or "hurt me somehow." Of the thirty-seven women who could have stopped the tenure clock (because such policies existed on their campus), only nine (24 percent) opted to do so.

Several respondents indicated that they were fearful about the effect that taking a leave or stopping the tenure clock would have on their careers. Officially (and legally) the time one has off as part of an official leave or officially stopped tenure clock (regardless of reason) is not supposed to count as part of a faculty member's dossier when she goes up for tenure. In practice, however, this is hard to implement, and it is also hard to document how it does affect someone's tenure bid. One faculty member very eloquently spoke to this issue:

> Statutorily you are supposed to be able to stop the tenure clock when you have kids. However, I don't think any slack is being cut based on your having kids. I personally feel like expectations here are very high. You can take the time you need to be with your kids as long it doesn't interfere with your output at all. It is sort of your time management problem—if you want to take three months off to stay at home with your baby that's fine, but down the road, you can't say "I spent time with my kids and I only published four papers."

Officially this faculty member had taken a leave and slowed the tenure clock; however, it was not without repercussion or at least the fear and threat of it. Part of this fear comes from concerns about how external tenure reviewers would view the gap in productivity. Outside reviewers play a particularly important role in the evaluation of tenure-track faculty, especially at research universities. At top-tier institutions, in particular, faculty are expected to be national experts in their field by the time they go up for tenure, and the external review process is in place to contribute to the assessment of their emerging role as expert. In relationship to stopping the tenure clock, the general perception was that "People writing letters nationally, which here is the biggest weight, don't cut any slack for any reason." Those at the other institutional types worried about how to cover their classes and about how colleagues would perceive their choices. As a result of this fear, many women faculty members decided not to use any leave, even if it was potentially available to them.

THE ROLE OF THE DEPARTMENT

The presence of a policy is a start, but how this policy is negotiated with the department head is essential to the use of the policy. We found that departmental-level responses to women faculty were very influential in determining whether and how policies were utilized. The department chair is particularly important when campus parental leave policies are minimal and/or vague (Raabe 1997; Hollenshead et al. 2005). And department chairs were especially critical in negotiating a workable leave, because most specifics about how the leave would be implemented are determined at the departmental level. Indeed, we found the local departmental context to be essential to creating a climate where policies, if available, are free to be utilized. We found two types of departmental contexts: first, those imbued with vague and reactive ideas about how to help faculty negotiate work and family; and second, those that were creative, proactive, and open about helping faculty get what they need to help them succeed as parents and as professors.

For faculty members with a supportive chair, using the available policy was not a problem, and the choice to use the policy was somewhat free. A handful of participants talked about their department heads as open and accommodating to suggestions, although again it was often the faculty member who took the lead in the conversation, which of itself requires a certain amount of agency. This could be inhibited in an environment that is not viewed as open and welcoming to deviations, and in which utilizing policy could be viewed by colleagues and administrators as a deviation. Several faculty members felt that their departments were supportive and that there was positive communication with the department chair and dean regarding policy options. As one professor indicated: "My department chair mentioned it [stopping the clock] to me because of pregnancy; she saw that for me and where I was in my career that it would be a bad idea for me *not* to take a leave and stop the clock." This same professor went on to say, "I obviously want to get tenure, but I wasn't one of those people who wanted to get it as fast as I can. . . . It's a natural step whether I get it in five years or ten years."

On those campuses where policies were minimal and the department chair was not particularly creative, the power of the department chair presented a greater challenge. Sometimes the chair wanted to help, but was unaware of institutional policies. What this meant for faculty was either going without accommodation of any sort or coming up with a plan and then "selling it to the department head." In these instances, many faculty members simply opted not to take a leave or use the stop-clock policy. Many of the department chairs mentioned by respondents were not unhelpful per se, they just didn't seem to know how they could be of assistance. This left one faculty member in our study to wonder, "Should I take the semester off or should other folks be responsible for this? I felt totally responsible."

Having a downright noncooperative department chair, on the other hand, complicated the situation further. Under these conditions, women, and certainly women with children, are in many ways viewed as anomalies, so that their cases must be dealt with privately. Accommodations in such a situation are "problems" to be resolved on an individual basis rather than institutionally. The onus is on the woman, not the institution, to fix the problem—an orientation that needs to shift if real change in work and family policy creation and utilization is to come about.

One of the things that exacerbate the problems faced by women faculty in terms of negotiating work/family policy is the culture of silence that surrounds work and family in higher education. This silence was especially pronounced in our interviews with department chairs and senior colleagues, who felt uncomfortable talking to their colleagues about having children. Of course, niceties are exchanged and baby showers are planned, but straight talk about what type of leave arrangement a faculty member may need or how having a baby might impact productivity at work is a conversation that is avoided by all involved.

Not all chairs were silent and, in fact, some were quite helpful. Some of the women in our study talked about very helpful and open department chairs who lead progressive departments where family and work seemed more easily combined—we call these "new-generation" departments. While still relatively rare, some women in our study reported a shift occurring in their academic departments caused by the retirement of senior faculty members and the opening of the academic labor market. The makeup of these new-generation departments included senior faculty members with young children, department chairs and other senior colleagues with their own grown children dealing with work and family issues, along with male faculty members who are more involved with their families. The openness of these new departments was often the result of having more than one faculty member in the department who was dealing with work and family balance concerns. Together, these individuals put the concerns "on the table," which resulted in a more proactive stance for the whole department. Although it is still unusual to have a departmental discourse cognizant of work family issues, where it was present it made for a smoother transition between work and family for the women in the study. Children and parenthood were normalized, and the decisions to use policies and to be up front about needs to accommodate work and family were more open. For example, a faculty member in such a department talks about how she handles weekend work commitments: "I have taken my son to every retreat. . . . I decided from the beginning if my department wanted me at a [department] retreat then they get my consort and me. I didn't really ask if it was ok. . . . If you are going into my weekends and my evenings, that is time that is allocated for my family I am going to take as much of that with me as I can."

Other faculty members mentioned departmental functions that included families and also the scheduling of meetings with specific mention of having them at times that were amenable to families. Again, these new-generation department contexts were generally more open about work and family issues, in contrast to departments where faculty kept their family life invisible. It is in these new-generation departments that the climate starts to move beyond specifically binary constructions—man/woman; work/family; junior/senior; public/private—to a space where these constructions are blurred. This makes *everyone* more cognizant of their multiple roles, making it feasible for faculty members to more easily balance the demands of work and children. The presence of children does not automatically make things easier or smoother for departmental functioning or for individual women; however, awareness of the tensions is a first step.

What we found from looking at policy and its use, as well as the culture of different types of departments, is that policy is really enacted at the department level. Yes, the campus needs to have the policies to provide the impetus, but it is in the department that faculty members have to organize and enact the taking of the leave. If people feel leave is a "bad choice," one that will be looked at askance and as inconvenient, the faculty members faced with decisions about taking leave are likely to either opt not to take the leave or to do so in ways that call as little attention to the leave as possible.

Here we have discussed how the department and chair shape choices about leave. We now turn to a discussion of the policy orientation within different types of campuses. As we have emphasized throughout this study, how work and family are experienced varies considerably not only by department but also by institutional context and culture.

Policy Perspectives from Different Institutional Types

When we talk about policy context we are doing so inclusively. Interviews included questions about policies available for faculty having children (such as parental leave or stopping the tenure clock) and also about the larger campus environment and how it supports or inhibits family life (such as the presence of daycare facilities and how using policy is talked about). Overall, we found that the experience of being an academic and a mother is one that shows significant commonality across campuses. The focus here, however, is to tease out the different nuances that exist with regard to the work/family policy context at each campus type included in the study. The findings here emanate primarily from the early-career interviews, when policy utilization was more of a focus, as well as from what we found in the policy documents we gathered from each campus.

Research Universities

The content analysis of the policy documents at the ten research universities included in the study reveal that FMLA is universally mentioned as the primary policy vehicle that allows for maternity leave. Nine of the ten research universities in the study had university policies in addition to FMLA policies. Stopping the tenure clock was mentioned at eight universities, with seven of the universities having the faculty member take the initiative to request the stop clock. Three research universities mentioned paid leave, one as short-term disability pay and another as using sick or vacation leave. Most policies only focused on the woman having the baby. However, three research universities listed policies for the spouse of the woman giving birth; in two cases, the other parent was also allowed to take twelve weeks of leave, and in one case the other parent was also allowed to stop the tenure clock. Because of the limited availability of paid leave, we were not surprised that a majority of the research university faculty members in the study did not use any type of leave and, in fact, went to great lengths to avoid using leave.

Most of the women in the study, it turns out, did not even know what policies were available, nor was this information made readily available to them. As one respondent indicated, "I blazed the trail. No one knew what to do [with regard to leave] when I became pregnant and wanted to take time off." Such comments were quite typical among the research university respondents. We heard repeatedly from the early-career faculty members that their chairs and deans did not really know what to do because people had not used leave previously. One reason for the lack of awareness is the prevalence of nine-month contracts. As we learned at one campus, when a faculty member called her human resource department about taking a leave she was greeted with the response, "you are on a nine-month contract, with limited leave. I guess you are supposed to have a baby in the summer." It's easy to think leaves are unnecessary for faculty members, given their short-term contracts. Another reason for the lack of awareness was the time period in which this study took place. The early-career interviews were done in the late 1990s, when work and family conversations were just increasing and not long after FMLA became law. Not to pardon campuses for not having policies with regard to work and family, but it was not as much of a focus as it is today. Findings from the mid-career interviews suggest some progress in this area, but there is still a general lack of awareness about policy availability and use.

In sum, the predominant finding for faculty at research universities was the pressing concern about what impact using leave policies would have on research productivity and ultimately tenure decisions. Faculty wanted to avoid being perceived of as needy while on the tenure track. Fear emanating from using policies related to parenthood was a prevalent theme throughout the interviews at all institutions, but the focus on how this fear would impact tenure was most pronounced at research universities. There was a general preoccupation with how using leave would be viewed by colleagues (on campus and nationally) and department chairs, and, especially at research universities, how it would figure into the tenure decision.

Comprehensive Colleges and Universities

As we have discussed, comprehensive colleges and universities are a diverse group of institutions, with some more focused on gaining a national reputation and others more regionally focused. When viewed from a policy perspective, however, we found that the concerns of faculty with young children were fairly consistent regardless of the focus of the institution within this category. Faculty members at comprehensive colleges and universities, like those at research universities, also had concerns with how having a baby would impact the tenure decision and the faculty career as a whole. The predominant theme in the interviews at the comprehensives, however, had to do with the extremely informal nature of the policy context, which left the women we interviewed feeling unsure of what policies were available, and how to go about using them if they were.

The policy documents from the comprehensives in the study show that the majority of the campuses in the study offered only the provisions provided by the FMLA. Of the seventeen comprehensive universities in the study, ten mentioned FMLA provisions, and two had unknown leave policies (policies were not included in human resource information, the faculty handbook, or the campus Web site). Five institutions mentioned policies for both parents, four of which provided twelve weeks of for each parent and one that provided thirty days of paid leave for each parent. Only one comprehensive university mentioned stopping the tenure clock, and in this case it was a given unless the faculty member requested the clock not stop. Generally, the comprehensive institutions in our sample were not very progressive on the work and family policy front.

The informal atmosphere with regard to work and family is probably an outgrowth of the limited availability of policies. We were initially surprised by the number of faculty who simply did not know what family-related policies were available—the assumption was that no policies were available and that any existing policies would not be useful. Examination of the policies shows that these assumptions were well founded. What this meant for the women in the study was the need to organize one's own maternity leave and to work with the department chair in doing so. On these campuses, department chairs played a pivotal role in helping study participants figure out how to make taking a leave work within the strictures of the semester schedule. This typically meant department chairs agreeing to or fine-tuning plans that the women faculty themselves came up with in working out the logistics of a parental leave.

In contrast to faculty at research universities, where the main preoccupation with leave and tenure revolved around research, the preoccupation for faculty at comprehensive colleges was with arranging course schedules. Given the informal policy situation, most departments had no methodical way of covering classes in the event of an extended absence. Of all the interviews we conducted, only one faculty member mentioned that the department chair simply took care of hiring an adjunct to cover classes while she took a six-week leave when her baby was born. Other faculty members spoke of "asking friends to cover classes," "only teaching on Wednesdays so I wasn't away from the baby much," "my TA covered the last two weeks of the semester after the baby was born," and "banking courses until next semester." These were all devices faculty used to cover courses, since adjuncts were generally unavailable. Again, with a semester schedule of fifteen weeks, it can be very difficult to figure out how to take a six-to-twelve-week leave.

In addition to the challenge of handling logistics for sometimes as many as four classes a semester, faculty mentioned how awkward it was to have to make such arrangements with colleagues to cover classes. One faculty member talked of this situation:

It's really yucky [to ask people to cover classes] because they don't like
to hire people [i.e., adjuncts] here. What ends up happening is that you
have to ask your fellow colleagues. Here, they are all wonderful and I was
lucky and did it happily. But, I just think it is a horrible position to put
someone in if they don't have as good of a group around as I did.

Faculty new to the institution and also having a baby found this situation
to be particularly awkward. These women were in vulnerable situations and
often didn't know the culture of the institution well enough to determine
an acceptable or reasonable accommodation. A faculty member who had a
baby in the first semester of a new faculty job talked about it this way:

I asked about maternity leave and was told there is no maternity leave
here, there is no policy for it and what faculty women do is take sick
leave, but you can't do that because you have to be employed at least six
months before you can take sick leave or disability. And, of course, there
was no sick leave accrued anyway [since I was new]. . . . I didn't really
think that much about just going along with the flow and they did give
me a course reduction for that first semester from three to two so I was
teaching two new courses for me, one at the master's level and one at
the undergraduate level. I started right in when the semester started and
then three weeks later, on September 22, I had the baby. I had the baby
on Friday and so I had my classes that week on Tuesday and Wednesday
online and then I was back in the classroom the next week.

This professor went on to say, "I must have been crazy" and "now I'm a little
resentful that no one even mentioned taking time off." Such sentiment was
commonly expressed in the mid-career interviews by faculty who did not
take leave when they were early in their career. We don't want to suggest that
people were not kind to this faculty member and to others having children, as
babies tend to bring out kindness in people. Faculty in the study at all types
of institutions talked about baby showers, elaborate gifts, people helping,
and month-long provision of food. Personal kindness abounds when it
comes to babies. What it does say, however, is that the policy environments
at these comprehensive colleges were ill equipped to handle the basic needs
of faculty women as new mothers.

In summary, the focus for faculty members at comprehensive institutions was on how having a baby would work around teaching schedules. There was little mention of stopping the tenure clock or of how having a baby would affect research productivity. Further, in general, faculty members felt that their institutions were open to them taking time off, but the time off would be without pay (which few could afford), and arranging course schedules and replacements was up to the faculty member taking the leave, not the institution or its representatives. This meant that for some, taking leave was not worth the hassle, negotiation, and potential repercussions.

Liberal Arts Colleges

Policy statements at the liberal arts colleges reveal that on the whole they are the most progressive institutional type when it comes to parental leave policies. Of the thirteen liberal arts campuses included in the study, two had no leave policies specified, and two used only FMLA policies. Eight colleges mention the possibility for paid leave, either as the university policy (six colleges) or through the use of sick leave (two colleges). Tenure stop-clock options were listed by six of the colleges. Family leave policies for the other parent (not the woman giving birth) were specifically listed at five colleges. Seven colleges mentioned the ability to take more than the FMLA-mandated twelve weeks of leave, anywhere from one full semester to a whole year of leave. While all liberal arts college campuses mentioned FMLA, a majority of them went beyond the minimum required by law. In general, the more selective liberal arts colleges in the study were more progressive in their policies; we surmise that this is a function of greater campus financial health and therefore the ability to pay for more comprehensive policies.

The predominant finding from the women we interviewed at liberal arts colleges is that the family orientation does help shape a more "family-friendly" environment in terms of policy. Like women at other colleges, those who did not take a semester-length leave still had to do quite a bit of negotiating to arrange for covering missed classes and the like. However, haggling with department chairs was not as predominant a theme as it was at the comprehensive colleges. Given the more highly evolved nature of the policy environment, the interview comments about policy were not so much focused on how to cover classes when having a baby as on concern with things like adding adoption to the leave policies and changing times for faculty meetings to accommodate families better. Once more basic needs are met, faculty can and do focus on those needs that are more advanced.

The contrast of the liberal arts college campuses with work/family policies to campuses without strong policies is stark. A faculty member from a liberal arts campus without a policy that goes beyond FMLA had this to say: "I was up on my feet and teaching in front of the classroom the first day of classes, which was ten days after a C-section. I was two weeks into the semester where I remember thinking I had made the biggest mistake that I had ever made in my life." This faculty member works in a policy environment that did not provide any type of paid leave, and she could not afford to take an unpaid leave. Her experience stands in contrast to another faculty member in our sample who had modified duties in the semester after she had a baby, which meant she "took a half-time parent leave at full salary yet taught only one course." The half-time parental leave offered by her campus allows faculty members to either take off the semester they have a baby for 50 percent of salary or to work a modified load (which is roughly half time) for full salary. Such a leave led this faculty member to say, "I had no problem at [my campus]"—a statement that was unique among those offered by the women in the study regardless of institutional type. In short, on campuses where leave must be negotiated, the onus is on the faculty member to do the arranging to cover classes and other responsibilities. In contrast, on campuses with formal leave policies, the process of negotiating and figuring out how to cover faculty responsibilities tends to rest with the department chair.

The general tenor of the interview findings from the faculty at the liberal arts colleges was more focused on children and family in general than on birth and babies. We interpret this to mean that when institutions have more progressive policies, women feel less threatened about the viability of their jobs when they decide to have a baby, which allows them to be concerned about things like campuswide faculty meetings at 4:30 that "always run over, creating a real problem for daycare pick up." Further, there was concern about things like coordinating the college's schedule with the local school district or providing affordable, accessible child care—again, issues that have more to do with families in general than with having a baby.

Other policy findings from the liberal arts college faculty members had to do with campus culture and campus expectations for women who have children while working there. Two expectations were prevalent: first, that a woman having a baby will do so in May to save the campus from having to deal with leave (whether paid or unpaid); and second, that a woman will have only one baby while on the tenure track. The preoccupation with pregnancy timing is not unique to liberal arts college faculty (timing was a preoccupation of nearly everyone in the study), but this was the only institutional type in which women faculty suggested that it was the culture of the campus that encouraged women to time the arrival of their babies in May. As one faculty member explained, "Faculty are expected to have children in May, thus allowing them to take the summer off to avoid time off for maternity leave and then to just come back in the fall." While this faculty member did have her baby in May, she told us it was not planned, "it just worked out that way." This professor noted that her colleagues and department chair complimented her on her timing.

The expectation and campus lore about having only one baby were also expressed as a part of the culture at many liberal arts colleges. We found, for example, that on campuses with paid leaves it was easy to use the leave policy for baby number one but more difficult to use the policy for subsequent pregnancies. Faculty members thinking about having a second baby while on the tenure track did so with trepidation about how it would be viewed to stop the tenure clock twice and to take two leaves. We learned from the interviews that faculty felt that one baby is tolerated, but having two might just push one's luck to the limit. One faculty member relayed a conversation she had with her department chair about taking a second leave: "She [my department chair] said it was unprecedented to ask for two [maternity leaves and clock delays]. People haven't had two kids pretenure before." Ultimately, this faculty member got a new chair who granted a second leave without fanfare, but the point remains that the policy environment does shape a woman's decision to have a child, when to have it, and how many to have.

Community Colleges

Though all of the eighteen community colleges in the sample are covered under FMLA, five did not have specified leave policies. For the thirteen community colleges with a stated leave policy, the majority (seven) kept to the twelve-week maximum from FMLA as the only policy relevant to employees who are seeking assistance related to work and family. Eleven of the institutions listed the possibility of using sick leave when taking family leave; this was the only mention of paid maternity leave policies. Three community colleges specifically listed less than the FMLA-mandated twelve weeks of leave, with two colleges allowing only ten weeks of leave, up to four weeks before and up to six weeks after the birth of the baby; one community college allowed the use of the lesser of either the accrued sick leave or the number of days the doctor says is needed for the pregnancy. Only one institution listed anything other than FMLA or sick leave, offering a provision to allow probationary faculty to stop the tenure clock for childbirth. And only one community college mentioned any policies for the other parent.

Faculty members at community colleges experience fairly controlled environments when it comes to work and therefore family. The women we interviewed painted a picture of the work environment as one that does not allow for much flexibility or autonomy, due to the demands of heavy course loads and required office hours. Community college faculty members in the study were required to teach between 24 and 32 credit hours, or their equivalent, per contract year. Most were required to be on campus a minimum of thirty-five hours per week, including teaching, office hours, advising, and providing service to the department and institution. The birth of a child required faculty members to figure out how to cover their classes during the semester in which they had a child; this was a concern for the eleven women in our community college sample who had their children while in the probationary period. The other women in the sample had their children before beginning their full-time employment as faculty and thus were less concerned about maternity leave policies and more concerned about the general climate of the campus as it pertained to balancing work and family.

It is important to note that the probationary period for full-time community college faculty is typically three years, and that professors are granted tenure based primarily on their classroom performance. Earning tenure was typically not an intense concern for the faculty we interviewed, as most believed that they were good teachers and would be granted tenure as a matter of course. Nonetheless, some of the women did express trepidation about the effect that having a baby might have on their eventually earning tenure. As one faculty member explained, "You know, even with my feeling fairly confident about the tenure system here . . . I do wonder if I should just make sure I get the tenure first and then have the other baby." Another faculty member advised new colleagues to "wait until they're not probationary [to have a baby] because I could see how [maternity leave arrangements] could come back and slap them in the face."

When asked about the maternity-related policies on their campus, half of the participants mentioned the options of using sick leave, catastrophic illness leave, or disability leave, and about half indicated that the option open to them was unpaid leave through FMLA. Some faculty also mentioned that they understood that it was best to time the arrival of children for summer or semester break, as there was no workable institutional policy for them to utilize. On the more progressive end of the spectrum, several women suggested that they were offered a reduced teaching load, or worked with colleagues or department chairs to cover their classes in their absence, or taught online course that allowed more flexibility to accommodate the birth of their child, or negotiated arrangements with their chair that made taking a leave unnecessary.

The use of sick leave in lieu of maternity leave was perceived to be problematic; most of the women were less worried about the tenure implications then they were about what would happen during subsequent illnesses of the child or themselves. Further, they did not like the association of parental leave with sick leave or catastrophic illness because of the negative connotations implied by such a connection. One woman expressed these concerns accordingly: "They make you use up all your sick leave . . . so when you are done having a child, you have no sick leave and that's very hard because . . . I have to use sick leave to take him to the doctor. The fact that they bundle you into a medical emergency just like somebody who broke a leg or had a heart attack or something is awful."

The use of any kind of leave from teaching was a concern for many of the faculty members in the study. They suggested that while the leave (either unpaid or sick leave) was offered, there was a subtle implication that you ought not to use it. One professor explained, "I feel a sense of support from my department . . . everyone has been very supportive and very generous and has been really excited about the pregnancy and about the baby . . . but I do kind of feel as if there's this underlying tension about making certain

I hold up my end of the bargain." Still another professor told us that when she approached her division chair about going on maternity leave he said, "You can go on leave, but please don't take it." And a third professor who used sick leave for maternity leave told us that her dean asked, "'When are you coming back?' It was very much this business thing: 'What kind of burden are you putting on me and the department?'"

Interestingly, although most of the campuses were unionized, very few of the women talked about the role of faculty unions in addressing work/family concerns, let alone mentioning the union's role in advocating for such policies. One faculty member suggested that the union was more concerned with salary than with quality-of-life issues. Still, given the presence of faculty unions on these campuses, we were surprised at the ad hoc nature of maternity-related accommodations. It appeared that some departments and division heads were sympathetic and accommodating, while others created an extremely hostile work environment. The most extreme case was a woman whose department chair created a building policy barring children (for "liability reasons"); this chair also told this faculty member that she could not use a breast pump in the building nor bring a cooler to the office to store breast milk as that would "make this building appear to be a cafeteria." A more helpful department chair told his new faculty member that instead of taking a leave she ought to teach her courses online. The faculty member was told, "I don't know how I would feel about an adjunct walking in week 8 of the semester and taking over. What about we do this deal: you stay home and still do them [online courses] and I won't take as much sick leave out of your pay." The professor figured she didn't have any other options and that this was a workable, though difficult solution given the workload associated with online classes.

Beyond the need for maternity leave, faculty at community colleges expressed the need for policies related to both child care and support for breastfeeding mothers. The faculty members were unanimous in their request for affordable child care on campus that was available to faculty members. Some added that it would be helpful for the institution to offer child care allowances for faculty, child care visitation, and extended child care hours. The need for support for breastfeeding mothers seemed a unique concern among community college faculty—a concern that stems from the fact that many of the faculty members didn't have their own offices, and had difficulty finding a private place to use a breast pump. Most made do with this issue—pumping in the restroom or making arrangements with office mates. One woman discovered that OSHA requires workplaces to provide pumping rooms and requested that her dean comply. Another woman describes how her colleagues made a sign with a picture of nursing puppies on it that said: "New mother inside. Please knock." Another stated: "I pumped in my office . . . my office mate was sympathetic but it was still inconvenient. I had to think of putting a Post-it on the door before I did it. You know, you can hear the noises in the hallway, while I have my boobs exposed at my desk, the pumping machine going, I hoped she saw the Post-it before she came in after class." Another faculty member was told that she shouldn't store her breast milk in the department refrigerator because someone might mistake it for creamer. Each of these women wanted some space, acceptance for their decision to breastfeed, and acknowledgment that this was a necessary accommodation that should be easy to fulfill and ought to be a nonissue.

POLICY PERSPECTIVES AND CHOICE: SOME THEORETICAL CONSIDERATIONS

There is an underlying concept of choice that is inherent in the findings related to policy. That is, faculty members choose to utilize (or not) the work/family policies on their campus. Faculty members even choose where to work on the basis of environments they believe are (or will be) family friendly. On the surface such choices seem like ones that are free and unfettered. With regard to policy, faculty members should be free to choose whether they will utilize the policies on their campus (or not). Is simply choosing to use a policy such a simple matter? Our findings clearly suggest not. We use feminist and poststructural theoretical perspectives, in particular the work of Allan (2011), Allan et al. (2010), and Ball (2002), to more fully understand the nuances of choice and the choices faculty make when it comes to the workplace and work/family issues.

Choice is a cornerstone of a liberal feminist perspective and is one that women should be "free" to exercise. In particular, a woman should be free to make choices about reproduction and careers without constraint of societal and workplace expectations about what a woman "should" do based on gender roles or work norms. A liberal feminist perspective suggests that the work to be done is to add policies and then people will use them (i.e., "if you build it, they will come"). However, the findings from our study suggest that although many campuses have added policies, faculty do not feel free to use the policies and, department chairs do not feel free to offer them. Clearly, choice is hindered considerably when it comes to policy utilization. Simply having a policy is not enough.

The idea that utilizing policy is a matter of personal choice and preference puts the responsibility to use the policy on the user (in this case female faculty members) and not on the institution. The institution's responsibility is to create the policy, and the faculty member's responsibility is to use the policy. In such a view, if a person does not use the policy it is her choice. Institutions typically absolve themselves of responsibility, and we certainly heard this from department chairs in our interviews. As one said, "She [referring to a female faculty member in his department] had it all worked out. She didn't need to use any policies." The faculty member opted to not take a leave, as an individual she exercised her choice to do so, and the department chair thought it was a choice that met the faculty member's needs. From his vantage point, she made a "choice" that worked for her and certainly for his department. The campus did its job—had a policy available—and the faculty member did her job, too, in choosing not to use the policy. A poststructural view of this interchange suggests that the policy utilization is primarily the responsibility of the individual and not the institution (Ball 2002).

Many campuses, although not all, have heeded the call over the last dacade to be more responsive to work and family issues for faculty by creating policies. But is the creation of policy enough? A poststructural analysis of our findings suggests the need to look not only at the particular policies but also the discourse that surrounds the policy to critically examine power, language, and practice. Absent such an analysis, it is too easy to focus on the individual and her choice to use policies or not. Poststructuralism offers the tools to do a comprehensive and critical analysis of the language used in the policy and the discourse that surrounds it. The women in the study who assumed there were no polices, or that the policies the campuses had would not be useful, were making that assumption on the basis of existing campus norms, the experience of those who had gone before them, in addition to what they had heard from their colleagues and institutional leaders about policies. These conversations and practices are just as important to an examination of policy as looking at the actual polices. The discourse surrounding the policy is powerful, maybe even more powerful than the policy itself. Needless to say, the faculty member making choices about using policy are doing so in very constrained environments, and under these conditions, choice is illusory.

The choice to use or not use a policy is not a free choice. In thinking about this issue, it is interesting to go back to our initial stories in chapter 2 about our own experiences as academic mothers. You can see from our narratives that we both felt the need not to use policies so as not to hurt our own chances of success, but also to not let our parenting issues inconvenience those around us. We didn't make those choices because we were "superwomen" who didn't need assistance—we made those choices because we didn't feel the alternatives were viable. This is particularly telling, given that both of us are experts on work and family and faculty, and both of us should have "known better" and felt freer to make different choices. But the truth is that workplace norms affect us all. Workplace norms in academic environments that dictate a singularity of purpose, a "sink or swim" mentality, and "up or out" consequences, do not create an environment in which one can make a free choice about a policy that will take one away from work.

We found in our study that the women we talked to were making the choice, for the most part, to not use a policy in a constrained environment. Yes, the option to use the policy was present (although often not very clearly), but to use it required deviating from the work norms that call for success. Combine all this with workers that have diminished agency based on their position as new to the institution, as tenure-track faculty members, and as women in male-dominated environments, and it is easy to see how complicated it is to simply have a policy and then expect people to use it. Campuses do need to have policies and the choice needs to be present, but the policy discourse needs to be understood as imbued with norms that do not make the choice to use a policy a free one. It is also not a choice that should be put on the faculty member alone. For the choice to use a policy to be free calls for organizational actors at different levels to be cognizant of the policy and, more important, of the policy environment. It is not possible to look at a policy separately from the norms and cultures in which the policy is created and enacted.

Another element of choice that merits discussion is to what extent individual women had the cultural capital to exercise the choice to use policies. There were some women in our study, although they were in the minority, who did use policies and did so without obvious fear. What makes these women different? Our observation and analysis is that those that did exercise the option to use the policies were those who had cultural capital or what O'Meara and Campbell (2011) refer to as professional capital. Faculty with professional capital typically had some circumstance that made them privileged. They were specialists in their fields, were heavily recruited to come to campus because they were up-and-coming "academic stars," or they had already established themselves in some special way, and so felt freer to use policies without fear of repercussion. Those with capital felt they could use the policies and those without capital felt they could not (as discussed in chapter 8).

The sense of agency and entitlement was also experienced as a function of cultural capital. Faculty members with spouses that had lucrative careers felt freer to use the policies. These women had a financial safety net that provided them the means and the agency to choose to take the leave. If they took the leave and it, in turn, affected their bid for tenure or they weren't successful in their positions, they would not be left without economic means, which helped them to feel freer to take a leave. Choice is clearly tied to the presence of cultural capital (Ball 2002): those with economic and educational backgrounds that gave them the sense that their use of the policy was not linked to their self-worth or workplace effectiveness used their own agency to make choices.

Conclusions

The findings suggest a rather tenuous policy environment with regard to work and family at all institutional types. We found three themes with regard to policy needs: first, concerns related to the birth of a child, including the need for maternity leave or the need to stop the tenure clock; second, needs related to being a parent in the long term, including access to child care and concerns about scheduling classes and meetings; and third, the policy environment as a whole and how people use policies. Most institutions focus their policies, however inadequate, on the first set of needs—those involving birth. Only a handful of campuses extend their policies to respond to the second set of needs. To be sure, faculty members themselves bear significant responsibility to figure out how work and family can be combined, yet from a policy perspective many faculty in our study believed it was the institution's responsibility to have viable options available for women to consider and for department chairs to be aware of the policies.

The findings and our analysis also suggest that simply having policies is not enough. Campuses need to also focus on how people talk about policies, how chairs present the policies to their faculty, and how people using policies are received and reviewed by their colleagues. If faculty members find the leave policies on their campus useful, use leaves, and stop their tenure clock, and do so without repercussion and snide remarks by their colleagues, this sends a message that using work and family policies is a good choice. The opposite is also true: if people take leave and then are talked about as not serious or not doing their share in the department, and are ultimately unsuccessful as faculty members, this sends the message that policy use is a bad choice.

In spite of the shortcomings many campuses face with regard to policy, it is still necessary to have policies available for faculty to use. In the next chapter we discuss the types of policies that campuses can and should have available, as well as the discourse necessary to convey that policies are present, useful, and meant to be used.

CHAPTER 11

Conclusions, Recommendations, and Parting Thoughts

The findings from this project suggest that family plays a role in how people develop in their academic careers, just as careers play a role in how people evolve in their family. The intent of this project, and subsequently this book, is to show that these paths can be integrated in ways that are meaningful and gratifying. There is no need to either work as a tenure-track faculty member *or* have a family, as has often been prescribed for women in the past. In our work, we have found that women can have both work and family, and do so in ways that are not always without challenge (of course) but are impassioned and joyful. For such integration to occur, individuals who seek to combine work and family need to be thoughtful about their careers. And, perhaps more important, institutions need to be thoughtful about their expectations of faculty, the enactment of their mission, and the creation and enculturation of policy environments that support faculty at all stages of their career.

In this chapter we focus on the types of policies that can help facilitate the integration of work and family, basing our recommendations on a review of the literature, a review of current practices, our understanding of the utilization of policies, and analysis of the data from different aspects of our research. Although the focus of our research has been on faculty women, many of the policies we propose would also help male faculty members integrate work and family. For work and family policy to be integrated, utilized, and normalized calls for an examination of workplace norms for all members of the academic workplace. Policy discussions also call for examining larger questions surrounding gender and work norms that shape how people approach their work and family lives and also shape how they might think about using policy for work and family needs.

What has to take place on college campuses for administrators to create and implement policies *and* for faculty to feel free to use such policies? If policies are underutilized, there is little impetus for administrators to expand the policy agenda. Moving the policy conversation to a centralized position calls for an examination of existing policies to see if they are complete. It also calls for particular actors to critically examine what they can do to advance a policy agenda so it is useful and utilized. Faculty members with children and graduate students, the future faculty members, need to be part of the conversation about policy, for they are the people who will use the policy. The intent of this chapter is to address all three of these areas—policy making, administrators and faculty who implement policy, and faculty (and prospective faculty) who utilize policy.

POLICY RECOMMENDATIONS TO FACILITATE THE INTEGRATION OF WORK AND FAMILY

Throughout our research, the people we talked to at all levels were quick to make recommendations to assist faculty attempting to balance work and family. The recommendations for policies from our respondents and from prior literature fall into several categories: policies that allow for time off; those that deal with tenure; those that create services to support parents; and cultural changes to the institution that support the use of such policies. Together, these recommendations can help to make higher education more family friendly and conducive to people living holistic and integrated lives.

Go Beyond FMLA to Offer Leave and Release Time Options That Are More Focused on Meeting the Needs of Faculty Who Are Having Children

The creation and implementation of the Family Medical Leave Act (FMLA) has helped put the concerns of families on the policy map in higher education and other sectors of work, and in this way has been invaluable to work and family policy. However, the FMLA is only a start; it is not a policy end by itself, yet many campuses use it that way. Campus policy makers need to look closely at the FMLA and what it provides and then fill in the gaps.

Provide Paid Leaves That Are Separate
from Sick Leave or Disability Leave

By relying on sick or disability leave as the primary vehicle for faculty to take paid leave, campuses juxtapose pregnancy and childbirth with sickness. This is problematic on two fronts: first, pregnancy is not a sickness, and second, if a parent or child does get sick, there is limited ability to use sick leave as it is intended—for illness. We recognize that offering paid leave for faculty members to cover childbirth and recuperation is expensive. Yet offering such a provision communicates that campuses value faculty members and that pregnancy is distinct from sickness. These policies should be offered on an opt-out basis rather than an opt-in one. An opt-out approach sends the message that the institution expects faculty members to use the policies that are made available to them. An opt-out approach also avoids situations in which faculty members feel uncomfortable asking for permission to use the available policies.

Consider Modified Duty Policies

The findings from our research suggest that faculty members sometimes don't feel that they need a full leave to accommodate having child. Modified duties can provide a "win-win" situation for faculty and the institutions where they work. Typically, faculty members with modified duties get full pay but have some type of reduction or reorganization of workload. For example, if a faculty member has a child in September, for the fall semester she may only teach one course instead of two, limit involvement in service obligations, and maintain involvement in research but forgo travel to conferences. Modified duty might also call for faculty members to serve in some type of administrative capacity or to engage in a project for the department in lieu of other types of work obligations. Such options keep the faculty member on campus (and therefore can quell fears about being out of sight and out of mind) and keeps her active in her work, albeit in a limited way. The modified duties approach recognizes the rhythms of the faculty career, where some times in the career are more productive than others. Most institutions take account of the ebb and flow of the faculty career. A modified duties policy recognizes that these ebbs and flows can happen concurrently with childbirth and other family concerns.

Modified duties can also be used for mid-career faculty members as a means to regenerate their academic careers and to help them shift their priorities. For institutions wanting to encourage mid-career faculty members to consider promotion to full professor, a modified duty policy could be used to help them prepare for promotion. This could mean allowing limited teaching for a semester or a year to reestablish a research program, or requiring no service commitments for a year as a way to encourage research or teaching productivity. Sabbaticals serve this renewal process and are available on many campuses, but we found that many faculty members in the study took their sabbaticals shortly after receiving tenure, and thus were not eligible for another leave even though they were eligible to be considered for promotion. A modified duty policy for mid-career faculty would keep faculty members on campus and focused on activities that would help them with their promotion to full professor.

Provide Tenure Clock Extensions and Communicate Their Use

Temporarily stopping the tenure clock is one of the most common ways that institutions accommodate junior faculty who face circumstances, like childbirth, that can cause a setback in productivity (Sullivan et al. 2004). Unfortunately, research demonstrates that faculty members do not feel free to stop their tenure clock for fear of repercussions. Campuses not only need to provide the opportunity to stop the clock but they also need to let faculty know it is safe to use such a policy. Policy makers need to provide clear directions on how the policy can be used and be clear with both the faculty member using the policy and, more important, those who will judge her productivity come review time, on how a tenure extension will be evaluated. It can be useful to provide examples and scenarios so faculty can see how an extension can work as part of a successful tenure process. Provisions to stop the tenure clock should also be an opt-out policy rather than opt-in. If faculty members have to take the initiative to stop the clock, existing research suggests these policies are underutilized due to fear. Faculty members, both mothers and fathers, on the tenure clock should automatically be granted a tenure extension unless they choose to opt out of the tenure extension.

Develop a List of Possible Accommodations for Faculty Members
to Utilize in Relation to Family Leave and Communicate
Those to Department Chairs and Faculty Members

Many campuses are quite creative in how they accommodate faculty members who have children while on the tenure track, yet many of these accommodations are negotiated informally and privately. We recommend that campuses provide a lot of examples of how faculty might manage having a child while maintaining their career. By providing examples, policy makers can show faculty members, their department chairs, and their colleagues possible scenarios for taking a leave, given timing of the birth and stage of career.

Create Flexible Tenure Clocks

In 2000, Bob Drago and Joan Williams suggested that institutions of higher education create part-time tenure-track options for faculty. They suggested that parents (either mothers or fathers) should be allowed to request to work half time while remaining on the tenure clock as a way to accommodate work and family. The faculty member would receive half of their pay for the time period in which they worked half time, while the affected department would get the other half of the salary to arrange for courses to be covered. The faculty member would receive half of their retirement benefits, but still receive full health insurance. The tenure time clock would be adjusted to run half as fast as for someone who was employed full time. The actual tenure requirements would remain the same—just the time frame to achieve tenure would be extended. Part-time tenure options could be made available as a permanent option (for the duration of one's career) or as a temporary option that combines part-time leave with a tenure clock extension. This type of approach has not gained much popularity, but individual institutions have offered the option on a case-by-case basis. For example, the University of Washington implemented a part-time tenure clock option, but there were few people who opted to take advantage of it, largely due to fear about the repercussions of such a choice, combined with the financial cost to the faculty member—it is difficult to live on half of a salary.

Innovation with regard to tenure is particularly risky in an era when academic credibility is often challenged and the very practice of tenure is threatened. Administrators do not feel they can protect the sanctity of tenure while simultaneously arguing for its alteration. Ideas for changing tenure call for maintaining its sanctity but making changes to the process of acquiring it to make it less rigid. Although there is promise in such an approach, it has yet to be realized. We still propose it as a policy option because it does provide faculty members with children the option to integrate work and family more holistically.

Offer Mentoring and Support for Faculty Members throughout Their Career

Faculty members who had access to mentoring in their early career mentioned this as part of the reason for their success with the tenure process. Mentors can help offer guidance and feedback about the promotion and tenure process and, when available, play a key role in professional preparedness for tenure. Mentoring and related support systems, however, tend to focus solely on junior faculty. The findings from our study suggest that mentoring should continue beyond tenure to help faculty members be mindful of how they are spending their time and thinking about their career advancement. Many campuses have clear goals for the advancement of women to the senior faculty and administrative ranks. Formalized mentoring should be available to help faculty members prepare for these senior roles as a way to help individuals continue to move through the faculty and administrative pipeline.

Provide Clarity about Tenure Expectations and Expectations for Promotion to Full Professor

The tenure process is known for its ambiguity. Many campuses have developed mentoring programs, faculty handbooks, and professional development materials to help guide faculty through its ambiguities. Still, many early-career faculty members wish for more clarity about the process. We also found from the second-phase interviews that promotion to full professor is fraught with ambiguity as well, yet there is even less information available to help faculty members decode this process. It is not unusual for faculty handbooks to provide detailed information about when and how to prepare for tenure, but little information about the timing or requirements for promotion to full professor. Campuses wanting to provide guidance for faculty members at all stages of their careers would do well to help them with more detailed information about when faculty are eligible for full professor and what is required. This information should appear in faculty handbooks, be part of the annual review process, and be the subject of professional development workshops so tenured faculty members can be prompted to think about career advancement, like early-career faculty.

Adopt Holistic Perspectives about the Faculty Career

Findings from both phases of the study suggest that there is strong emphasis on productivity during the tenure-track years, leaving people burned out and sometimes disenchanted with what it takes to be successful as a faculty member across the lifespan of their career. Although we do not advocate lack of productivity for new faculty, we do suggest that campus leaders think about the tenure process as a time for faculty members to show their potential and their productivity and to take a long view of the faculty career. The goal is for faculty to be productive throughout their careers, and hyper-productivity during the tenure process has the potential to burn out faculty and limit ongoing productivity which, in turn, can foil ongoing attempts to maintain a high-quality and diverse faculty.

Offer Professional Development Opportunities for Administration

Many campuses have specified goals to diversify their administrative ranks in terms of race and gender. One of the findings from the second interviews is that the female faculty members are generally not interested in moving into formal administrative positions beyond their particular programs. In part, this is because of their family responsibilities, but also because of their concerns about dealing with campus politics, conflict, and difficult personalities. Professional development programs could help provide greater understanding of administrative roles and could help faculty as potential administrators learn more about administration. These programs could also provide part-time opportunities for faculty to try out administration under the guidance of an administrative mentor. Although there are national-level programs, like the American Council on Education Fellows Program, the problem with these is that they typically require the fellows to do an internship at an institution different from their own. This can be difficult when one has family responsibilities and cannot just pick up and leave campus for long periods of time. As such, many campuses have developed programs to "grow their own" administrators, and the findings from our research suggest that such programs are a helpful way to expose people to administrative careers without requiring faculty to be gone for long periods of time.

Communicate Policies and Conduct Ongoing Evaluation of Available Policies

The findings from the study make it clear that the majority of campuses in the study have attempted to develop and revise policies to help accommodate faculty as parents, especially during the early stages of their career. Unfortunately, another finding is that a majority of faculty members in the study did not use these policies due to concern that taking a leave or delaying the tenure clock would have a negative consequence. There was also a general lack of awareness about what works, and what family policies were available. Based on these findings, we suggest that campuses continually revisit their policies to monitor their use and to monitor how the policies are communicated to the faculty. As campuses strive to be more "family friendly," they need not just to adopt policies but also be attentive to who uses the policies and how they are communicated. Attention to the faculty culture and lore about what policies and practices are "okay" to be used and what should be avoided also needs some attention.

Provide Daycare Options

While not a policy per se, the provision of quality and accessible daycare for faculty is essential to a comprehensive policy package. Too often, new faculty members are faced with quality daycare shortages, leaving them in a difficult spot about how to best care for their children and do their job. This is particularly important in small towns where there are few options for daycare. On some campuses with daycare there are often priority slots for students. There needs to be awareness about the importance of accessible daycare for tenure-track faculty. Across the board in our study, we learned that finding affordable and accessible daycare was a major challenge for faculty with children. While it is may not be realistic that all campuses provide daycare centers to meet the needs of faculty, campuses do well to identify and make available these services. Such policies can also involve modifying teaching and meeting schedules so as to allow parents to work with daycare centers and local schools.

Consider the Needs of Dual-Career Couples

Dual-career issues often go hand-in-hand with family leave policies. Not all couples have children, and not all parents are part of a couple, but we found that the needs of dual-career couples have to be considered when looking at family policies as a whole. Campuses need to have staff and administrators who are aware of the nuances of dual-career couples and be prepared to address their needs as part of recruitment and retention of faculty. Dual-career assistance can take a number of forms, including, but not limited to, creating a spousal/partner relocation office to help the "accompanying" spouse or partner find work in the local area; having a formalized process or protocol to assist accompanying spouses/partners in securing an academic position at the institution (either tenure track or nontenure track); providing funding incentives and bridge programs to assist departments in hiring accompanying spouses or partners; allowing couples to share a tenure-track academic position; advertising positions through Higher Education Resource Consortia (HERCS) to make it easier for couples to find work in the same geographic region; educating deans, department chairs, and search committees about ways to broach dual-career issues and assist couples; and, finally, evaluating these programs to determine if they are effective.

Educate Deans and Department Chairs about the Range of Options and Policies Available, and Make Sure That They Communicate This to Their Faculty

An important component of any comprehensive work and family policy agenda is the communication of the policies and suggestions for their use. Too often faculty and administrators are ill informed about available policies and how they can be used. Campuses need to have comprehensive policies, as suggested here, and have administrators in place who can promote their use.

Attend to the More Long-Term Concerns
of Faculty Members with Children

Dealing with faculty members when they have a baby is only the first step to helping them manage work and family concerns. Institutions need to take into consideration that families continue to evolve, and the needs of children and families go beyond those that exist at birth, the current focus of most policy discussions. The mid-career faculty members were largely unaware of policies available on their campuses to help faculty manage work and family. In part, this is because the policy arena tends to focus on the needs of new parents and on helping faculty manage tenure-track expectations with having a new child. Both of these issues—childbirth/infancy and tenure track—are issues that tend to come up during the early career. More established faculty with older children (and possibly aging parents) can also benefit from a comprehensive policy environment that includes accommodations such as information about elder care, camps for older children, wellness in families, and the awareness that policies are available that cover the entire career and that recognize that work and family integration are concerns that continue beyond the tenure track and beyond small children.

Designate a Staff Person to Oversee Work/Life Issues on Campus

Increasingly policy makers and practitioners in the American workplace, including colleges and universities, recognize that efficient workplaces and effective workers are those that are able to manage the needs of both their jobs and their families. Family care ranges from the birth of children, to care of aging parents, to managing daycare for either. Having a designated staff person on college campuses to help employees manage the intersection of work and family can be very beneficial. This is particularly the case for new faculty members, whether they are early or later in their careers, who are often relocating to a new community and may not be certain about the resources that are available. Having a contact person with information about work and family concerns can be crucial to help faculty adapt to new workplaces or new family realities.

Recognize That Faculty Have Lives Outside of Work

The focus of this chapter is creating policy (and campus environments, in general) that more fully support the combination of work and family for faculty. Such an approach is not just about faculty members with families. Faculty of all ages, genders, and work stages have lives that extend beyond the workplace, whether it is related to family for not. Too often the academic workplace is consuming and geared toward a work ethic that thrives on constant work. Needless to say, such an approach is not good for any faculty member, and certainly not for those with young families. We would argue that it is also not good for campuses as a whole. Policy makers need to recognize faculty as people with divergent interests and demands that go beyond the workplace. Creating a campus culture that allows faculty members to combine work and family is good for everyone; it will enhance faculty recruitment and retention, lead to higher faculty morale, and it will, in the end, be good for the institution as well as its faculty.

ADDITIONAL POLICY CONSIDERATIONS

Creating appropriate and adequate institution-level policy is only the first step in creating a supportive work/family climate. As we have pointed out, our research demonstrates that tenure-track faculty members are frequently unaware of policies and, even if they know they exist, are hesitant to use them. The hesitancy is attributed to fear of being perceived as not serious, not committed, and not "up to" the level of faculty work needed to achieve tenure. Given the pervasiveness of this fear, institutions need to also adjust their climate and culture to be more receptive to faculty with work/family needs. Among other things, institutions ought to consider the following:

- Think about these issues as a way to recruit and retain the best faculty members. It is in an institution's best interest to be responsive to the work/family needs of their faculty members throughout the career.
- Adopt a life-course perspective. Work/family concerns affect faculty

members at all stages of life. Policies need to recognize the needs of new parents with infants, parents with older children, and the needs of faculty members who have caretaking responsibilities for their own parents. If we think of family concerns more broadly, it can create a more affirmative environment for everyone, not just those who have young children.

- Learn from the research and experiences of others. There is a burgeoning literature related to work and family in higher education that highlights individual and institutional best practices. This literature provides an important resource for individual faculty members as well as administrators who want to make thoughtful decisions related to work and family for faculty members.

- Publicize the existence of policies. What good is a policy if no one knows it exists?

  o Make a Web page dedicated to the topic with advice for faculty and department chairs. Provide links to policies, forms, and other related resources.

  o Establish a point person in human resources and the provost's office who is knowledgeable about policies and approaches to work/family concerns especially geared toward faculty. With nine-month contracts and the tenure track, policy use is often different for faculty than for other personnel on campus. Making sure there is a contact person knowledgeable about work and family issues is essential.

- Bring work/family concerns "out of the closet" and end the silence on these issues. Work/family policies and practices need to be included as part of the institutional culture, and not just thought of in terms of the presence or absence of policies.

  o Provide training for department chairs on how to address these issues with their faculty members.

  o Discuss work/family concerns and related policies at new faculty orientations.

  o Hold workshops, forums, and discussions across campus to educate the community about work/family concerns.

  o Educate and socialize graduate students to think about work/family balance concerns by including topics in graduate student orientation and future faculty workshops. Graduate students represent

the future of the academic profession, and if the campus culture
indicates an "either/or" approach to work and family, it is not good
for the future of the profession.

• Recognize that flexibility is needed in policy implementation. Although
we advocate the existence of centralized policies, we recognize the
importance of offering individual faculty members and departments
flexibility in responding to work/family needs. A one-size-fits-all model
is insufficient and is not appropriate, given the variations in institutional,
departmental, and individual needs.

• Address perceptions of inequity among different groups of faculty. Many
administrators are worried about implementing work/family policies
because they fear privileging one group over another. These concerns
include privileging women over men, privileging those with children
over those without children, and privileging newer faculty over their
more senior colleagues. This latter concern, expressed by some senior
faculty members (both male and female) who did not have access to
such policies in their careers, suggests that providing "extra" assistance
to newer generations of faculty higher education may be akin to "letting
them off easy" by not making them survive the rigors of tenure without
assistance. These types of concerns can stymie department chairs, deans,
and provosts in the creation and implementation of policies to help
parents, and need to be directly addressed.

• Stay current about policy discussions related to work and family. Given
the current expansion of work and family research and policy development, campus leaders need to stay aware and current about policy
and practice. For example, the *Chronicle of Higher Education* and *Inside
Higher Ed* routinely cover topics related to work and family and are a
vital resource. There is a work and family researchers' network at the
University of Pennsylvania that is a clearinghouse of current research
and practices with many helpful resources (http://workfamily.sas.upenn.
edu/index.html). The Council of Contemporary Families, a membership
organization, maintains up-to-date information about work and family
issues generally and also issues related to policy (http://www.contempo-
raryfamilies.org/). The College and University Work-Family Association
is an information source that looks specifically at contemporary issues
related to work and family in higher education (http://www.cufwa.org).

In addition, two recent publications provide useful information to guide campus conversations and to offer practical advice. These books, Philipsen and Bostic's *Helping faculty find work-life balance* (2010) and Lester and Sallee's edited volume *Establishing the family-friendly campus* (2009), should be available to campus leaders and human resource practitioners. These resources are just examples of the types of information that are helpful to have available for faculty facing the issues, leaders wanting to guide practice, and human resource practitioners charged with carrying out policies.

CREATING A CULTURE OF USE: SUGGESTIONS FOR ADMINISTRATORS, GRADUATE STUDENTS, AND FACULTY

Our research and that of many others suggests that having policies in place is not enough. Given campus norms to work more and work often, faculty do not always feel free to take advantage of policies like parental leave or tenure extension as a way to manage work and family. There also needs to be a culture that supports the creation and use of family-friendly policies. We now turn to a discussion of how different campus actors can create cultures that support work and family integration and support the policy environment. Throughout the duration of this project, we often heard from well-meaning administrators that they want to do the "right thing" with regard to supporting faculty with work/life integration, but they don't know what being supportive entails. The suggestions we offer here are in the spirit of helping leaders do the "right thing" when it comes to helping faculty lead integrated and holistic lives.

Advice for Provosts and Presidents

Senior leaders play a crucial role in setting the tone and creating a culture that supports the overall policy environment of their campus. Top-level academic administrators need to do their part by creating the climate for work and family. They need to make the campus aware of shifting faculty demographics and how the presence of more women faculty (which is the case on almost every campus) can call for the need to rethink accepted processes and policies. Provosts need to make sure policies are in place, educate deans and department chairs about their use, and provide examples of how policies can work; they need to set the tone for their utilization. Of course, this also means providing line items in the budget to cover adjuncts for parental leaves so department chairs are more apt to present them as an option.

Gappa and MacDermid, in a working paper entitled "Work, family, and the faculty career (1997)," suggest that academic leaders should conduct ongoing assessments of work/family concerns; engage in campus dialogue about these concerns; appoint task forces to consider ways to create and implement policies; and tap into existing networks to find solutions to deal with specific work/family–related situations. It is also important to provide resources that support work and family. Investing financially in a work/family consultant within human resources is another way to send a clear message to the campus community that work and family issues are important. The senior leadership's support for work and family needs to be expressed "early and often" to let people know that the campus is truly a family-friendly environment.

Questions about the financial implications of adopting certain work/family policies can lead administrators to decide to forgo the implementation of such policies. But financial costs are not the only concern; some well-meaning administrators also fear that creating an institutional policy or policies will limit their ability to respond creatively to unique situations. They worry about the rigidity of written policies, and feel that it is better to respond to work/family situations as they occur. Unfortunately, flexibility can also translate into disparity between how individuals are accommodated, with some being granted much more than others.

Further, some administrators worry about the cost to institutional reputation if they implement policies that are perceived to lower the bar for achieving tenure. Creating policies that might be perceived as reducing the standards for achieving tenure might lead to perceptions that the institution itself doesn't "measure up" to the standards of the most prestigious institutions. Institutional theory put forth by DiMaggio and Powell (1991) suggests that while the most prestigious institutions in the country (e.g., Duke, MIT, Berkeley) are free to create innovative policies, campuses that are upwardly aspirational will be more reluctant to tinker with their policies because it could affect their ability to achieve academic legitimacy. It is the role of the provost and presidents to lead their campuses to better policies as well as to think about how to deal with financial issues. Creating a climate to foster the integration and use of policy requires financial support and personnel as well as academic leadership.

Advice for Deans

While presidents and provosts do a lot to set the tone at the campus level, deans set the tone at the school and college level. Faculty life is enacted locally, with deans and department chairs playing a vital role in communicating to faculty the importance of different aspects of their positions. The promotion and tenure process is primarily a department and college-level process. Deans are often on the front line communicating these policies and processes. Laying out the array of possibilities with regard to work and family policy and practice during new faculty orientation makes it clear what policies and practices are in place at the institution and conveys the importance of this information. If deans talk about and normalize these options as ones that faculty members have exercised, then new faculty members will feel more confident about using these policies.

Deans play a key role with regard to how policies are used and how faculty members are evaluated. Deans also play an important role in terms of career development and creating an information stream to let faculty members know about the overall climate with regard to promotion, tenure, and career advancement. Mentoring programs enacted at the college level can be put in place to help junior faculty with the tenure process and to help associate professors maintain focus on career advancement and achieving full professor rank. Mentoring programs should be thought of broadly as part of the whole career path and not just for the early career.

Advice for the Chair

Given that so much of what we found points directly to departmental contexts, we thought it important to offer suggestions to chairs for effectively dealing with work and family issues among their faculty members. Although colleagues play an important role in creating the environment where policies are used, department chairs play probably the most important role in helping faculty negotiate work and family. Chairs need to know policies, apply them fairly, and educate faculty members about their use. This education needs to be extended to those who may use the policies as well as to those who evaluate the faculty members who use them. When faculty members are new to an institution, they tend to be cautious about how they move forward in their decisions about having a child and using available policies. Chairs can play a mentoring role in talking about how leave works and how to make use of available policies. Department chairs need to be proactive in maintaining a climate that is open, where policy issues regarding work and family are talked about forthrightly. Below we provide some specific suggestions for chairs to consider.

- Be aware of and advocate for institution-wide policy. Chairs need to be aware of what policies exist on their campuses. If there are no policies, then chairs need to be leaders in creating them. Campuses are becoming increasingly competitive when it comes to offering leaves as part of a recruitment package, and those campuses with more progressive policies stand to recruit and retain more qualified faculty than those that do not.
- Call for department chair training. The widespread lack of awareness regarding work and family policy suggests that the topic is not brought up at meetings of department chairs and new chair orientations. Chairs would do well to be leaders among their peers in starting the conversation.
- Break the silence. A major finding of our study is that no one talks about work and family issues, especially with the person having the baby. Department chairs need to take the lead in talking about work/family issues with their departmental colleagues. The silence is often well meant in terms of not wanting to tread in an area where conversation is not welcome, but creating a hospitable climate for work and family issues calls first and foremost for talking about it.
- Share the wealth. Creative solutions for helping faculty make arrangements to manage work and family need to be shared. Part of sharing the wealth is talking about work and family within the department and with chair colleagues. The other aspect of sharing the wealth is becoming familiar with the topic.

• Adopt a life-course perspective. One of the reasons work and family issues are "loaded" and thereby lead to fear and silence is that they often come up during the tenure-track years—a critical period of time for junior faculty. By adopting a life-course perspective, chairs can help normalize life events. There are different phases to the academic career, and adopting a life-course perspective can shift the emphasis of work and family as being the concern of only a few to being a concern of many. We have heard from chairs that they are nervous about providing accommodation to junior women faculty with children and not to others. Adopting a life-course perspective can show that people may need accommodation at any time and for a variety of health and family issues. Anyone can get sick at any time and need accommodation. Faculty members might find themselves caring for aging parents and therefore in need of accommodation. And a junior faculty member may become pregnant while on the tenure track and be in need of accommodation. Such a perspective can help chairs deal with concerns about equity.

• Recognize power differentials. Chairs sometimes do not know their own power. One of the reasons junior faculty are fearful to ask department chairs for "help" is their awareness of the power chairs have to make decisions that can affect their career. By recognizing their own power, chairs might be better able to understand why a new assistant professor is reluctant to come to the chair and ask to modify duties to have a baby. Understanding this power relationship may help both parties come to beneficial solutions.

• Assist with options for covering classes. Typically, research is a preoccupation of tenure-track faculty members, especially at research universities. However, across institutional types, a significant concern for faculty members in our study was how to cover classes during the semester in which a baby is born. Opting for an unpaid leave (as provided by the Family Medical Leave Act) is often not an affordable option for many faculty members, and the twelve-week leave provided does not account for the length of a typical academic term. Similarly, many new professors do not have sufficient sick leave to compensate for missing a semester's worth of teaching. In helping faculty respond to work/family demands, department chairs need to think carefully about what needs to be taught, when, and by whom. There are a number of ways that chairs can help with this concern (depending on the specific policies of the institution):

- o Allow faculty members to go on a modified duty status, where they continue to engage in service or research obligations, but are relieved from teaching responsibilities for a term. Courses taught by faculty members on modified duty would be canceled or taught by someone else.
- o Allow faculty members to bank courses (teach an overload in a different semester) so that they can be free from teaching during the semester in question.
- o Let faculty members team-teach a course with another professor, adjunct, or graduate teaching assistant.
- o Consider offering the courses in alternative formats (online, condensed, and so on).

- Recognize that one size does not fit all. We are strong advocates for centralized policy offerings, but we also recognize that no one policy scenario can meet all faculty needs. Chairs must recognize that they may need to be creative with how they translate policy options for individual faculty members. A faculty member with a baby born with complications may need different accommodation from a faculty member with a trouble-free pregnancy.

We offer these suggestions, hopeful that department chairs will take a proactive stance in working with members of their faculty who have immediate work and family concerns. Departments that are aware of and open about meeting faculty needs and make reasonable accommodation are likely to be healthier in the long run and are more likely to recruit and retain high-quality faculty.

Advice for Senior Colleagues

One of the things we established in our findings is that it takes more than the presence of a policy to create an affirmative and family-friendly environment. Our research and other studies have confirmed that there is great trepidation about using policies to assist in making work and family life more bearable because to do so signals weakness, neediness, and a lack of commitment to the field (Drago & Colbeck 2003; Hochschild 1995). The ideal worker norms come from somewhere—and their presence is largely a product of institutional and departmental climate. In turn, climate is set by the senior faculty in the department, and how these individuals respond to the needs of their colleagues will determine the extent to which the environment is perceived to be family-friendly or hostile. The extent to which senior colleagues convey a family-friendly environment determines whether such an environment is present. To be fair, many of these senior colleagues came of age in a time in which "family friendly" wasn't an option. Some of these individuals might have had stay-at-home spouses or were single, or just made their own family lives mesh with work out of sheer grit and determination. They didn't have policies to assist them and perhaps, as a result, they believe that this younger generation is too coddled, too spoiled, and needs to "suck it up" and deal with the requirements of the profession without assistance. In this case, they are just passing on the socialization that they received and are expecting their newer colleagues to do the same.

The trick is for senior colleagues to see that what was available to them was inadequate and that an equitable workplace is one that does better than what they might have been offered. By whatever means possible, we need to move beyond the self-referential mentality of: "I did it without help, so my new colleagues should do it too." One means of convincing senior faculty that this is the case is to talk about work/family policies and climates as being appropriate and necessary for faculty members at all stages of the career and life cycle. One means of appealing to senior faculty, for example, is to acknowledge their out-of-work needs. Do they have elderly parents who need assistance? Do they have high school-aged children that need additional attention? Do they have grandchildren who need care? By making the workplace more family friendly for new colleagues, it might become more family friendly for everyone, including the senior faculty.

Senior faculty members have a lot of sway in terms of how family friendly a campus feels. It therefore becomes crucial for institutions to bring senior faculty into the discussion of work/family climates. Senior faculty who did manage to balance work and family should talk about it with their younger colleagues and graduate students. Engaging in the mentoring process will help show colleagues the various ways that they managed their multiple roles. Part of this goes back to what we wrote in chapter 1 about the faculty career mystique and the fear that all faculty have about admitting that there are benefits to the academic lifestyle. To avoid being seen as unproductive deadwood, faculty members have a tendency to posture and therefore to perpetuate idealized worker norms, creating a fictional standard that cannot be achieved. Senior colleagues owe it to themselves and their junior colleagues (not to mention their students) to move beyond the posturing and to be more honest about the joys and tribulations of academic life. Senior colleagues are an especially important part of this equation because they are the ones who will evaluate the junior faculty when they come up for promotion and tenure. They will determine how a leave of absence is to be evaluated or how a stop-clock policy is to be enacted (and whether or not it is safe to use such policies).

Advice for New Faculty and Graduate Students

Although we have written a lot about the need for institutional and cultural changes to take place in order to make the academic workplace more family friendly, the truth is that it will probably always be a matter of personal agency—choices, options, and actions that make combining work and family in an academic setting viable. As such, this next section offers some advice and guidance for graduate students considering an academic career and for faculty members who have already embarked on their careers.

We are often asked by eager graduate students and concerned new faculty about the best time to have a baby, what policies to use, and how to convey their needs to their colleagues and supervisors. Often our answer is "it depends," but we do try to offer some wisdom based on our interviews, personal experiences, and knowledge of the field. We have organized the first section of advice as answers to frequently raised questions. The second part of this section is framed as pieces of advice in the personal and professional realms. Note that we didn't divide up this section by career stage; rather, we believe that the advice is relevant to individuals across the stages as they seek to balance work and family.

- When should I have a baby? Timing was clearly a preoccupation for many of the women in our study. Most spent a lot of time thinking about when in their career to have a child—In graduate school? Early on the tenure track? Mid-tenure? Post-tenure? Certainly, many talked about aiming their due dates for the summer or the end of a semester. So did we determine that there is a best time to have a child and be a successful faculty member? The answer is no. There is no "right time"—so our advice is that people should have a baby when they are ready, on the basis of personal clocks and not on the basis of what they feel an academic career dictates. It is always possible to find a reason why the timing is bad—financial, personal, professional—and the decision to have a child is extremely personal. When faculty members feel they are at a point in life when they want to start or expand their family, they should make that decision without putting undue pressure on themselves about tenure or work expectations.

Respondents chose a variety of timing strategies. Some believed that graduate school was the ideal time, as long as their graduate advisor was flexible and supportive. If in graduate school, some suggested that it is better to wait until one was done with coursework. Some chose to wait until they had secured a tenure-track position; others waited until they were farther along on the tenure track. All of these choices came with pluses and minuses and different kinds of challenges and triumphs. One of the most important considerations in terms of timing is that control and timing of fertility can be elusive. Sometimes it takes longer to have a child than planned. Sometimes people miscarry. Sometimes people get pregnant earlier than they had planned. The truth is that some things cannot be controlled—a truism that becomes more apparent with parenthood. The timing of a child is not an exact science, and since there is no "right time," faculty members should follow their instincts and do what feels best for their family. To some degree, the psychic energy spent on figuring out an exact timing scheme might better be used for other pursuits.

- How many babies should I have? Once again, the answer to this question is "it depends." This is an interesting question, because there is certainly lore and beliefs about how many children are too many, not just in academic circles, but in society in general. The conventional wisdom is that it is okay to have one child, and perhaps two—but any more than that would make having a full-time tenure-track job too difficult. Interestingly, many of the tenure stop-clock policies limit the number of "stops" that can be utilized to two. Many of our respondents said that they were told that having more than two children was not okay. However, we had several faculty members in our sample who defied such norms and had more children; the maximum number of children anyone in our sample had was four. How many children to have is a difficult question to wrestle with, and the answer comes down to how many children the faculty member can handle and still be a productive faculty member and a "good" parent. The faculty member will need to decide how many compromises she is willing to make personally and professionally. Having a stay-at-home parent, a luxury afforded to a few people in our sample, made having more children an easier proposition. Two working professionals who both make their careers a priority might find it difficult to have more children. There is not one single equation for success in these situations. What works best for one academic mother depends on individual factors of personality, family constraints, work constraints, and so forth. Although this question is often asked, we find it interesting that such a question is even part of the academic discourse, given how personal it is to determine how many children are "right" for a particular family.

- Is there an ideal spouse/partner out there to make this more workable? The ease with which women make balancing work and family possible is facilitated by the qualities of their spouse/partner and the strength of their relationship. Who a person chooses as a life partner is certainly one of the most important decisions to make. While making this choice, discussions and decisions about careers, about gender roles, about sharing responsibilities are essential. The happiest people we interviewed were those with stay-at-home husbands who handled the family responsibilities, leaving the women to focus on their work. This isn't always economically feasible- nor might it fit the personality of the person with whom the faculty member is committed. However, it is worth noting that those who choose this option were better able to achieve in both domains than those in dual-career relationships. Our research did show that there are many benefits to being part of a dual-career couple—not the least of which includes more financial stability. But a couple in which both members feel their career should be the most important consideration are likely to face challenges. At some point in time, someone is going to end up feeling like the "trailing spouse" and may have to compromise his or her career. Discussions in advance about how to deal with careers and family responsibilities help to avoid a lot of problems.

The other thing worth mentioning here is that the more egalitarian the home setting, the easier it was for an academic woman with children to "have it all." This was particularly difficult to maintain when her spouse had a less flexible position (e.g., shift work, significant travel) than when both members of the couple were in positions with autonomy and flexibility. What we found was that if the father had no flexibility in his work, the mother was the one who picked up the slack. It is important to note that egalitarian relationships require more negotiation because they don't rely on traditional gendered roles and expectations. Whom a faculty member partners with is a personal choice, but discussing the road blocks ahead is a wise choice that can help avoid pitfalls in the road.

• Can I have it all? When people talk about whether it is possible to "have it all," the answer depends on what a person means by "all." If "all" means having a productive, intellectually stimulating successful career and also have a loving family to spend quality time with, then the answer is yes. If, however, a person wants to fulfill both of those roles and always have a clean house, home-cooked gourmet meals, attend every child's activity, be recognized as the school volunteer of the year, spend lots of quality time engaging in personal hobbies, be the perfect wife, regularly host charming dinner parties, win the MacArthur genius award, publish a groundbreaking book every year, win multiple teaching awards, travel to every relevant conference, and otherwise be perfect at both home and work, then the answer is no. Doing the best of one's abilities in both realms of life can be accomplished, but always doing so perfectly will not happen, and some things will have to fall by the wayside. Being busy means redefining priorities at home and work in ways that make having it all possible. One of the things that helps is understanding that no particular moment of the day will be "balanced"—at any one time, energies may be invested in one aspect of life more than another. Balance itself is a term rejected by most of the people we interviewed. What they suggested is that rather than seeking balance between work and family, people strive for harmony and understand that at any one point in time their lives won't feel balanced, but may instead feel integrated.

Family-Related Strategies

There are some strategies to assist women academics that come from the findings of our study. We thought it would be helpful to share some of the suggestions and ideas from faculty who seemingly have it all.

- Satisfice and find perspective. As indicated, having it all is a matter of setting priorities and figuring out what must get done versus what could get done. This piece of advice may be easier said than done, but the best way to find balance is to distinguish tasks that are priorities from those things that would be simply nice to do. Also, determine what must be done immediately, versus what can wait. Try to break tasks into smaller, reasonable chunks rather than only working toward the end goal. Does the birthday cake need to be homemade, or will a store-bought cake suffice? Do the Halloween costumes need to be original, or can you purchase one at Target? There is an art to figuring out what can be good enough versus what has to be perfect. Practice this art form.

- Seek support from others. If you feel as if everything is yours to handle alone, then it will be much more difficult to get everything done. Seek support from a host of sources—informal social support can come, for example, from a partner, from other family members, and from friends. Many people don't live in the same vicinity as their extended family and so do not have the luxury of relying on them for help. In such cases, find other sources of support. Seek help from mentoring programs, counselors, discussion lists, electronic social networks, and so on. Faculty members shouldn't feel they are in this alone or that their problems are unique and not shared with others. Sometimes, misery loves company. And sometimes we need to just vent and share our frustrations and joys with someone else. Suffering in silence will not serve a faculty member well. Support is especially important when things are not going as planned and a safety net is needed.

- Share responsibilities. In addition to the moral support that comes from our social networks, it is also important to share actual responsibilities. As such, whenever possible, faculty members can find ways of sharing the jobs that need to be done. They can share with a spouse/partner, other family members, other parents, and colleagues. But whatever faculty members do, they should attempt to share the load so that the second shift does not make work/family life more difficult. When a faculty member isn't the only person responsible for everything, then it is much easier to get things done.

• Outsource. A variation on the above suggestion comes in the form of hiring people to help with the housekeeping, the cooking, running errands, lawn care, and child care. From our interviews, we found that people who hired others to assist with these tasks had an easier time engaging in those things that were most important to them and brought them the most joy. We recognize that might not be an option for some, given limited resources, but it was an option many women used to help manage work and family.

• Take care of yourself. In the hustle and bustle of life, faculty members themselves are the ones that end up getting neglected. It is important for individuals to take care of themselves through eating right, getting some exercise, getting enough sleep, spending time with friends, and spending time relaxing. It is easy to move taking care of yourself off the to-do list in favor of other things, but it is not a wise solution. Taking care of oneself allows for the ability to do everything that needs to be done. Make yourself a priority.

• Take care of your relationship. It is really important for faculty to spend some quality time with their spouse or partner (think date night). Divorce rates are high among academics, and the pressures of work and family can take its toll on a relationship. Time spent together (apart from children) is the only way to maintain a relationship and block the road to divorce.

• Let go of the guilt. Working mothers have a tendency to spend a fair amount of time feeling bad about themselves and their ability to juggle everything. There is a significant amount of guilt that comes either from external sources or from within. This guilt doesn't help—it doesn't make anything better and, in fact, it makes things worse. Faculty members need to spend their psychic energy on something more productive than worrying. Everything (children, family, work) will be fine. Faculty members need to give themselves a bit of a break and do the best job they can—it is all anyone can ask of them and it is all they should ask of themselves.

Work-Related Strategies

In addition to making life on the home front more manageable, there are things to consider with regard to work as well.

- Find the right fit for you and your interests. In this book we have talked a lot about opting in and opting out and making choices—some of which are constrained by the circumstances and contexts in which women find themselves. We have attempted to problematize the notion of choice and talk about the ways in which the academic environment might be restructured as to make the choice of having a successful academic career and a happy family life both possible. We have also talked about institutional types and their various priorities. Here, we wish to suggest the best way to find happiness and success in both work and family life is for faculty members to choose to work at a type of institution that matches their interests and passions. There is a great diversity of institutional types, and a great variety of institutional missions—so, to the extent possible, faculty members should try to find a workplace that matches their interests. This is difficult because faculty members are trained at research universities. They are socialized by their faculty to believe that a successful academic career is one that takes place at the most prestigious institutions. We often do a poor job of letting our graduate students know about other institutional types and introducing them to what academic life might be like in other settings. Graduate students owe it to themselves to find that match. What we are loath to see, however, are women who love research but who opt out of a research university setting for fear that it won't be family friendly. If a faculty member chooses another institutional type she should make sure that choice is a product of following passion and not of avoiding problems that might or might not be present with other options. Academic life is driven by internal motivation, and to choose to work at a place where there isn't a fit is a recipe for unhappiness.
- Ask for what you need. Whether a newly hired faculty member or someone who is more senior, the onus is still on the faculty member to ask for what is needed. A faculty member needs to know the work family policies available at institution and to negotiate with the department chair and the dean about how to handle maternity leaves, stop the tenure

clock, find mentoring, and proceed through the various faculty ranks. A faculty member cannot wait for someone else to do these things, she has to take it upon herself (no matter how scary or daunting), and offer solutions to her own concerns. It is in the institution's best interest to help the faculty member be successful—and sometimes administrators just need guidance on how best to do this. To quote the Rolling Stones, "You can't always get what you want, but you may find sometimes that you get what you need."

• Find allies and support. The truth is that the faculty member isn't in this alone. There are other faculty members at the institution or in the research field who have made this work. Talk to them. Find out what they did and how they did it. Brainstorm with others and ask about the range of possible forms of assistance. It is always helpful for faculty members to know that they aren't alone and it is also helpful to find out what the pitfalls, obstacles, and success points are as they venture forward. Allies come in many forms—it may be a senior colleague, it may be a department chair, it may be a faculty member from across campus, it may be a formal mentor, it may be a colleague at another institution, or it may be from a chance encounter. Talking to others about the choices they have made and the paths they have followed is the best way for faculty members to figure out how to navigate their path. It is important to not rely on a single person to pave the way because there are lots of different answers that can be combined to make the best decision for each faculty member. Think about mentoring as a mosaic.

There are also resources for support that go beyond particular campuses or disciplines. It can be helpful to read blogs about work and family to glean support and also to refer to books like *Professor mommy* (Connelly & Ghodsee 2011) as a way to garner support for different aspects of managing (or thinking about managing) work and family.

• Do your work. This may seem obvious, but it is really important for faculty to not abuse the system and to get their work done. The workplace doesn't owe each faculty member a permanent pass on being a productive member of the organization just because she is a parent. The faculty member is hired with the expectation that she would do a good job and be a contributing member of the department, school, and university. That doesn't mean that the faculty member has to do everything she is asked and do it all perfectly. But she does need to do what she was hired to do. If the faculty member does this most of the time, then in times when she needs a break or needs extra help, her colleagues will be more willing to cut her some slack.

- Set reasonable priorities and satisfice. When one becomes a parent new priorities need to be established. Our respondents talked a lot about how they refocused their research agendas after having children in ways that were more conducive to having a family. Faculty at a research university will still have to publish, but the kind of work they do may need to shift to be more manageable and still important. These decisions need to get made in all aspects of the academic career—in teaching, in advising, in research, and in service. Faculty members have to figure out what can be done "well enough" and what has to be done at a really high level. This is a tricky thing to figure out, but it is important. For example, one of the things that may be affected by parenthood is the ability to travel. It may be that the faculty member will have to cut back on travel to professional conferences somewhat when her children are young. Cutting out all professional travel is not wise, however, as professional networking is valuable, and presenting seminars at other universities is a very useful way of building visibility and making connections with people who will write promotion letters.

- Manage time wisely and efficiently. One of the things that we learned from our interviews and from personal experience is that there are ways to be more or less efficient. When time is a precious commodity, then one needs to figure out ways to do things efficiently. This means breaking down tasks into reasonable parts and doing them when time is available. People spend a lot of time not getting things done and fretting over how much they have to do. This a classic form of procrastination. It is better to make lists and figure out what needs to get done, prioritize that list, and figure out how to do it as best as you can.

- Plan and anticipate. Some people we interviewed commented on the need for advance planning and not leaving things for the last minute. If something needs to get done, there is a tendency to work toward the deadline (this is a natural thing to do). However, given the unpredictable nature of parenthood, leaving really important things for the last minute is more risky. Our interviewees, for example, all had stories about a child who wakes up sick and has to be taken to the doctor the day of a major presentation. One unplanned illness and that spare time to prepare the lecture disappears. When possible, things need to be done in advance because a faculty member can't count on the hours to be there on any particular day. The exception to this, of course, is if the partner or other family member (or reliable neighbor and friend) is the first line of defense against unexpected events of this type.

- Be a good colleague. In contrast to the advice above about efficiency, we suggest that faculty not neglect the personal side of the workplace. Being at work isn't always about being productive. It is important to be a good colleague—so it is important to attend departmental meetings and departmental functions and to be there for those events that are important in the program, department, school, and university. These types of things aren't efficient, but they are an important part of academic life. As with the other areas of academic responsibility, faculty members don't need to do it all or do it perfectly, but they do need to make an effort. Being a good colleague will pay off in a lot of ways throughout the academic career and beyond.

- Pay it forward. When faculty members are pretenure and feeling vulnerable, they tend to have limited power to change things at their institutions. But as soon as that power is bestowed and the faculty member feels she has that power, then she owes it to the larger campus community to make the campus more family friendly. If an institution doesn't have a tenure stop-clock policy, then a faculty member should work to have one implemented. If there are no spaces available to use a breast pump, then faculty members should lobby for such spaces to be created. If the campus doesn't provide adequate daycare support, then the faculty member should work to make it more accessible. As a parent who might have had to suffer through some difficulties, faculty members have an obligation to try and make it better for the next person. Although they may not singlehandedly be able to change the campus climate or policy environment, they can make it better for those who follow behind them.

On a related theme, it is really important for faculty women to be a role model for graduate students and new faculty with regard to work/family. Academic women with children need to demonstrate how it is possible to be both a successful academic and a successful mother without perpetuating super worker norms. One accomplishes this by talking about experiences, sharing triumphs and struggles, and generally being honest about how she made it work. Be honest, frank, and human about sharing experiences so that the next generation of faculty will see this as a possible and viable career option.

• Take a life-course perspective. We have written a lot in this book about the greedy institutions of academic life and motherhood and the all-consuming nature of both. We have also tried to express the belief that the demands of career and family vary over time. Sometimes the faculty role may take precedence—say, for example, on the eve of a major deadline—and sometimes family life will be the priority—on the eve of a major life event, like a birthday or a graduation. To be successful as both an academic and a mother calls for individuals to take a life-course perspective. Rather than seeking to balance out any particular moment in time, we suggest that people recognize that both an academic career and being a parent bring with them obligations and responsibilities that evolve over time and that involve considerable give and take. While any one particular moment might not feel balanced in one direction, there will undoubtedly be a moment that takes you in the other direction. The trick is not neglecting either realm, but being true to both, and understanding how the realms interact and evolve and going with that flow.

As we move into the future, faculty members and administrators need to consider the research, policies, and dilemmas presented by work/family issues. Although it is easy to think of combining work and family as women's problems, and private ones at that, given the basic logistics of earning an advanced degree, landing a tenure-track position, and seeking promotion and tenure, it is important to consider existing research done on women faculty and family issues in an effort to understand the phenomenon and what is being done about it. As higher education moves into a new century, work/family issues need to focus on policy and research agendas. These initiatives are good and necessary returns on the investment that institutions make in their faculties.

Issues related to work and family are of increasing concern for faculty.

Conceptions of the academic career that are viewed as either/or propositions—that is, that faculty members can have a career or a family, but not both—do not bode well for the future of the academic profession. Recent research suggests that concerns about the ability to combine work and family are a major concern for graduate students considering academic careers (cf. Austin 2002; Golde & Dore 2001; Mason et al. 2009). At research universities, in particular, where most graduate students are socialized to what it's like to be an academic, students see their professors firsthand encountering the policy environments and work norms discussed throughout this book. Graduate students see faculty members in their departments grappling with decisions about their careers and how to combine them with the needs of a spouse and the desire to have a child. Faculty members, like those who are the focus of this book, are role models to the graduate students and newer faculty in their midst. If they have a child, take a leave, stop the tenure clock, and then get on with their career without repercussion, this leaves one message; whereas if they choose not to have a baby because of tenure, or if they opt to take time off and then are the subject of negative hallway conversations, this sends another, and far more indelible, message. It is this latter message that we hope can be remediated as campuses attempt to look more forthrightly at work and family policy so that talented faculty can make the combination of a successful career and a personal life that includes children possible.

FINAL CONCLUSIONS

The rewards of an academic life are many. The work is intellectually stimulating. The career provides faculty with the satisfaction of knowing that they can make a contribution to their field and that they are educating the next generation of students and scholars in their discipline. It is a demanding career that feeds on internal motivation. It is also a flexible career. To a large degree, faculty have the self-determination that comes from having no boss, and from choosing what to work on, how to work on it, and when to work on it. Although the work itself may never end and the expectations for performance are high, the rewards of being an academic are also numerous.

So what do we want people to take away from this book? What are the grand messages? First, there are women out there who are managing to combine being mothers with being tenure-track faculty. They exist, and they are role models for others. Not every day is perfect and not everything they do is done "successfully"—but all in all, they are making it work in the best way they can. These women exist in different fields and at different institutions, and their stories show common themes of joy, satisficing, perspective making, and resilience. These women don't offer up a single pathway to managing work and family, but they do demonstrate ways to make it work. These women serve as everyday examples of the counternarrative that we want to highlight in this book—they show that it is possible to be a successful tenure-track academic woman and raise a family.

Choice is a theme that permeates this study. People make choices about whether to go to graduate school, where to go to graduate school, whether to pursue an academic career, where they would consider working, whether to have children, when to have children, whether they should seek accommodation and support for family leave and assistance with tenure, what they decide to do once tenured, whether they stay put or pursue other positions, whether they advance to full professor, whether they pursue an administrative post, and how they chose to juggle all of this with the demands of being a parent. Clearly, personal choices abound. But, what is equally clear is that these choices are constrained by societal and organizational expectations of what women should do in the best interests of their families and their careers. Societal expectations about gendered norms at home and what it means to be a good mother combine with institutional expectations reflecting faculty mystique and ideal worker norms and what it means to be a good professor. These norms make what might seem to be free and unconstrained not so free. How one navigates these choices is a function of the capital that people bring with them as well as the expectations they hold of themselves and the expectations of significant others who surround them. Our intent is not to judge the choices people make, but to call attention to the contexts in which those choices are made.

Similarly, another major point we would like to make is that for an institution to have work/family policies is not enough. The constrained choices mentioned above are enacted at the institutional level. Although there are choices that women can make with regard to their own careers, there are also things the campus (and the higher education system as a whole) can do to make combining work and family more possible and more manageable. This involves going beyond creating policies to creating environments that are conducive to using policy.

Another take-away message here is that the academic career and motherhood are shaped by each other—work life is shaped by home life, and vice versa. This is true for all faculty members, regardless of their parental status, but given the focus of this book on academic mothers it is certainly true for women with children. Larger life-course perspectives shape the academic career and the choices that are made with regard to it. Further, there is more to an academic career than just the probationary period, and there is more to parenthood than just infancy. Both are lifelong propositions. Adopting a life-course perspective is not just about women, and it is not just about having babies; it is about recognition that if we want to have creative, imaginative research and teaching environments in which everyone is doing their best work, then we need to pay attention to creating work/life family-friendly institutions.

We want to encourage women academics to not be afraid of academic life or motherhood as possible life choices. Despite the faculty mystique, ideal worker and ideal motherhood norms, the academic profession is one that allows flexibility and autonomy such that engaging in the dual roles of mother and professor are possible. You need to navigate the choices that come to you and make those decisions that you feel are in your best interest (and the best interest of your family and career). You need to chart the path that you want to take and empower yourself to make the most of your career and family life.

For institutions of higher education (and those who lead them), you must work harder to become truly family friendly. Establish policies and practices and a culture that encourages all faculty members to be productive, successful, happy institutional citizens. This is necessary in order to recruit and retain the most qualified, generative, diverse, and productive faculty. It is the individual and the institution that together make academic motherhood a viable combination.

REFERENCES

Acker, J. (1987). Sex bias in job evaluation: A comparable worth issue. In C. Bose & G. Spitze (Eds.), *Ingredients for women's employment policy* (pp. 183–196). Albany: State University of New York Press.

Acker, J. (1990). Hierarchies, jobs, bodies: A theory of gendered organizations. *Gender and Society*, 4(2), 139–158.

Aisenberg, N., & Harrington, M. (1988). *Women of academe: Outsiders in the sacred grove*. Amherst: University of Massachusetts Press.

Allan, E. J. (2011). Women's status in higher education. *ASHE Higher Education Report*, 37(1), 1–163.

Allan, E., Iverson, S., & Ropers-Huilman, R. (Eds.) (2010). *Reconstructing policy in higher education: Feminist post-structural perspectives and policy analysis*. New York: Routledge.

Allen, H. L. (1998). Faculty workload and productivity: Ethnic and gender disparities. *NEA 1998 Almanac of Higher Education* (pp. 19–24). Washington, D.C.: National Education Association.

American Association of University Professors. (2001). Statement of principles on family responsibilities and academic work. http://www.aaup.org/AAUP/pubsres/policydocs/contents/workfam-stmt.htm.

American Association of University Professors. (2006). *AAUP faculty gender equity indicators 2006*. http://www.aaup.org/AAUP/pubsres/research/geneq2006.

Armenti, C. (2000). *Women academics blending private and public lives*. Unpublished dissertation. University of Toronto.

Armenti, C. (2004). May babies and post-tenure babies: Maternal decisions of women professors. *Review of Higher Education*, 27(3), 211–231.

Astin, H. S., & Davis, D. E. (1985). Research productivity across the life and career cycles: Facilitators and barriers for women. In M. F. Fox (Ed.), *Scholarly writing and publishing: Issues, problems, and solutions*. Boulder, Col.: Westview.

Astin, H. S., & Milem, J. F. (1997). The status of academic couples in U.S. institutions. In M. A. Ferber & J. W. Loeb (Eds.), *Academic couples: Problems and promises*. Urbana, Ill.: University of Illinois Press.

Austin, A. E. (1990). Faculty cultures, faculty values. *New Directions for Institutional Research*, 68, 61–74. doi: 10.1002/ir.37019906807.

Austin, A. E. (2002). Preparing the next generation of faculty: Graduate school as socialization to the academic career. *Journal of Higher Education*, 73(1), 94–122.

Baez, B. (2000). Race-related service and faculty of color: Conceptualizing critical agency in academe. *Higher Education*, 39, 363–391.

Bailyn, L. (2003). Academic careers and gender equity: Lessons learned from MIT. *Gender, Work and Organization*, 10(2), 137–153.

Bailyn, L. (2011). Redesigning work for gender equity and work—personal life integration. *Community, Work, and Family*, 14(1), 97–112.

Baldwin, R. G. (1990). Faculty vitality beyond the research university: Extending a contextual concept. *Journal of Higher Education*, 61(2), 160–180.

Baldwin, R. G., & Blackburn, R. T. (1981). The academic career as a developmental process: Implications for higher education. *Journal of Higher Education*, 52(6), 598–614.

Baldwin, R. G., Lunceford, C. J., & Vanderlinden, K. E. (2005). Faculty in middle years. *Review of Higher Education*, 29(1), 101–118.

Ball, S. J. (2002). *Class strategies and the education market: The middle classes and social advantage*. New York: Routledge Falmer.

Barbezat, D. (1988). Gender differences in the academic reward system. In D. W. Breneman & T. I. Youn (Eds.), *Academic labor markets and careers* (pp. 138–164). New York: Falmer.

Barnett, R. C., & Hyde, J. S. (2001). Women, men, work and family: An expansionist theory. *American Psychologist*, 56(10), 781–796.

Bassett, R. H. (Ed.). (2005). *Parenting and professing: Balancing family work with an academic career*. Nashville, Tenn.: Vanderbilt University Press.

Becher, T. (1994). The significance of disciplinary differences. *Studies in Higher Education* 19(2), 151–161.

Becher, T., & Trowler, P. (2001). *Academic tribes and territories: Intellectual enquiry and the cultures of disciplines* (2nd edition). Bristol, Penn.: Open University Press/SRHE.

Belkin, L. (2003, October 26). The opt-out revolution. *New York Times Magazine*, 42–47, 58, 85–86.

Bellas, M. (1992). The effects of marital status and wives' employment on the salaries of faculty men: The (house) wife bonus. *Gender and Society*, 6(4), 609–622.

Bellas, M. L., & Toutkoushian, R. K. (1999). Faculty time allocations and research productivity: Gender, race, and family effects. *Review of Higher Education*, 22(4), 367–390.

Berdahl, R. (1985). Strategy and government: U.S. state systems and institutional role and mission. *International Journal of Institutional Management in Higher Education*, 9(3), 301–307.

Bielby, D., & Bielby, W. T. (1992). I will follow him: Family ties, gender role belief and reluctance to relocate for a better job. *Journal of Sociology*, 97, 1247–1267.

Birnbaum, R. (1988). How colleges work: The cybernetics of academic organization and leadership. San Francisco: Jossey-Bass.

Blair-Loy, M. (2005). *Competing devotions: Career and family among women executives*. Cambridge: Harvard University Press.

Boice, R. (1992). Lessons learned about mentoring. *New directions for teaching and learning*, 50, 51–61.

Bourdieu, P. (1977). *Outline of a theory of practice*. New York: Cambridge University Press.

Braskamp, L. (2003). *Fostering faculty development through student development:*

A national survey of chief academic officers at church-related colleges. Project report, Loyola University of Chicago.

Braskamp, L., Trautvetter, L., & Ward, K. (2006) *Putting students first: How colleges develop students purposefully.* Bolton, Mass.: Anker.

Britton, D. (2009). Engendering the university through policy and practice: Barriers to promotion to full professor for women in the science, engineering, and math disciplines. Paper presented at conference on Gender change in academia: Re-mapping the fields of work, knowledge, and politics from a gender perspective. International Conference at the Georg-August-Universität Göttingen.

Budig, M. J., & Hodges, M. J. (2010). Differences in disadvantage: Variation in the motherhood penalty across white women's earnings distribution. *American Sociological Review, 75*(5), 705–728.

Ceci, S. J., & Williams, W. M. (2011). Understanding current causes of women's underrepresentation in science. *PNAS Early Edition.* http://www.pnas.org/content/early/2011/02/02/1014871108.full.pdf.

Clark, B. R. (1983). *The higher education system: Academic organizations in cross-national perspective.* Berkeley: University of California Press.

Clark, B. R. (1987). *The academic life: Small worlds, different worlds.* Princeton, N.J.: Carnegie Foundation for the Advancement of Teaching.

Clark, S. M., & Corcoran, M. (1986). Perspectives on the professional socialization of women faculty: A case of accumulative disadvantage. *Journal of Higher Education, 57,* 20–43.

Cohen, A. M., & Brawer, F. B. (2008). *The American community college* (5th edition). San Francisco: Jossey-Bass.

Colbeck, C. L., & Drago, R. (2005). How faculty members respond to bias against caregiving . . . and how departments can help. *Change: The Magazine of Higher Learning, 37*(6), 10–17.

Cole, J. R., & Zuckerman, H. (1987). Marriage, motherhood, and research performance in science. *Scientific American, 256*(2), 119–125.

College and University Work and Family Association. (2011). *http://www.cuwfa.org/.*

Connelly, R. & Ghodsee, K. (2011). *Professor Mommy: Finding Work-Family Balance in Academia.* Lanham, Md.: Rowman & Littlefield.

Cooney, T. M., & Uhlenberg, P. (1989). Family-building patterns of professional women: A comparison of lawyers, physicians, and postsecondary teachers. *Journal of Marriage and the Family, 51,* 749–758.

Cooper, J. E., & Stevens, D. D. (Eds.). (2002). *Tenure in the sacred grove: Issues and strategies for women and minority faculty.* Albany: State University of New York Press.

Coser, L. (1974). *Greedy institutions: Patterns of undivided commitment.* New York: Free Press.

Creamer, E. (1998). Assessing faculty publication productivity: Issues in equity. *ASHE-ERIC Higher Education Report, No. 26.* Washington D.C: ASHE-ERIC/George Washington University.

Crosby, F. J. (1991). *Juggling: The unexpected advantages of balancing career and home for women and their families.* New York: Free Press.

David, M., Davies, J., Edwards, R., Reay, D., & Standing, K. (1996). Mothering and education: Reflexivity and feminist methodology. In L. Morley & V. Walsh (Eds.), *Breaking boundaries: Women in higher education*. London: Taylor and Francis.

Didion, C. J. (1996). Dual careers and shared positions: Adjusting university policy to accommodate academic couples. *Journal of College Science Teaching*, 26(2), 123–124.

Digest of Educational Statistics (2010). http://nces.ed.gov/pubsearch/pubsinfo. asp?pubid=2011015.

DiFuccia, M., Pelton, J., & Sica, A. (2007). If and when sociology becomes a female preserve. *The American Sociologist*, 38(1), 3–22.

DiMaggio, P. J., & Powell, W. W. (Eds.). (1991). *The new institutionalism in organizational analysis*. Chicago: University of Chicago Press.

Donovan, J. (2000). *Feminist theory: The intellectual traditions*. New York: Continuum.

Drago, R. W. (2007). *Striking a balance: Work, family, life*. Boston: Dollars & Sense.

Drago, R. W., & Colbeck, C. (2003). *Final report from the mapping project: Exploring the terrain of U.S. colleges and universities for faculty and families*. New York: Alfred P. Sloan Foundation.

Drago, R., Colbeck, C. L., & Stauffer, K. D. (2006). The avoidance of bias against caregiving. *American Behavioral Scientist*, 49, 1222–1247.

Drago, R., Colbeck, C. L., Stauffer, K. D., Pirretti, A., Burkum, K., & Fazioli, J. (2005). Bias against caregiving. *Academe*, 91(5). http://www.aaup.org/AAUP/ pubsres/academe/2005/SO/Feat/drag.htm.

Drago, R., & Williams, J. (2000). A half-time tenure track proposal. *Change*, 6(6), 46–51.

Dwyer, M. M., Flynn, A. A., & Inman, P. (1991). Differential progress of women faculty: Status 1980–1990. In J. Smart (Ed.), *Handbook of theory and research*, Vol. 7 (pp. 173–222). New York: Agathon.

Eddy, P., & Cox, E. (2008). Gendered leadership: An organizational perspective. *New Directions for Community College*, 142, 69–79.

Ely, M., Vinz, R., Anzul, M., & Downing, M. (1997). *On writing qualitative research: Living by words*. London: Falmer Press.

Etzkowitz, H., Kemelgor, C., & Uzzi, B. (2000). *Athena unbound: The advancement of women in science and technology*. New York: Cambridge University Press.

Evans, E., & and Grant, C. (Eds.). (2008). *Mama, PhD: Women write about motherhood and academic life*. New Brunswick: Rutgers University Press.

Fairweather, J. S. (1996). *Faculty work and public trust: Restoring the value of teaching and public service in American academic life*. Boston: Allyn and Bacon.

Ferber, M. A., & Kordick, B. (1978). Sex differentials in the earnings of Ph.D.'s. *Industrial and Labor Relations Review*, 31, 227–238.

Ferber, M. A., & Loeb, J. W. (1997). *Academic couples: Problems and promises*. Urbana : University of Illinois Press.

Finkel, S. K., & Olswang, S. G. (1996). Child rearing as a career impediment to women assistant professors. *Review of Higher Education*, 19(2), 123–139.

Finkel, S. K., Olswang, S., & She, N. (1994). Childbirth, tenure, and promotion for women faculty. *Review of Higher Education,* 17(3), 259–270.

Finkelstein, M. J. (1984). *The American academic profession: A synthesis of social science inquiry since World War II.* Columbus: Ohio State University Press.

Finkelstein, M. J. (1987). Women and minority faculty. In M. Finkelstein (Ed.), *ASHE reader on faculty and faculty issues in colleges and universities* (2nd edition) (pp. 66–97). Lexington, Mass.: Ginn.

Finkelstein, M. J., Seal, R. K., & Schuster, J. H. (1998). *The new academic generation: A profession in transformation.* Baltimore: Johns Hopkins University Press.

Finnegan, D. E., & Gamson, Z. F. (1996). Disciplinary adaptations to research culture in comprehensive institutions. *Review of Higher Education,* 19(2), 141–177.

Fox, M. F. (1985). Publication, performance, and reward in science and scholarship. In J. C. Smart (Ed.), *Higher education: Handbook of theory and research,* Vol. 1 (pp. 255–282). New York: Agathon.

Fox, M. F. (1991). Gender, environmental milieu, and productivity in science. In H. Zuckerman, J. R. Cole, & J. T. Bruer (Eds.), *The outer circle: Women in the scientific community* (pp.188–204). New Haven: Yale University Press.

Fox, M.F. (1995). Women in scientific careers. In S. Jasanoff, et al. (Eds). *Handbook of science and technology studies* (pp. 205–223). Thousand Oaks, Cal.: Sage.

Gappa, J. M., Austin, A. E., & Trice, A. G. (2007). *Rethinking faculty work: Higher education's strategic imperative.* San Francisco: John Wiley & Sons.

Gappa, J. M., & Mac Dermid, S. M. (1997). Work, family, and the faculty career. *New Pathways Working Paper Series,* no. 8. Washington, D.C.: American Association for Higher Education.

Ginther, D. K., & Hayes, K.J. (2003). Gender differences in salary and promotion for faculty in the humanities 1977–95. *Journal of Human Resources,* 38(1), 34–73.

Glazer-Raymo, J. (1999). *Shattering the myths: Women in academe.* Baltimore: Johns Hopkins University Press.

Golde, C. M., & Dore, T. M. (2001). *At cross purposes: What the experiences of today's doctoral students reveal about doctoral education.* http://www.wcer.wisc.edu/phd-survey/golde.html.

Goulden, M., Frasch, K., & Mason, M. A. (2009). Staying competitive: Patching America's leaky pipeline in the sciences. Berkeley: Center for American Progress. http://www.americanprogress.org/issues/2009/11/women_and_sciences.html.

Grant, L., Kennelly, I., & Ward, K. B. (2000). Revisiting the gender, marriage, and parenthood puzzle in scientific careers. *Women's Studies Quarterly,* 1–2, 62–85.

Grundy, E., & Henretta, J. C. (2006). Between elderly parents and adult children: A new look at the intergenerational care provided by the "sandwich generation." *Ageing & Society,* 26(5), 707–722.

Gunderson, M. (1989). Male-female wage differentials and policy responses. *Journal of Economic Literature,* 27(1), 46–72.

Hagedorn, L. S., & Sax, L. J. (2003). Marriage, children, and aging parents: The role of family-related factors in faculty job satisfaction. *Journal of Faculty Development,* 19(2), 65–76.

Hall, R. M., & Sandler, B. (1984). *Out of the classroom: A chilly classroom climate for women.* Washington, D.C.: Project on the Status and Education of Women, Association of American Colleges.

Hamovich, W., & Morgenstern, R. D. (1977). Children and the productivity of academic women. *Journal of Higher Education,* 48(6), 633–645.

Han, S.-K., & Moen, P. (1999). Work and family over time: A life-course approach. *Annals of the American Academy of Political and Social Science,* 562, 98–110.

Hargens, L. L., & Long, J. S. (2002). Demographic inertia and women's representation among faculty in higher education. *Journal of Higher Education,* 73, 494–517.

Hargens, L. L., McCann, J. C., & Reskin, B. F. (1978). Productivity and reproductivity: Fertility and professional achievement among research scientists. *Social Forces,* 57(1), 154–163.

Harper, E. P., Baldwin, R. G., Gansneder, B. G., & Chronister, J. L. (2001). Full-time women faculty off the tenure track: Profile and practice. *Review of Higher Education,* 24(3), 237–257.

Henderson, B. B., & Kane, W. D. (1991). Caught in the middle: faculty and institutional status and quality in state comprehensive universities. *Higher Education,* 22(4), 339–350.

Hensel, N. (1990). Maternity, promotion and tenure: Are they compatible? In L. Welsh (Ed.), *Issues for women in higher education* (pp. 3–11). New York: Praeger.

Hensel, N. (1991). *Realizing gender equality in higher education: The need to integrate work/family issues.* ASHE-ERIC Higher Education Report No.2. Washington, D.C.: The George Washington University, School of Education and Human Development.

Herr, J. L., & Wolfram, C. (2009). Work environment and "opt-out" rates at motherhood across high-education career paths. Cambridge, Mass.: National Bureau of Economic Research. http://www.nber.org/papers/w14717.

Hill, C., Corbett, C., & St. Rose, A. (2010). *Why so few? Women in science, technology, engineering, and mathematics.* Washington, D.C.: American Association of University Women.

Hochschild, A. R. (1975). Inside the clockwork of male careers. In E. Howe (Ed.), *Women and the power to change* (pp. 470–480). New York: McGraw-Hill.

Hochschild, A. R. (1989). *The second shift: Working parents and the revolution at home.* New York: Viking.

Hochschild, A. R. (1995). The culture of politics: Traditional, postmodern, cold-modern, and warm-modern ideals of care. *Social Politics,* 2(3), 331–346.

Hochschild, A. R. (1997). *The time bind: When work becomes home and home becomes work.* New York: Henry Holt.

Hollenshead, C. S., Sullivan, B., Smith, G. C., August, L., & Hamilton, S. (2005). Work/family policies in higher education: Survey data and case studies in policy implementation. *New Directions for Higher Education,* 130, 41–65.

Jacobs, J. A., & Winslow, S. E. (2004). Overworked faculty: Job stresses and family demands. *Annals of the American Academy of Political and Social Science,* 596(1), 104–129.

Jarvis, D. K. (1992). Improving junior faculty scholarship. In M. D. Sorcinelli & A. E. Austin (Eds.), *Developing new and junior faculty* (pp. 63–72). San Francisco: Jossey-Bass.

Kalleberg, A. L., & Reskin, B. (1995). Gender differences in promotion in the United States and Norway. *Research in Social Stratification and Mobility*, 14, 237–264.

Kaplan, S., & Tinsley, A. (1989). The unfinished agenda: Women in higher education administration. *Academe*, 75(1), 18–22.

Kelly, R. (2007). Now is the time to prepare for millennial faculty." *Academic Leader* 23(2), 1, 6.

Kezar, A. J., & Sam, C. (2010). Understanding the new majority of non-tenure-track faculty in higher education: Demographics, experiences, and plans of action. *ASHE Higher Education Report*, 36(4).

Kulis, S., & Sicotte, D. (2002). Women scientists in academia: Geographically constrained to big cities, college clusters, or the coasts? *Research in Higher Education*, 43, 1–30.

Kulis, S., Sicotte, D., & Collins, S. (2002). More than a pipeline problem: Labor supply constraints and gender stratification across academic science disciplines. *Research in Higher Education*, 43(6), 657–691.

Lazear, E. P. (1989). Symposium on women in the labor market. *Journal of Economic Perspectives*, 3(1), 3–7.

Lester, J., & Sallee, M. (2009). *Establishing the family-friendly campus: Models for effective practice*. Sterling, Va.: Stylus Publishing.

Long, J. S. (1990). The origins of sex differences in science. *Social Forces*, 71, 159–78.

Long, J. S., & Fox, M. F. (1995). Scientific careers: Universalism and particularism. *Annual Review of Sociology*, 21, 45–71.

Lovitts, B. E. (2001). *Leaving the ivory tower: The causes and consequences of departure from doctoral study*. Lanham, Md.: Rowman and Littlefield.

Marcus, J. (2007). Helping academics have families and tenure too: Universities discover their self-interest. *Change: The Magazine of Higher Learning*, 39(2), 27–32.

Marotte, M. R., Reynolds, P. M., & Savarese, R. J. (Eds.) (2010). *Papa, Ph.D.: Essays on fatherhood in the academe*. New Brunswick: Rutgers University Press.

Mason, M. A. (2009, February 6). A bad reputation. *Chronicle of Higher Education*. http://chronicle.com/article/A-Bad-Reputation/44843.

Mason, M. A. (2011, March 9). The Pyramid Problem. *Chronicle of Higher Education*. http://careernetwork.com/article/The-Pyramid-Problem/126614/.

Mason, M. A., & Ekman, E. M. (2007). *Mothers on the fast track: How a new generation can balance family and careers*. New York: Oxford University Press.

Mason, M. A., & Goulden, M. (2002). Do babies matter? The effect of family formation on the lifelong careers of academic men and women. *Academe*, 88(6), 21–27.

Mason, M. A., & Goulden, M. (2004). Do babies matter (Part II)? Closing the baby gap. *Academe*, 90(6), 10–15.

Mason, M. A., & Goulden, M. (2009). Marriage and baby blues: Redefining gender equity in the academy. *Annals of the American Academy of Political and Social Science*, 596(1), 86–103.

Mason, M. A., Goulden, M., & Frasch, K. (2009). Why graduate students reject the fast track: A study of thousands of doctoral students shows that they want balanced lives. *Academe*, 95(1), 11–16. http://www.aaup.org/AAUP/pubsres/academe/2009/JF/Feat/maso.htm.

Mavriplis, C., Heller, R. S., Beil, C., Dam, K., Yassinskaya, N., Shaw, M., & Sorensen, C. (2010). Mind the gap: Women in STEM career breaks. *Journal of Technology Management & Innovation*, 5(1), 140–151.

Merton, R. K., & Rossi, A. S. (1968). Contributions to the theory of reference group behavior. In R. K. Merton (Ed.), *Social theory and social structure* (pp. 229–235). New York: Free Press.

Misra, J., Lundquist, J., Holmes, E. D., & Agiomavritis, S. (2011). The ivory ceiling of service work. *Academe*, 97(1). http://www.aaup.org/AAUP/pubsres/academe/2011/JF/Feat/misr.htm.

Moen, P. (1992). *Women's two roles: A contemporary dilemma*. Westport, Conn.: Greenwood.

Moen, P., & Roehling, P. (2005). *The career mystique: Cracks in the American dream*. Lanham, Md.: Rowman and Littlefield.

Monosson, E. (Ed.). (2008). *Motherhood, the elephant in the laboratory: Women scientists speak out*. Ithaca: Cornell University Press.

Moore, K. M., & Sagaria, M.A.D. (1991). The situation of women in research universities in the United States: Within the inner circles of academic power. In G. Kelly & S. Slaughter (Eds.), *Women's higher education in comparative perspective* (pp. 185–200). Dordrecht: Kleiwer Academic Publishers. Reprinted in J. S. Glazer, E. M. Bensimon, & B. K. Townsend (Eds.), *Women in higher education: A feminist perspective*. Needham Heights, Mass.: Ginn Press, Simon & Schuster.

Morphew, C. C. (2002). A rose by any other name: Which colleges became universities. *Review of Higher Education*, 25(2), 207–224.

Munn-Giddings, C. (1998). Mixing motherhood and academia—a lethal cocktail. In D. Malina & S. Maslin-Prothero (Eds.), *Surviving the academy: Feminist perspectives* (pp. 56–68). Philadelphia: Falmer.

National Center for Education Statistics. (2010). *The condition of education 2010* (NCES 2010–028). Washington, D.C.: U.S. Department of Education.

Nettles, M., Perna, L. W., Bradburn, E. M., & Zimbler, L. (2000). *Salary, promotion, and tenure status of minority and women faculty in U.S. colleges and universities* (NCES 2000–173). Washington, D.C.: U.S. Department of Education.

Neumann, A, (2009a). *Professing to learn: Creating tenured lives and careers in the American research university*. Baltimore: Johns Hopkins University Press.

Neumann, A. (2009b). Protecting the passion of scholars in times of change. *Change: The Magazine of Higher Learning*, 41(2), 10–15.

Neumann, A., & Terosky, A. L. (2007). To give and to receive: Recently tenured professors' experiences of service in major research universities. *Journal of Higher Education*, 78(3), 282–310.

Nippert-Eng, C. (1996). *Home and work*. Chicago: University of Chicago Press.

O'Laughlin, E. M., & Bischoff, L. G. (2005). Balancing parenthood and academia: Work/family stress as influenced by gender and tenure status. *Journal of Family Issues*, 26, 79–106.

O'Meara, K. A. (2007). Striving for what? Exploring the pursuit of prestige. In

J. C. Smart (Ed.), *Higher Education: Handbook of Theory and Research*, Vol. 22, 121–179.

O'Meara, K. A., & Campbell, C. M. (2011). Faculty sense of agency in decisions about work and family. *Review of Higher Education*, 34(3), 447–476.

O'Meara, K., Terosky, A. L., & Neumann, A. (2008). Faculty careers and work lives: A professional growth perspective. *ASHE Higher Education Report*, 34(3). San Francisco: Jossey-Bass.

Perna, L. W. (2000). Understanding the decision to enroll in graduate school: Sex and racial/ethnic group differences. *Journal of Higher Education*, 75(5), 487–527.

Perna, L. W. (2001a). Sex differences in faculty salaries: A cohort analysis. *Review of Higher Education*, 24, 283–307.

Perna, L. W. (2001b). The relationship between family responsibilities and employment status. *Journal of Higher Education*, 72(5), 584–611.

Philipsen, M. I. (2008). *Challenges of the faculty career for women: Success and sacrifice*. San Francisco: Jossey-Bass.

Philipsen, M. I., & Bostic, T. B. (2010). *Helping faculty find work-life balance: The path toward family-friendly institutions*. San Francisco: Jossey-Bass.

Raabe, P. H. (1997). Work-family policies for faculty: How "career-and family-friendly" is academe? In M. A. Ferber & J. W. Loeb (Eds.), *Academic couples: Problems and promises* (pp. 208–225). Urbana: University of Illinois Press.

Rapoport, R., Bailyn, L., Fletcher, J. K., & Pruitt, B. H. (2002). *Beyond work-family balance: Advancing gender equity and workplace performance*. San Francisco: Jossey-Bass.

Rice, R. E., Sorcinelli, M. D., & Austin, A. (2000). *Heeding new voices: Academic careers for a new generation*. Washington, D.C.: American Association for Higher Education.

Richards, A. (2008). *Opting in: Having a child without losing yourself*. New York: Farrar, Strauss and Giroux.

Ridgeway, C. & Correll, S. (2004). Unpacking the gender system: A theoretical perspective on gender beliefs and social relations. *Gender and Society* 18(4), 510–531.

Roehling, P. V., Roehling, M. V., & Moen, P. (2001). The relationship between work-life policies and practices and employee loyalty: A life course perspective. *Journal of Family and Economic Issues*, 22(2), 141–170.

Ropers-Huilman, B. (1998). *Feminist teaching in theory and practice: Situating power and knowledge in post-structural classrooms*. New York: Teachers College.

Ropers-Huilman, B. (2000). Aren't you satisfied yet? Women faculty members' interpretations of their academic work. In L. S. Hagedorn (Ed.), *What contributes to job satisfaction among faculty and staff*, issue 27(1) of *New Directions for Institutional Research* (21–32). San Francisco: Jossey-Bass.

Rosser, V. J. (2004). Faculty members' intentions to leave: A national study on their work life and satisfaction. *Research in Higher Education*, 45(3), 285–309.

Ruscio, K. P. (1987). The distinctive scholarship of the selective liberal arts college. *Journal of Higher Education*, 58(2), 214.

Sallee, M. W. (2010, November). The ideal worker or the ideal father: Organizational structures and culture in the gendered university. Paper presented at the annual meeting of the Association for the Study of Higher Education, Indianapolis.

Schiebinger, L., Davies Henderson, A., & Gilmartin, S. (2008). *Dual career couples: What universities need to know.* Michelle R. Clayman Institute for Gender Research, Stanford University. http://gender.stanford.edu/dual-career-academic-couples-what-universities-need-to-know.

Schor, J. B. (1992). *The overworked American: The unexpected decline of leisure.* New York: Basic Books.

Schuster, J. H., & Finkelstein, M. J. (2006). *The American faculty: The restructuring of academic work and careers.* Baltimore: Johns Hopkins University Press.

Scott, J. W. (1988). Deconstructing equality versus difference: Or, the uses of post-structuralist theory for feminism. *Feminist Studies,* 14(1), 33–50.

Simon, H. A. (1981). *The sciences of the artificial.* Cambridge: MIT Press.

Smart, R., & Peterson, C. (1997). Super's career stages and the decision to change careers. *Journal of Vocational Behavior,* 51, 358–374.

Smith, K. E., & Bachu, A. (1999). Women's labor force attachment patterns and maternity leave: A review of the literature. U.S. Census Bureau, Population Division Working Paper 32. http://www.census.gov/population/www/documentation/twps0032/twps0032.html.

Solomon, B. (1985). *In the company of educated women: A history of women in higher education in America.* New Haven: Yale University Press.

Somerville, J. (2000). *Feminism and the family: Politics and society in the UK and USA.* New York: Palgrave Macmillan.

Sonnert, G., & Holton, G. (1995). *Gender differences in science careers: The project access study.* New Brunswick: Rutgers University Press.

Sorcinelli, M. D., & Near, J. P. (1989). Relations between work and life away from work among university faculty. *Journal of Higher Education,* 60(1), 59–82.

Spalter-Roth, R., & Merola, S. (2001). Early career pathways: Differences among moms and dads, childless men, and childless women in sociology. Paper presented at the annual meeting of the American Sociology Association, Anaheim, Cal.

Stack, S. (2004). Gender, children and research productivity. *Research in Higher Education,* 45(8), 891–920.

Stone, P. (2007). *Opting out? Why women really quit careers and head home.* Berkeley: University of California Press.

Stone, P., Kohler, J., & Ackerly Hernandez, L. (2010). Opting out. In S. Sweet & J. Casey (Eds.), *The work and family encyclopedia.* http://wfnetwork. bc.edu/encyclopedia_entry.php?id=17303&area=All.

Stout, P. A., Staiger, J., & Jennings, N. A. (2007, Fall). Affective stories: Understanding the lack of progress of women faculty. *NWSA Journal,* 19(3), 125–144.

Sullivan, B., Hollenshead, C., & Smith, G. (2004). Developing and implementing work-family policies for faculty: Balancing faculty careers and family work. *Academe,* 90(6), 24–27.

Super, D. E. (1992). Toward a comprehensive theory of career development. In D. Montross & C. Shinkman (Eds.), *Career development: Theory and practice* (pp. 35–64). Springfield, Ill.: Charles C. Thomas.

Taylor, M. C. (2010). *Crisis on campus: A bold plan for reforming our colleges and universities.* New York, NY: Alfred Knopf.

Tierney, W. G., & Bensimon, E. M. (1996). *Promotion and tenure: Community and socialization in academe.* Albany: State University of New York Press.

Toutkoushian, R. K. (1998). Sex matters less for younger faculty: Evidence of disaggregate pay disparities from the 1988 and 1993 NCES surveys. *Economics of Education Review,* 17(1), 55–71.

Townsend, B., & Turner, C. (2000, March 27). Reshaping the academy to accommodate conflicts of commitment: Then what? Paper presented at the Shaping a National Agenda for Women in Higher Education Conference. Minneapolis.

Townsend, B. K., & Twombly, S. B. (2007). Community college faculty: Overlooked and undervalued. *ASHE Higher Education Report,* 32(6). San Francisco: Jossey-Bass.

Trower, C. (2010, Summer). A new generation of faculty: Similar core values in a different world. *Peer Review,* 12(3).

Twombly, S., & Townsend, B. K. (2008). Community college faculty: What we know and need to know. *Community College Review,* 36(1), 5–24.

U.S. Department of Labor. (2010). Wage and Hour Division. Family and medical leave act. http://www.dol.gov/whd/fmla/.

Valian, V. (1998). *Why so slow? The advancement of women.* Cambridge: MIT Press.

Valian, V. (2005). Beyond gender schemas: Improving the advancement of women in academia. *Hypatia,* 20(3), 198–213.

Van Vooren, N., & Spalter-Roth, R. (2008, November). Success of women with children in sociology. *Footnotes,* 36(8). http://www.asanet.org/footnotes/novo8/women.html.

Varner, A. 2000. The consequences and costs of delaying attempted childbirth for women faculty. University Park: Department of Labor Studies and Industrial Relations, Pennsylvania State University.

Varner, A., & Drago, R. (2001) Fertility and work in the United States: A policy perspective. Report for the National Institute of Population and Social Security Research, Japan.

Ward, K. (2003). *Faculty service roles and the scholarship of engagement.* San Francisco: Jossey Bass.

Ward, K., & Bensimon, E. M. (2002). Engendering socialization. In K. Renn & A. Martinez Aleman (Eds.), *Women in higher education: An encyclopedia* (pp. 431–434). Santa Barbara: ABC-CLIO.

Ward, K., & Grant, L. (1996). Gender and academic publishing. In J. C. Smart (Ed.), *Higher education: Handbook of theory and research,* Volume 11 (pp. 172–212). New York: Agathon Press.

Ward, K., & Wolf-Wendel, L. E. (2004a). Fear factor: How safe is it to make time for family? *Academe,* 90(6), 28–31.

Ward, K., & Wolf-Wendel, L. (2004b). Academic motherhood: Managing complex roles in research universities. *Review of Higher Education,* 27, 233–257.

Weedon, C. (1997). *Feminist practice and post-structuralist theory* (2nd edition). Malden, Mass: Blackwell.

Wilde, E. T., Batchelder, L., & Ellwood, D. T. (2010). The mommy track divides: The impact of childbearing on wages of women of differing skill levels. NBER Working Paper 16582. http://www.nber.org/papers/w16582. pdf?new_window=1.

Williams, J. (2000a, October 27). How the tenure track discriminates against women. *Chronicle of Higher Education*, B10.

Williams, J. (2000b). *Unbending gender: Why family and work conflict and what to do about it*. New York: Oxford University Press.

Williams, J. C. (2003, April 14). The subtle side of discrimination. *Chronicle of Higher Education*, 49(32), C5.

Williams, J. C. (2004). Hitting the maternal wall. *Academe*, 90(6), 16–20.

Williams, J. C. (2010). *Reshaping the work-family debate: Why men and class matter*. Cambridge: Harvard University Press.

Williams, W. M. (2001, July 20). Women in academe, and the men who derail them. *Chronicle of Higher Education*, B20.

Wilson, R. (2001, April 13). The backlash against hiring couples. *Chronicle of Higher Education*, A16.

Wilson, R. (2010, May 10). Many full-time instructors prefer working off the tenure track. *Chronicle of Higher Education*. http://chronicle.com/article/Many-Full-Time-Adjuncts-Prefer/65465/.

Wolf-Wendel, L. E., Twombly, S., & Rice, S. (2000a). Dual-career couples: Keeping them together. *Journal of Higher Education*, 71(3), 291–321.

Wolf-Wendel, L. E., Twombly, S., & Rice, S. (2000b, November). Dual career couple accommodation policies in higher education: Dilemmas of balancing institutional and individual needs. Paper presented at the Association for the Study of Higher Education annual meeting, Sacramento, Cal.

Wolf-Wendel, L. E., Twombly, S., & Rice, S. (2003). *The two-body problem: Dual career couple hiring policies in higher education*. Baltimore: Johns Hopkins University Press.

Wolf-Wendel, L., & Ward, K. (2006). Academic life and motherhood: Variations by institutional type. *Higher Education*, 52(3), 487–521.

Wolfinger, N. H., Mason, M. A., & Goulden, M. (2009). "Stay in the game": Gender, family formation, and alternative trajectories in the academic life course. *Social Forces*, 87, 1591–1621.

Yoest, C. (2004). *Parental leave in academia*. Report to the Alfred P. Sloan Foundation and the Bankard Fund at the University of Virginia. http://www.faculty.virginia.edu/familyandtenure/institutional%20report.pdf.

Zuckerman, H. (1987). The careers of men and women scientists: A review of current research. In L. S. Dix (Ed.), *Women: Their underrepresentation and career differentials in science and engineering* (pp. 127–156). Washington, D.C.: National Academy of Sciences, National Academy Press.

INDEX

academic drift, 118, 119
academic profession, background information on, 3–7
accumulative disadvantage. *See* cumulative advantage and disadvantage
administrative careers, 80–84, 116, 117–118, 218–219
Aisenberg, Nadya, 9–10
agency, personal: and choice, 151–152, 162, 163–164, 165–166, 172, 177; and opting out, 165–166, 172, 178; and service work, 124–125; and work and family policies, 186, 189–191, 193–194, 207–210, 213, 215
Allan, Elizabeth, 36–37, 207
American Association of Colleges and Universities (AACU), 160–161
American Association of University Professors (AAUP), 4, 187
American Association of University Women (AAUW), 21
American Council on Education Fellows Program, 218–219
assistant professor rank, 3–4, 8, 14–15, 26, 33, 34, 62, 180, 229
associate professor rank, 5, 8, 26, 33, 34–35, 41, 75–78, 103, 125, 227

Baldwin, Roger, 34–35, 130
Bassett, Rachel Hile, 98
Belkin, Lisa, 165
bias avoidance, 41–42, 191–193
biological clock, 7, 40–41, 56, 57–58
Birnbaum, Robert, 111
Blackburn, Robert, 34–35
breastfeeding and work and family policies, 206–207
buffering, 43–44
burnout, 35, 66, 78–79, 86–87

Campbell, Corbin, 190, 210
capital, cultural and socioeconomic: and choice, 151–153, 162–163, 210; and cosmopolitan orientation, 152; inherited, 149–150, 163
career mobility, 64, 67, 68–69, 70–71, 121, 126, 152, 159, 161–162, 175
career mystique, 30, 31, 104–105, 145, 231–232, 244, 245
"career recycling," 79
career stages, academic, 34–35. *See also* assistant professor rank; associate professor rank; early-career stage; full professor, advancement to; mid-career stage
childbirth. *See* pregnancy and childbirth
child care: dual-career couples and, 155–157, 158, 159; local orientation and, 152–153; second shift and, 41, 70, 157; traditional norms and, 146, 159; work and family policies and, 142, 182, 187, 202, 206, 210–211
choice: family and work strategies and, 234, 235, 238; feminist perspective on, 176–178, 207–208; gendered and workplace norms and, 2, 11, 147–148, 190–191, 209, 211, 244; opting out and, 173, 176–178; personal agency and, 151–152, 162, 163, 165–166, 172, 177, 210; and work and family policies, 77, 123, 186, 189–191, 192, 193–194, 196, 207–210, 244–245. *See also* "free choice"
Clark, Burton, 110–111, 113, 118, 119, 129–130, 138, 152
Clark, Shirley, 44–45
College and University Work-Family Association, 224
commonality of experience, 49, 88, 111, 196

community colleges: early-career faculty at, 134–138, 144–145; flexibility of, 140–141, 204; and ideal worker norms, 146–147; local orientation and, 152–153; mid-career faculty at, 138–143, 144; mission of, 144–145; satisfaction at, 136–137, 138, 140–141, 144–145, 147; teaching emphasis at, 137–138, 140, 144–145; and tenure, 204–205; vignettes, 134–136, 138–139; work and family policies at, 142–143, 144, 203–207

comprehensive institutions: and academic drift, 118, 119; and career advancement, 125–126; early-career faculty at, 143–144; and expectations, 126–127; and ideal worker norms, 146–147; in institutional hierarchy, 118–119; mid-career faculty at, 123–127, 144; mission of, 118, 119, 121, 122–123, 127, 144; as "regional comprehensives," 119, 122–123, 124; as "striving comprehensives," 118–121, 123, 124, 143–144, 146; service and agency at, 124–125; tenure at, 121, 123, 124, 143–144, 198–199; vignettes, 119–121, 122–123, 123–124; work and family policies at, 198–201

Corcoran, Mary, 44–45

Coser, Lewis, 41

cosmopolitan vs. local orientation, 152–153

Council of Contemporary Families, 224

counternarratives vs. existing narratives, 1–2, 10, 28–30, 32–46, 244. See also gendered norms and expectations; poststructural feminism

cultural capital. See capital, cultural and socioeconomic

cumulative advantage and disadvantage, 40, 44–45, 150

daycare needs, 219–220

demographic inertia, 8–9

dependent-care leave, 69, 96, 182

disability leave, 184–185, 197, 200, 205, 214

disciplinary cultures, 88, 108–109

Drago, Bob, 216

dual-career couples: career mobility in, 159, 161–162; hiring policies for, 160–161; and impact on career and family, 9, 149, 154; mother as breadwinner in, 155–159; and opting out, 171–175; poststructural feminism and, 163–164; research on, 153–155; traditional gender

norms in, 158–159, 163–164; vignettes, 155–156, 157–158, 159–160; and work and family policies, 220. See also "trailing spouse"

early-career stage: and academic workload, 54–55; "career mystique" and, 145; commonalities among faculty in, 49; at community colleges, 134–138, 144–145; at comprehensive institutions, 143–144; differences between mid-career and, 34–35; focus of, 69, 85–86, 113–114; and flexibility and autonomy, 52–54; and greedy institutions, 146; at liberal arts colleges, 127–130; and perspective, 59–62, 113–114; professional and personal roles in, 49–52, 113; at research universities, 111–115; and satisficing, 60–62, 114; tenure clock and, 56, 57–59, 69, 75, 85–86, 182; vignettes, 47–48, 111–113, 127–128, 134–136; and work and family policies, 180, 181–182, 197, 221

faculty career stages. See assistant professor rank; associate professor rank; early-career stage; full professor, advancement to; mid-career stage

faculty productivity, studies on, 153–154

"family-friendly" institutions and policies: and choice, 17, 148, 207–208; and faculty perspectives, 139; and feminist theory, 36–37, 163; and liberal arts colleges, 128–129, 132, 133–134, 144, 201–202; NSF and, 96; and research universities, 182

Family Medical Leave Act (FMLA), 182–184, 197, 198, 201–202, 203–206, 213, 229

feminist theory, 29–30, 35–38, 162–164, 176–178. See also liberal feminism; poststructural feminism

FMLA. See Family Medical Leave Act (FMLA)

"free choice," 151, 162, 163–164, 177, 178, 190, 207–208, 209, 213, 215

full professor, advancement to, 73–78, 86–87, 125–126, 217–218

gender: in academic hierarchy, 42, 46; and demographic inertia, 8–9; and feminist theory, 35–38; and ideal worker norms, 6–7, 8, 39–40, 145–146, 148; and opting out, 171–172, 176–178;

research productivity and, 154; tenure clock and, 40–41. *See also* gendered norms and expectations

gendered norms and expectations: and choice, 2, 11, 147–148, 176–178, 190–191, 209, 244; and dual-career couples, 158–159, 163–164; and ideal worker norms, 6–7, 30–32, 38–45; and separate sphere notion, 31–32, 166; and work and family policies, 212–213

gender schemas, 39–40

"greedy institutions," 41, 44, 49, 52, 146, 190–191, 41

Harrington, Mona, 9–10

Hochschild, Arlie, 6

humanities, women in: career demands for, 98–101; career options for, 101–102; vignette, 96–98

ideal mother norms, 31, 245

ideal worker norms: and choice, 147–148, 190–191, 209, 244; and gender, 6–7, 8, 39–40, 145–146, 148; and greedy institutions, 41; and institution type, 145–148; and stereotypical faculty, 5–6; and tenure, 30–31, 148, 175–176, 190–191; and time constraints, 145–147

institutional expectations, 11–12, 126–127, 244. *See also* gendered norms and expectations

institutional hierarchy, 118–119

institution type: and commonality of experience, 111, 196; and dual-career hiring policies, 161; and early-career faculty, 62, 111–115, 127–130, 134–138, 144–145; and ideal worker norms, 145–148; key findings on motherhood and, 143–148; local orientation and, 152–153; and mid-career faculty, 73, 115–118, 123–127, 138–143, 144; and research and publication demands, 153–154; research on, 110–111, 118; and tenure, 2–3, 4; and work and family policies, 196–207. *See also* community colleges; comprehensive institutions; liberal arts colleges; research universities

Kelly's story. *See* Ward, Kelly, story

leave, paid vs. unpaid, 47–48, 182–183, 183–184, 191, 202, 203, 205, 229. *See also* Family Medical Leave Act (FMLA)

leave, types of, 181–188

liberal arts colleges: career advancement at, 132–133; early-career faculty at, 127–130; family and workplace norms at, 128–129, 132, 133–134, 144, 146, 201; mid-career faculty at, 130–134, 144; mission of, 132; research on, 129–130; service work expectations at, 129–130, 130–133, 144; vignettes, 127–128, 130–131; work and family policies at, 201–203

liberal feminism, 30, 36–37, 38, 163–164, 207–208. *See also* poststructural feminism

life-course perspective on work and family, 2, 23, 25–26, 29, 32–35, 65–66, 85, 168, 242, 245

Lisa's story. *See* Wolf-Wendel, Lisa, story

literature on work and family, 28

Lovitts, Barbara, 145–146

male time clocks, 40–41

marital status, 149, 153, 154, 162

maternity leave: FMLA and, 197, 201, 203–206; and work and family policies, 112, 182, 188–189, 190, 192, 199–200, 210–211; and work-related strategies, 238–239. *See also* pregnancy and childbirth

"Matthew effect," 45

mentoring and support systems, 84–85, 87, 217

methodology in academic motherhood research, 22–27

mid-career stage: and administrative careers, 80–84, 116, 117–118; and burnout, 35, 78–79, 86–87; at community colleges, 138–143, 144; at comprehensive institutions, 123–127, 144; differences between early-career and, 34–35; and full professorship, 73–78, 86–87, 125–126, 217–218; at liberal arts colleges, 130–134, 144; mentoring and support systems for, 84–85, 87; and opting out, 167–170, 171–175; and perspective, 66–73, 79, 86, 167–168; and research productivity, 116–117, 125, 126–127; at research universities, 115–118; and tenure denial, 167–170; vignettes, 63–65, 115–116, 123–124, 130–131, 138–139; and work and family policies, 142–143, 144, 182, 197–198, 221

modified-duty policies, 182–183, 185–186, 214–215, 230

Moen, Phyllis, 31
"motherhood penalty," 39–40

"narrative of constraint," 28
National Science Foundation (NSF),
    95–96
Neumann, Anna, 28, 35, 79

O'Meara, Kerry Ann, 28, 190, 210
online teaching, 140, 141–142, 144, 206
opting out: defined, 165–166; in dual-
    career couples, 171–175; for family
    needs, 170–171, 175–176; and gendered
    norms, 176–178; impact of, 178; as
    involuntary, 166–170; and personal
    agency, 165–166, 172, 176–178

"parenthood lens," 67, 69
Peterson, Marvin, 79
"place bound," 68, 125, 159. See also career
    mobility
policies, work and family: advice for
    administrators on, 225–230; advice
    for faculty and graduate students on,
    230–235; awareness of, 188–189, 197–198,
    199, 221, 222; breastfeeding and,
    206–207; and cultural capital, 210; and
    daycare needs, 219–220; departmental-
    level role in, 180, 191, 193–196, 199, 202;
    and dual-career couples, 220; and
    early-career faculty, 180, 181–182, 197,
    221; faculty perspectives on, 188–193;
    and family-related strategies, 236–237;
    and institutional culture, 187–188,
    200, 202–203, 204–206, 209–211, 219,
    222–225, 245; and institution type, 182,
    142–143, 144, 196–207; and mid-career
    faculty, 142–143, 144, 182, 197–198, 221;
    and personal agency, 186, 189–191,
    193–194, 207–210; and recommenda-
    tions for work/family integration,
    213–222; and tenure, 187, 188, 190–191,
    191–192, 198, 201, 204–205; types of,
    181–188; and unions, 139, 142, 206;
    usage of, 181, 197, 198, 199, 205–206,
    208–211, 219, 222; vignette, 179–180; and
    work-related strategies, 238–242. See
    also Family Medical Leave Act (FMLA);
    tenure stop-clock policies
poststructural feminism, 30, 36, 37–38,
    163–164, 207, 208–209. See also liberal
    feminism

pregnancy and childbirth: and bias
    avoidance, 41–42, 191–193; biological
    clock and, 7, 56, 57–58; Family Medical
    Leave Act and, 183–184, 197, 205, 209;
    and gendered and workplace norms, 7,
    8, 145–146; and life-course perspective,
    168, 229; and "motherhood penalty,"
    39–40; sick leave for, 47–48, 97, 184–185,
    200, 205, 206, 214; and tenure, 187,
    191–193; timing of, 15, 47, 57–58, 203,
    216, 232–233
Pregnancy Discrimination Act, 185
primary caregivers, women as, 6, 31,
    39–40, 57
private and public spheres, notion of,
    31–32, 33, 38–39, 43, 85, 155–156, 166, 168,
    175–176
professional fields, women in, 105–108
publishing demands, 100–101, 153–154

"quasi-administration," 72–73, 126,
    135–136

reference group theory, 147
research productivity, 116–117, 125,
    126–127, 130, 154, 198, 199
research universities: dual-career hiring
    policies at, 161; early-career faculty at,
    111–115; and ideal worker norms, 146;
    mid-career faculty at, 115–118; mission
    of, 116; publishing demands at, 153–154;
    and role modeling, 114, 143; and tenure,
    114–115, 116, 182, 197, 198; vignettes,
    111–113, 115–116; work and family poli-
    cies at, 182, 197–198

satisficing, 38, 42–43, 44, 60–62, 114, 116,
    236, 240, 244
sciences, women in. See STEM fields,
    women in
"second shift," 6, 41, 52, 57, 63–64, 70,
    157–158, 237
service work: at comprehensive
    institutions, 124–125, 144; at liberal
    arts colleges, 129–130, 130–133, 144;
    and mid-career faculty, 72–73, 77, 118,
    124–125; at research universities, 182,
    197–198
sick leave, 47–48, 97, 120, 182–183, 184–185,
    197, 200, 201, 204, 205–206, 214
Smart, John, 79

social sciences, women in: generational differences among, 104–105; growth of, 103–104; vignette, 102–103

socioeconomics, 32, 149–153, 163

spheres. *See* private and public spheres, notion of

STEM fields, women in: and disciplinary culture, 109; and disciplinary identity, 95–96; and lab research, 93–95; and marital status, 153; underrepresentation of, 91–93; vignette, 89–91

stereotypes, faculty, 5–6, 31

"striving comprehensives," 118–121, 123, 124, 143–144, 146. *See also* comprehensive institutions

tenure: ambiguities related to, 217–218; benefits of, 3, 4, 30, 176; and bias avoidance, 41–42, 191–193; biological clock and, 7, 56, 57–58; and buffering, 43–44; and burnout, 35, 78–79, 86–87, 117, 218; at community colleges, 204–205; at comprehensive institutions, 121, 123, 124, 143–144, 198–199; denial of, 167–170; dual-career couples and, 161, 171–175; early-career faculty and, 52, 54, 56, 57–59, 69, 75, 82, 85–86, 113–114, 182; and gender, 38, 39, 40–41; and ideal worker norms, 30–31, 148, 175–176, 190–191; and mid-career faculty, 116–117, 167–170; and opting out, 165–166, 166–170, 171–176; process of, 3–5; and promotion to full professor, 77–78; and publication demands, 100–101; and research universities, 114–115, 116, 182, 197, 198; and satisficing, 42, 43, 61, 116; and work and family policies, 182–183, 187, 188, 190–191, 197, 203, 204–205, 219. *See also* tenure stop-clock policies

tenure stop-clock policies: at comprehensive institutions, 198–199; department-level role in, 194; at liberal arts colleges, 201; opt-in vs. opt-out, 186–187; recommendations for, 216–217, 232, 241; at research universities, 182, 197; usage of, 191–192, 193, 233–234

Terosky, Aimee LaPointe, 28

theoretical frameworks, 29–30, 45–46

"trailing spouse," 9, 154–155, 162, 163, 234–235. *See also* dual-career couples

unions, 139, 140, 142, 206

unpaid leave. *See* leave, paid vs. unpaid

Valian, Virginia, 39, 45

Ward, Kelly, story, 17–22

"web of interdependence," work and family, 32–33, 85, 168

Williams, Joan, 216

Wolf-Wendel, Lisa, story, 13–17

women faculty, research on, 9–10

ABOUT THE AUTHORS

KELLY WARD earned her Ph.D. from Penn State in 1995. She has held administrative and faculty positions at the University of Montana and Oklahoma State University. She is currently serving as chair and professor in the Department of Educational Leadership and Counseling Psychology at Washington State University. Kelly's research addresses issues associated with academic careers, including how faculty members manage work and family, and faculty involvement in community engagement. She is author of *Faculty Service Roles and the Scholarship of Engagement* and coauthor of *Developing New Faculty as Teachers and Scholars.*

LISA WOLF-WENDEL is a professor in the Department of Educational Leadership and Policy Studies at the University of Kansas (KU). She earned her Ph.D. from the Claremont Graduate School and her undergraduate degree from Stanford University. Lisa's expertise centers on faculty concerns and equity issues in higher education. She is the coauthor of several books including *The Two-Body Problem: Dual Career Couple Hiring Policies in Higher Education* (2003) and *Taking Women Seriously: Lessons and Legacies for Educating the Majority* (1999).

CPSIA information can be obtained at www.ICGtesting.com
Printed in the USA
BVOW03s0137250713

326810BV00001B/16/P